Praise for Previous Editions from Your Peers

"To say that I read the book would be a serious understatement: I devoured it! The plain truth is that Kathie Hightower and Holly Scherer have compiled the most comprehensive text for how to successfully navigate through the military world while keeping the better part of your identity intact…The authors have challenged me to think more creatively about how I plan to achieve my own goals as I face the reality of military life."
—*Therese Mancevski*

"As a military spouse and former bookseller, I've come across lots of books in this subgenre, ranging from the dense to the superficial. It's with great pleasure that I discovered this gem of information. I've never recommended a 'military spouse' book before. I find that a lot of such books are either quickly outdated, written from the perspective of a particular branch, or full of 'suck it up and deal with it' attitudes. The strength of this book lies in the authors' willingness to acknowledge that military life has endemic challenges and that, as human beings, we're allowed to whine…sometimes. But it's also a book that emphasizes that your happiness is under your control. Highly recommended to military spouses of all branches; the resource sections alone are worth the price to own the book." —*Lindsey*

"Hightower and Scherer have crafted a fine tool for military spouses that will help people make their dreams come true! This great resource is full of practical advice as well as real-world examples that will empower spouses to have a life of their own while supporting their partners in the military lifestyle. This book belongs on the shelf of every military family who wants to get more out of their new life!"
—*Ellie Kay, Air Force spouse, international speaker,*
media personality, and author of more than a dozen books,
including Heroes At Home, *www.EllieKay.com*

"I attended the workshop Holly and Kathie put on here in Japan. It was the best and most useful workshop I have attended. This book is based on that workshop information PLUS more resources, shared experiences, and other insights I was thrilled to read! I read the book from cover to cover in two days (which is quite a task with four kids and a part-time job)! I believe every command should present this book to their service members' wives when they marry." —*S. E., Marine wife*

What Your Peers Say about the Workshop on which this Book is Based

"Eleven years married to the military, and I walked away with more in three hours than I did in all the time before this class."

—*Janelle Abbott, Hohenfels, Germany*

"If any of you hear of their workshop coming to your base RUN, don't walk, to sign up! They are wonderfully supportive, informative, and funny ladies! I had a wonderful time and learned a lot even though I thought I knew a lot before I went!" —*blog posting on Military Spouse Support Network after a workshop in Kaiserslautern, Germany*

"You were fantastic speakers. It is so nice to hear from people who have lived the life and who have walked the walk."

—*Carol Stone, Hohenfels, Germany*

"This workshop really helped me change my mindset from what am I missing, to what can I do to improve my life, and how to go about it."

—*Shauna Attaway, Korea*

"Wunderbar! I have gained worthwhile and valuable information on how to turn my dreams into reality. I wish I had a seminar like this to attend fifteen years ago." —*Gwendolyn A. Williams*

"This would have saved me a year of crying at Parris Island." —*Susan M.*

Military Spouse Journey

Discover the Possibilities & Live Your Dreams

Completely revised and updated third edition of
Help! I'm a Military Spouse—I Get a Life Too!

Kathie Hightower and Holly Scherer

Elva Resa ∗ Saint Paul

Military Spouse Journey: Discover the possibilities & live your dreams
© 2013 Kathie Hightower and Holly Scherer

This book is a completely revised and updated third edition of *Help! I'm a Military Spouse—I Get a Life Too!* First and second editions © 2005, 2007 Kathie Hightower and Holly Scherer.

Also by the authors: *1001 Things to Love About Military Life*, with Tara Crooks and Star Henderson, Hachette Books, 2011.

Blue Ridge Mountains cover photo ©2004 Leslie Sheridan.
Cover design by Andermax Studios.

Library of Congress Cataloging-in-Publication Data

Hightower, Kathie, 1953-
   [Help! I'm a military spouse.]
   Military spouse journey : discover the possibilities and live your dreams
   / Kathie Hightower and Holly Scherer. — 3rd edition.
      pages cm
Summary: "Guide for military spouses to help you define and live your dreams, even when faced with frequent moves, separations, and other challenges of military life. Includes tips and exercises to help you explore your passions, strengths, and goals, and apply five keys to happiness"— Provided by publisher.
ISBN 978-1-934617-17-5 (pbk.)
1. Military spouses—United States—Conduct of life. I. Scherer, Holly, 1956-
   II. Title.
UB403.H54 2013
355.1'20973--dc23
                                    2013022258

Printed in United States of America.
10 9 8 7 6 5 4 3 2 1
Elva Resa Publishing
8362 Tamarack Vlg Ste 119-106, St Paul, MN 55125
www.ElvaResa.com
www.MilitaryFamilyBooks.com
www.MilitarySpouseJourney.com

To all the military spouses who have walked this journey with us.
—Holly and Kathie

To Jack,
What a ride! Simply put: If I had not married you, I wouldn't
have been a military spouse. I cannot imagine how boring life
would have been if I had not been able to ride this ride and see the
world with you. I feel so privileged to have experienced military
life and to be married to someone as wonderful as you. I wish all
Americans could see the integrity, intelligence, and commitment
to country I have seen close up. Thank you for your unconditional
love and support for me to continuously go for my dreams.
—Holly

To Greg,
For your never-ending patience with my many ideas (even if
you do say "Oh, no" every time I start a conversation with
"Greg, I've been thinking..."). My life would be pretty dull without
your sense of humor and fun, your great dancing...and I can't
imagine life without your cooking and your natural gift as the
ultimate host and listener. (And yes, you are a great chef...it's
NOT just because I can't cook.) My short answer to "How to be
happy being married to the military" is still:
"Marry a man like Greg!"
—Kathie

Contents

SECTION SIX: Pay It Forward

The Next Step

Authors' Note

Why Read This Book?

Here is what you'll find:

- Research-based information on key factors that increase your happiness in life, and how to apply that research to your own unique life within the military.

- Exercises and resources to help you clarify your own dreams and tools to help you move toward those dreams, no matter where you are stationed, no matter what your circumstances.

- Quick, easy tools to help you decrease your stress and increase your energy, especially when you "don't have the time."

- Key resources to be aware of, specific to you as a military spouse. Many resources are free to you, even though they can be expensive in the civilian community.

- What we (and many other military spouses) wish we'd known early on about how to approach this military life more proactively.

Updated Version

We chose not to simply update references, but to fully rewrite this book, incorporating key material from previous editions and adding new stories, resources, and ideas.

We've continued to do workshops for military spouses and to interview spouses, of all services, since our second edition came out in 2007. As we travel the world, meeting with military spouses, we learn new things all the time. Since 2007, much has changed in our world, especially in our military. The materials presented incorporate our past experiences with new information, reflective of changes in the military spouse community.

Why the Title Change?

Initially, we titled the book *Help! I'm a Military Spouse—I Get a Life Too!* because we specifically wanted to reach spouses who were struggling most. We knew there were many military spouses who didn't know about the resources available to them, and who were possibly distrustful of anything provided by the military. We envisioned unhappy spouses walking through the exchange, seeing this title, and thinking, "Hey, that's exactly what I'm thinking…I need help!" Well, many of those spouses did stumble on our book, or they stumbled on our web site when they Googled "help for a military spouse." And many wrote to tell us how much the book did help them.

However, some spouses told us they didn't read the book because they couldn't get past the title, which sounded too negative. Some said, "I loved the book, but I hated the title. It sounds so whiny, and I don't want to be whiny."

Then we saw this review by Roz Riley, one of the military spouses who had a hard time getting past the title. "Even with a lifetime with the military—Army brat, Army nurse, retired veteran, Army wife of twenty-eight years (still counting), and now Army mom—I had this book sit on my shelf for several weeks before I opened it to read. For some reason I couldn't get past the title. Once I turned past the title page, I found the book to be one of the best on the market today for military spouses. It is full of possibilities for this lifestyle, with resources, ideas, and stories of other military spouses who have made this lifestyle work for them. I have read this book and have turned down pages, underlined key points, made notes in the margins and a list of references to share with others, and given the book to others. It is easy to read, practical, encouraging, and full of possibilities! More importantly, the authors back up their points with research and shared stories of other military spouses who have been able to use the keys of happiness and make the most of this challenging yet enriching lifestyle."

That's when we decided, "We have to change the title. We don't want anyone missing out on this material just because of the title."

Why Purple on the Cover?

We chose the color purple because purple symbolizes "joint" in the military world, meaning "all services." In the world of color, if you combine Army green, Coast Guard blue, Air Force blue, Marine red, and Navy blue, you get purple.

Our material applies to all military spouses, both new to the military and the more seasoned. The search for authenticity, personal growth, meaning in life, and happiness cuts across all ranks, all services, both genders, and all ages.

Spouse Stories and Names

Throughout the book, we use a mix of first names and full names. Where we have permission to use a name, we use it. We know how excited we have been to see our names mentioned in books, and many of the spouses we interviewed said they wanted their full names used, too. In some cases, we share stories from the past where we use first names only because we didn't know we would need permission later, and we no longer know how to contact those individuals. For individuals who asked us not to use their names, we've made up a first name and changed other identifying information.

Male Spouses of Female Military Members

The information we share is helpful to all military spouses, male and female. However, we know full well that male spouses sometimes face different situations and challenges than female spouses. A few of the things we cover here will apply more specifically to wives. Over all these years of doing workshops, most of our audiences have been 100 percent women until more recently, so our stories and examples are mostly female. At the moment, 7.1 percent of military spouses are male.

The good news is that male spouses are becoming more visible and involved in the military spouse world. Many are writing about their unique trials and connecting with others.

Check out bloggers such as:

- Chris Pape, www.MachoSpouse.com
- Wayne Perry, www.Facebook.com/MANningtheHomefront
- Tim Blake, ArmySpouseAmI.blogspot.com

In 2012, Jeremy Hilton was the first male spouse to be selected as Armed Forces Insurance Military Spouse of the Year. We think you'll find more and more resources with the male spouse perspective in the future. And, by the way, if you are a male spouse and have stories to share, write us. We'd love to include them in our workshops and future books.

LGBT Partners

Our books and workshops until now fell under the Don't Ask Don't Tell time period in the military. That policy ended in 2011. Much of what we cover in this book applies to every spouse and partner. However, as we write this, LGBT partners don't yet have equal access to some of the military benefits and services we mention in the book. This is a legal distinction, but we expect that will change over time.

We want to be sure every partner is aware of and connected to The American Military Partner Association (AMPA), www.MilitaryPartners.org. Founded and led by same-sex military partners in 2009 as the Campaign for Military Partners, AMPA is leading the effort to support LGBT military families. This nonpartisan, nonprofit organization is committed to connecting LGBT military families, supporting them through the challenges of military service, honoring them for their commitment to our country, and serving them by advocating on their behalf.

Contact Us

Please don't think of this book as a one-time resource. Email or call or write us.

- Have a question we didn't answer here? We'll answer it or refer you to a resource. If it might apply to other military spouses, we'll do added research for you, too.
- Have a story or example to share? We might use it in future books, updates to this book, or in our workshops.
- Want to start a Dare to Dream Team and need ideas, help, or encouragement along the way? We love to brainstorm.
- Want us to present a workshop in your community? Check out our web site for current information, or contact us, and we'll send you an information packet for meeting planners.

Find us at www.MilitarySpouseJourney.com.

Introduction

Why We Wrote This Book

We've presented workshops for military spouses, of all services, for years. Because of that work, we speak with military spouses from all services, all over the globe. And, we also talk with civilians and civilian reporters. Here's a common question we get from civilian reporters: "Well, if you choose to marry into the military, you know what you are getting yourself into, right?"

Wrong! Our polite answer is, "No, most military spouses simply fell in love with someone in the military. We don't think there is any way to prepare someone for this life!"

What we feel like saying is:

Oh right...let's see, we set out thinking, "What kind of life would I like? I want a life where someone can move us at any time, with little notice, and we have no say in the matter—oh, and let's make that to some really godforsaken places just for fun.

...and oh yes, where they can send my spouse off for long periods of time, like for a year to Korea during peacetime, and I can't go—what's up with that?

...and into war, to dangerous places for a year or more...over and over and over!

...and oh yes, I wouldn't want that life to include much income, of course.

...and oh yes, where huge demands are placed on me because of my spouse's position, with no compensation and little thanks,

...and a life where I have to repeatedly give up everything—my friends, my church, my house, my garden, my job—that job that took me so long to find, to start all over again, not just once, but over and over and over again."

As one Navy spouse we interviewed said, "No one in their right mind would choose this life!"

But here's an interesting fact. When we interview spouses who've been married to the military for ten years or more, we ask, "Knowing what you know now about military life, would you do it again?" And the majority not only answer, "Yes!" but a very powerful, "Oh, yes!" Why? Because of so many things: the incredible life experience, personal growth, the chance to be part of something bigger than yourself, a close-knit community and deep friendships not so common everywhere else. The list goes on.

That is not usually the mindset of spouses new to the military, though. In fact, most military spouses don't even identify themselves as military spouses until they've been married to the military for five years. Before the five-year mark, spouses simply see themselves as being married and trying to fit their idea of married life into this added dimension of the military world, thinking it's going to be, it "should be," like marrying anyone.

Quite frankly, we first did the research that resulted in our workshop, and much later, this book, because of one simple fact. After our first few years of "honeymoon…everything's new and exciting" phase, we weren't happy with military life. Don't get us wrong. We love our husbands, we're proud of their service to our country, and we support that service…but we felt like we'd lost ourselves in the process. Think of it, your service member has a plan and a purpose. In fact, it's all spelled out for them—what assignments they need, what schooling and training they need, what to wear every day, for heaven's sake! We struggled with how we fit in, in a way that made sense to us based on who we are as unique individuals, not based on some outdated concept of "the perfect military spouse."

Consider this. If you are unhappy with military life, we figure you basically have four choices.

1.   You could get divorced. It is an option, but it wasn't one we wanted to entertain. We love our husbands and want to grow old with them. We realize divorce is the path some choose. Now, you know as well as we do, in some relationships a divorce makes sense, because it's a bad marriage, not because of the military. Sadly, some of the divorces that occur in the military happen because the spouse simply isn't happy and can't figure out how to make this life work.

2.   You could convince your spouse to get out of the military. But if your husband or wife is one of those whose dream is to serve in the military, who considers it a duty and honor to serve, who down to their toes believes in their service, do you really want to ask your spouse and best friend to give up their dream? Are you willing to live with the consequences?

3.   You could choose to do nothing. You could keep complaining and continue to be unhappy with the way things are. We know spouses who do

that. They are not the ones you want to be around. They make themselves miserable, their spouses and families miserable, and yes, they pull down many other folks around them with their complaining and negativity. They end up bitter and resentful after military life. You don't want to go that route. We complained for years before we chose to change.

4. You can change your attitude and approach. You can figure out how to make this life work for you, to see progress toward your dreams as well as your spouse's dreams. You can learn about and tap into the many resources available to you. As a couple, you need a joint plan, to figure out how

> *"When we are no longer able to change a situation, we are challenged to change ourselves."—Viktor Frankl*

to craft a life for both of you within this military lifestyle. It takes creative thinking and action, and yes, work. That's the route we chose to follow.

When we decided to make changes, we read a lot of research. We focused on research about what makes people happy in life, because isn't that what we all want? To be happy? Interestingly, there are thousands of studies on this subject. We pulled the key factors we saw in study after study.

It's not just happiness these factors impact. It's your sense of self, your sense of accomplishment, of mattering in the big picture. And, with added importance to us as military spouses, these key factors impact your resiliency, your well-being, your ability to deal with stress, and to handle change and challenges in life.

After pulling these factors from the research studies, we thought, "Well, that's great for normal people, but what about us?" Haven't you ever watched an *Oprah* show or read a self-help book and thought, "Well, that's great for you...you don't have to move all the time, your spouse isn't deployed..." It's true, as military spouses we deal with many life challenges that "normal" people never will. What works for us?

So we interviewed, and continue to interview, hundreds of spouses in all service branches to find out how they make this life work for them, how they carve out happiness and a sense of fulfillment within the challenges of military life. And that's what we share.

People often say, "When my spouse retires," or "When my spouse returns from deployment," or "When the kids are out of the house,"..."then it will be my turn."

You cannot give up on your dreams or wait twenty years or longer for your turn. We want you to live YOUR life NOW, not when. This life can be rich and abundant and full of possibilities. It takes an open attitude and a creative approach—along with good friends and lots of laughter!

The reality is: we do have extreme challenges as military spouses, and yes, we make sacrifices, as do our spouses. This is not an easy life! Our path can't be as straightforward as other people's paths might be. That's just the way it is. We have to accept that reality and move forward from there.

We want you to discover what is possible. We share strategies and stories of other military spouses who have managed to follow their own dreams as they move around, spouses who have rich, full lives now, not waiting for some future time.

Military spouses are all unique individuals. We may all have the military in common, but that's where our sameness stops. This is not a "one-size-fits-all life." There are many ways to live this military life. We each have different talents, interests, priorities, and lifestyle preferences. Some dive fully into military life on post/base, while others live their lives more connected to the civilian community. Some of us have wardrobes full of red, white, and blue with "Hooah!" or "Oorah!" pins to proclaim our military spouse status and patriotism; others feel just as patriotic and proud to be married to the military but express it in quieter ways. Our goal with this book is to provide tools for you to create your own unique life within this military life—to create and embrace your own journey.

Dive in!

Chapter 1

Our Journey

"Welcome to the adventure of life as a military spouse." We can just hear you sarcastically saying, "Ha! Yeah…right!" as you roll your eyes. That's certainly how we would have reacted to a statement like that early in our married lives.

We are the first to say that sometimes this lifestyle sucks. Yes, we sometimes get discouraged and entertain thoughts of what life would be like if we weren't married to the military. But, we've learned not to dwell on those thoughts when they hit.

Instead, we've learned to take steps and take action to live our lives to the fullest, despite military challenges. And, in the end, the result is richer than we could have imagined.

There ought to be a disclaimer when you marry someone in the military, spelling out the hardships you will face along the way. Of course, maybe it's better we don't know ahead of time.

Oh sure, many women know what this life entails, those who grew up with it perhaps, or who were in the military themselves.

However, if you were a military or civil service brat, and are now married to the military, wouldn't you agree there is a BIG difference between being a military child and being a military spouse? (Makes you want to call your mom to thank her, and tell her you didn't have a clue about all she managed to do, doesn't it?)

And if you are prior service and now married to the military, wouldn't you agree there is a BIG difference between being in the military and being married to the military? In many ways, despite the long hours and extreme challenges, wasn't it easier being in the military? Okay, maybe not easier, but with a clearer path and reward system built in?

Kathie's Story

I had experience with military life before I married into it, so you'd think I'd have known exactly what I was getting into and how to make it work. Wrong.

I grew up as a civil service brat in Germany and Virginia. I entered the Army myself right out of college. After three years on active duty, when my then-fiancé Greg and I were planning on marrying, we were told we'd be stationed in two different places. We decided we didn't want to start our marriage that way, so I left the service and became a "dependent" overnight. I'll never forget the first time I signed a check at Fort Rucker, Alabama, as a newlywed. The clerk asked me for "your last four." I gave her the last four of my Social Security number as I'd been doing for three years. "Well, that doesn't match what is on this check," she said. "Well, that's my husband's last four—you asked for mine." "Well," she said with a roll of her eyes and an exasperated voice, "Of course, I meant his last four." Suddenly, I'd lost my identity. I wasn't me anymore; I was a dependent. I obviously didn't count.

I struggled terribly with that dependent status. (And yes, that was our official designation back then…dependents.) I wanted respect and acknowledgment of me as an individual, not as a military wife. I wanted to be accepted as a person in my own right, not based on whom I was married to. I found it challenging to find decent jobs with each move. I didn't feel like I fit in as a "good military spouse," often feeling like a black sheep and outsider. I resented this life more and more.

Because I worked full time and traveled quite a bit on business, I couldn't be involved in Greg's units as much as other spouses were. (And yes, in many cases, I simply chose not to be. I admit to having a bit of an "I'm better than this" attitude that isolated me.)

We didn't have kids, so I didn't feel a part of most spouse conversations at unit functions. I found myself drawn to talk with the soldiers, sharing my own "war stories" about my military life—which, of course, didn't endear or connect me to the spouses. Because I wasn't involved, I didn't have friends when I went to those functions, something that made me feel even more alienated. To be quite honest, I dreaded going to unit functions.

During that time, I blamed my unhappiness on the military. I spent a lot of time complaining. Of course, the military is a bit hard to complain to, so guess whom I complained to? Actually, I complained to anyone who would listen to me, but my husband got the brunt.

See if this sounds familiar to you. I'd say things like, "If the military didn't move us so much, I'd be able to get that job I want." "If the military didn't move us so much, we could have a garden, but what's the use?" "If the military didn't move us so much, I could do what she's doing over there." I compared my life and myself with other people and came up short in my estimation. Greg used to say to me, "The grass is always greener elsewhere for you, isn't it?" It was. I wasted a lot of years wallowing in my negative attitudes about this life, rather than taking creative action to make changes.

I finally got it: the military wasn't going to change for me, or at least not as fast as I might want. I had to change. I needed to figure out how to make this life work for me—within the challenges of military life. I realized the blame didn't really fit totally on the military. I had to take some of the blame for lack of clarity on what I wanted and for my own lack of action. I had to take responsibility.

So I did a lot of research. I read self-help books, listened to tapes, and took a number of personal growth courses. I went for counseling. I learned things I could do to make changes to my life and started making those changes.

I can tell you, now I love my life, and I've been able to say that for a long time. The circumstances didn't change. I changed my attitude and my approach. It works.

Holly's Story

I met my husband, Jack, on a blind date when he was attending a military course in Washington, DC. I was working at Johns Hopkins Hospital in Baltimore, MD, and taking graduate courses at Johns Hopkins University. I considered myself intelligent and well educated, but I was totally ignorant about military life.

I fell head over heels in love with Jack. He was the smartest man I had ever met; his morals and ethics were impeccable. Fortunately, he fell head over heels for me, too, and asked me to marry him on our fourth date. Nine short months later, we were married.

I need to preface my story by saying, when I was dating Jack, he was attending a military school, and I only saw him on weekends. I had never seen his military uniform. I had zero experience with anything military. I was clueless. I didn't know when you marry someone in the military, it means you enter a new lifestyle. The military is not a job someone goes to forty to seventy hours a week. It is an entirely new lifestyle—a lifestyle I knew nothing about.

I want you to visualize Jack and me back from our honeymoon, living in a tiny duplex in Manhattan, Kansas, and it is my first morning as a military spouse far away from my former East Coast life. It was 4:00 a.m. and the alarm went off. Certainly, it was set for the wrong time, I thought. No, my husband jumped out of bed.

"What are you doing?" I asked.

"Getting ready for work," he said matter-of-factly.

"At 4:00 a.m.?" I gasped in disbelief. He proceeded to put on his camouflage uniform (BDUs, cammies, ACUs).

"Why are you wearing that jungle man outfit?" I asked curiously.

"This is what I wear everyday to work," he said seriously.

"You have got to be kidding! You wear a jungle man outfit to the office? No way!"

I started to laugh as he slipped on his combat boots and proceeded with the long process of tucking his pant legs into the boots and lacing the boots all the way up, and then so carefully tucking the ends of the laces into the boot. Who in the world wakes up at 4:00 a.m., unless you are a baker or early show TV personality? And certainly, no one would put on a jungle man outfit, carry a briefcase, and head to the office. Not only did he leave at the crack of dawn that morning, as he did every morning for years to come, he did not come home for dinner, and sometimes not at all, because he was working on a project or was off training or deployed for months on end.

I've always heard people are unhappy when their expectations do not meet reality. I admit I had expectations of what married life would be like.

This new reality was not even close to my expectations. Over the next few years, I grew unhappy with my life as a military spouse.

I was unhappy about the demands that were placed upon me because of my husband's position in his unit. I was unhappy the military could tell my husband to go somewhere without me for a year, and he had to go, sometimes to dangerous locations. (I understood this is what a soldier had to do, but that doesn't mean I was happy about it.) I was unhappy we had to move so often with no input or choice of where we would go next.

I knew I was responsible for my own happiness, and I could not expect my husband to be the source of my happiness. But I didn't know how to break this cycle of negativity, always blaming my unhappiness on everything and everybody else.

I was left with this thought: if people are unhappy when their expectations do not meet reality, they have to either change their expectations or change reality. I struggled with how I could change my expectations without feeling angry or bitter. That's when I met Kathie, and she shared what she had discovered to make this challenging lifestyle work. I began to make conscious choices and changes in my life, accepting responsibility for my choices. Lo and behold, my life started to change from just an okay life to a life full of joy and possibilities. I knew we had to share these discoveries with other military spouses. That's how the workshop and this book got started.

We write this book and present our workshops with the full understanding that we certainly do not have all the answers. Let us repeat that: We do not have all the answers. We constantly learn new things and grow in our own lives and delve into new research daily.

We write this book to share things we have learned over many years of research and interviewing other spouses—to share what we wish we had known earlier in our marriages. Think of this as a collection of ideas, possibilities, and resources to inspire you to create your own unique way of participating in this military life, to craft a life that truly works for you. It's not about how your life is wrong. It is about growing and learning and adding dimension.

Have fun with this military life and this process. Approach it all as an adventurous journey, and that's what you'll experience. Remember, this isn't a dress rehearsal. This is your journey, your life. Don't wait to start living it. Take charge now to create what works for you. Let's look at the research that can help.

Chapter 2

Five Keys to Happiness and What that Means to You

What the Research on Happiness Reveals About Your Life with the Military

Our workshop and this book are centrally based on research about what makes a person happy in life. Findings of the American Psychological Association's "Positive Psychology" movement, along with results of many other studies, point out keys to human happiness and a better quality of life. Happiness and well-being result from the fulfillment of cherished goals in valued areas of life, as well as from connectedness and positive relationships.

You can apply that research to your life with the military. We don't share this information because it happened to work for us. This is information backed up by research. That means it can work for you, too.

Don't get us wrong. As we mentioned in the previous chapter, we are not approaching this life with a Pollyanna attitude, nor do we think by any stretch of imagination that military life is always a magical fun journey. Absolutely not! Especially in the midst of war.

There is no doubt you will probably experience more stressful, life-changing events during the years you are a military spouse than most Americans experience in their entire lifetime.

FACT—Many aspects of military life are difficult. You choose how to deal with the challenges. You can either get sucked into the negativity that can surround this lifestyle, or you can choose to apply the principles from the happiness research and learn what other military spouses have discovered works to enhance your life experience. The bottom line is, YOU make the choice.

Key findings from the happiness research point out how greatly the following five areas impact your happiness and your overall quality of life. We'll discuss each in brief here; and in later chapters, we'll expand on each one to show you how you can make changes in each area to increase your own quality of life. There are other factors that impact your happiness, such as physical health, finances, and laughter. As you'll see, many of those come into play within these five.

- Action Toward What You Want
- Support—Relationships
- Faith, Hope, and Gratitude
- Simple Joys
- Strengths Used in Service

What if I'm a Pessimist?

When we first shared information about happiness in our workshops, people would say, "Isn't it simply genetic to a great degree? Aren't some people just plain happier, more easygoing, than others?" Simply look around at your friends and family, and you'll probably agree with this concept. It's true. We see it with the two of us. Holly is an optimistic, cheerful, playful, "glass is half full" kind of person, and always has been. Kathie comes from a pessimistic family, tending toward a negative, anxious, catastrophizing, "glass is half empty" approach to life.

When Kathie talks about her pessimistic background in our workshops, she says, "Of course, Mom always said to me, 'Kathie, we aren't pessimists, we are...'" She opens her hands to the audience at that point without completing the sentence, and a chorus of "REALISTS!" comes back at us. "See, many of you come from the same kind of family as me," she continues. "When something bad happens to us pessimists, we focus on the bad, we wallow in the negative. It's almost like we prize it in some way. But here's the true test of a pessimist. When something good happens to us, we will find the bad within it and point it out to you first thing." Heads nod in agreement.

Studies from the University of Minnesota conclude that 50 percent of one's satisfaction with life comes from genetic programming. Genes *influence such traits as having an easygoing personality, your ability to deal with stress, and whether you experience low or high levels of anxiety and depression (Lykken and Tellegen, 1996). Circumstantial factors such as income, marital status, religion, and education contribute about 8 percent to one's overall well-being. The remaining 42 percent can be influenced by your own thoughts and actions, your choice of focus, your attitude.*

So what our book and workshop go after is that 42 percent—the area you can make conscious choices to change.

The interesting thing is, as Kathie can attest, when you are aware of what you are doing as a pessimist, you can take steps to buffer that genetic impact. You can read positive books, surround yourself with positive signs and people, and listen regularly to self-hypnosis recordings that keep you centered in positive thinking. You can actually change your genetic programming to some degree. And, hey, when you put that pessimistic streak to work by always having a Plan B and Plan C ready, that's not such a bad thing!

Happiness Key: Know What You Want and Take Action to Achieve It

The happiest people know what they want their lives to be like, they have a vision for their lives overall, and they work to achieve that vision in some manner. What's really interesting about this aspect of happiness is that it's not achieving your big dream that brings the happiness.

What brings you joy is that you identify what you want in line with your values, and you take action to get it. You take control of and responsibility for your own destiny, instead of simply letting things happen to you. Rather than staying stuck, waiting for some future event or timing, waiting for "someday," waiting for deployment to be over, waiting for your spouse's retirement, or waiting for someone else to do something, you enjoy a real sense of your authentic unique self actively engaged in life. That's what brings the joy. It's the process itself, embracing the journey, engaging in life.

Understanding this concept and acting on it was the big turning point for us when we started our searches for a different life within this military lifestyle. Until that point, we had been letting life happen, not making conscious choices and not taking responsibility to change things that weren't working. We both used the military and those constant deployments and moves as the excuse for not pursuing what we really wanted in life.

People accepted that excuse. So did we. But when we looked at it more objectively, we each realized there were many military spouses doing what we said we wanted to do—and many of those spouses had bigger challenges than we did.

That's when we started to make conscious choices, set goals, and take action. We took responsibility, finding ways around all these obstacles we had allowed to stop us. We opened ourselves up to possibility thinking and abundance thinking rather than wallowing in impossibility and lack.

From Kathie's Journal

I gain a lot of life's lessons from fiction. One line in a very funny novel by Shannon Olson, titled Children of God Go Bowling, *really hit home to me. "I had not been going out to figure out what I wanted, I had only been complaining about what showed up." I realized that is what I'd been doing: complaining about the military and my current circumstances, rather than really figuring out what I wanted and taking action to move toward it. Once I made that shift, my life changed.*

Happiness Key: Seek Out Friends and Support

Ask any military spouse who has been through a deployment or other challenge of military life, "What helped you get through that time?" and you will probably hear the answer, "My friends." Spouses who have the hardest time with military life are those isolated by circumstances or who choose to isolate themselves.

Relationships are key to our happiness in life, during deployments and otherwise. A study conducted at University of Illinois (Diener and Seligman, 2002) found the most common characteristic shared by those who have the highest levels of happiness and the fewest signs of depression are those who have strong ties to friends and family and a commitment to spending time with them. All the research we found concluded the happiest people are those who have strong relationships and strong positive support structures. That can be your spouse, your family, your friends, a church group, your Bunco group, or other kinds of groups. Because of the importance of this, we'll look at how to make friends and stay connected with friends and family as you move with the military, along with ways to strengthen your relationship with your spouse.

Happiness Key: Faith, Hope, and Gratitude

Faith, hope, and gratitude are essential to your overall sense of happiness in life. Our interviews with military spouses, as well as the research on happiness, indicate that a belief in something greater than yourself provides a sense of hope that is key to overcoming challenges in life. Note: The research does not point to any specific religion—the focus is on having a belief in something greater than ourselves. This is the key factor that gives people a sense of hope, optimism, and purpose.

Individuals who have a strong faith, who allow themselves to get quiet and go within on a regular basis, find they touch a center of calm that helps carry them through the stormy times. We've talked to many military spouses who say their faith deepened during deployments and other challenges of military life. We'll look at ways military spouses access stillness. We'll share the findings from the research studies that look at the correlation between people of faith and their level of life satisfaction. We'll also consider the importance of gratitude in our daily lives as well as during times of challenge. Taking time to switch our focus to what we are grateful for can make a difference in how we experience and approach life.

Happiness Key: Discover Simple Joys

Our experience of happiness in life to a great degree is made up of simple daily joys. It's a matter of learning to "be in the moment" enough to enjoy simple pleasures as they occur. Many of us have a lot of joy in our lives, but often are racing right by what is good as we move right on to the next task, to the next item on our daily to-do list. We can greatly improve our overall quality of life—and our energy—by taking time to participate in and appreciate simple joys. We'll look at how you can do that in your life along with other ways to increase your daily energy and decrease your stress, especially when you don't think you have time.

Happiness Key: Work from Your Strengths to Serve a Greater Good

The research suggests and our experience, as well as interviews with many military spouses, confirms the greatest high in life comes from using your strengths to serve a greater good. There really is such a thing as a "helper's high" similar to the "runner's high," where the release of endorphins, the feel-good brain chemicals, increases our experience of happiness. The most lasting experience of happiness occurs from using our strengths in service to others. That can be one on one with a child, with coworkers in the workplace, in a volunteer situation, or with a stranger on the street. We will share ideas for how you can identify your strengths.

Apply the Keys to Your Own Life

Throughout the rest of the book, we'll look at these five key factors in greater detail for how you can apply this knowledge to your own life as you move and grow with the military. You'll also learn about important resources, some of which are specific and unique to military spouses.

Let's start with the happiness factor, where military spouses get stuck the most: knowing what you want and taking action toward it. Here's what we've discovered. When military spouses get stuck (as we both did), it's because of one or both of two realities:

1. You haven't taken the time or done the work to really figure out how you want your life to be, what you want out of life, what activities matter most to you, who you really are, and your true priorities.

2. You know what you want, but you don't think it's possible, either because of where you are stationed right now, or because of military life in general. You simply don't know how to move forward.

We start with this factor because it's so essential to your overall well-being. In-depth studies from the Gallup Association, reported on in the book *Wellbeing: The Five Essential Elements* by Tom Rath and Jim Harter, suggest this is the most essential: "If you don't have the opportunity to regularly do something you enjoy —even if it's more of a passion or interest than something you get paid to do—the odds of your having high well-being in other areas diminish rapidly."

We want to help you figure out what you want and find a way to move toward that vision right now, wherever you are stationed. Let's go!

Resources

Authentic Happiness: Using the New Positive Psychology to Realize Your Potential for Lasting Fulfillment by Martin E. P. Seligman, PhD (2004).

Creating Your Best Life: The Ultimate Life List Guide by Caroline Adams Miller, MAPP, and Michael B. Frisch, PhD (2011).

Flourish: A Visionary New Understanding of Happiness and Well-being by Martin E. P. Seligman, PhD (2012).

"Happiness is a Stochastic Phenomenon." *Psychological Science*, 7 (3), 186-189, by David T. Lykken and Auke Tellegen (1996).

14,000 Things to Be Happy About by Barbara Ann Kipfer (1990).

How Full is Your Bucket? Positive Strategies for Work and Life by Tom Rath and Donald O. Clifton, PhD (2004).

The How of Happiness: A New Approach to Getting the Life You Want by Sonja Lyubomirsky (2008).

Simple Abundance: A Daybook of Comfort and Joy by Sarah Ban Breathnach (2009).

StrengthsFinder 2.0 by Tom Rath (2007).

Quality of Life Therapy: Applying a Life Satisfaction Approach to Positive Psychology and Cognitive Therapy by Michael B. Frisch (2006). Note: this is an academic volume.

"Very happy people." *Psychological Science*, 13 (1), 81-84, by Edward Diener and Martin E.P. Seligman (2002).

Wellbeing: The Five Essential Elements by Tom Rath and Jim Harter (2010).

What Happy People Know: How the New Science of Happiness Can Change Your Life for the Better by Dan Baker, PhD, and Cameron Stauth (2004).

Chapter 3

Know What You Want and Take Action Toward It

The happiest people know what they want their lives to be like, they have a vision for their lives overall, and they work to achieve that vision in some manner. What's really interesting about this aspect of happiness is that it's not achieving your big dream that brings the happiness. What brings you joy is that you identify what you want in line with your values, and you take action to get it. It's the process itself, engaging in life!

So what do you want? What feeds your soul? Shouldn't that be easy to figure out? Shouldn't we naturally know what we want? Actually, it's not easy for most of us. As Oprah says, "Have the courage to follow your passion—and if you don't know what it is, realize that one reason for your existence on earth is to find it…Your life's work is to find your life's work—and then to exercise the discipline, tenacity, and hard work it takes to pursue it."

Do that, and you'll live in what psychologist Mihaly Csikszentmihalyi calls "flow." Flow is the enjoyment you experience when you do something that stretches you beyond where you were before—in an athletic event, an artistic performance, a good deed, a stimulating conversation, a learning situation. Flow leads to personal growth and long-term happiness. Flow doesn't happen sitting passively watching television or complaining about your circumstances. Flow takes action on your part.

We used to think we each had only one mission in life, and we needed to figure out that one thing. That's a bit scary. The more we talk to people, read, and experience life, we think passions change as life changes, as you get out and have new experiences and discover new things. It's important you find interests to get excited about during each stage of life.

Before we dive into your dreams and your purpose in life, we want to address two key concepts: whole-istic dreams and gratitude.

Develop Whole-istic Dreams

When we talk about following your dreams, we mean holistic dreams, or maybe we should call it "whole-istic" dreams. Consider all aspects of your life. Ask yourself: "How do I want my life as a whole to be?"

As Gregg Levoy, author of *Callings: Finding and Following an Authentic Life*, says, "Dreams are more interested in the design and quality of our lives than in making us rich and famous."

Why have a whole-istic approach? We've seen too many people (ourselves both included, at times) who focus on one dream. That might be a career dream, an education dream, maybe even a parenting dream. If you focus too narrowly on one area of your life—if you spend all of your time, energy, and attention on that one area to the total exclusion of others—you might achieve that one dream, but at what cost?

Everyone knows an individual who has done that, or who is doing that:

- Military members who devote every living minute and all their attention to their military career, constantly shorting family, friends, and themselves. Mind you, there are times they have no choice but to do that, such as during war and deployments and certain high-stress positions. We're talking of the ones who never manage to turn off that ramped-up, crisis-management mode, even when they are in a peacetime assignment or on vacation. Many carry that same nonstop, 24/7 work pattern into the civilian workforce after military life. Unfortunately, our military culture does a lot to promote that thinking. It takes conscious choice, and often tapping into resources like counseling, to fight that trend.

- Military spouses who get so caught up in a volunteer position that their family, spouse, and sometimes even their health suffer. Volunteering is a wonderful thing, and the military community benefits greatly from our many volunteers. But, it's not a good thing when it negatively affects your family and your health.

- Parents who can't make any time for their spouses, their friends, or themselves. Certainly, you make sacrifices in life for your children. But focusing all your time, energy, and attention solely on your children isn't good for you—or for them.

If you are like Kathie, a recovering workaholic and perfectionist, you might recognize this syndrome in yourself. At different times in Kathie's life, she managed to focus solely on one area—in her case, her career. At times, that career wasn't even her dream. When she did start working on her dream business, her single-minded, workaholic tendencies crept right back in. There's a danger in this. Unless your dream is something that can fully sustain you in all areas forever, you cut off other important aspects of life.

Another reason the whole-istic approach is so important is this. Say your career is everything to you. Then the military moves you to a place where you really can't pursue that particular career. If all you have is your career—if your whole sense of self is dependent on that position—you will be miserable for that assignment. But if you have whole-istic dreams, you can welcome that location as an opportunity to put your time and energy into another interest, another facet of your life. Over the long haul, this approach helps you create a richer, fuller life.

In fact, research shows that if one area of your life is not working well and is difficult for you to change, you can improve your overall quality of life—your happiness—by making improvements in other areas of your life.

In a whole-istic life dream, consider: health and physical fitness, self-esteem, finances, work, play, learning, creativity, helping, love, friends, children, relatives, home, spiritual life, neighborhood, community.

Live in Gratitude

The second important concept is to start out fully aware of your current abundance. Identify and be grateful for what you already have in your life. We know people who are so focused on future dreams and goals, they never stop to appreciate the joys staring them in the face. If you focus only on what's missing, your life becomes negative and narrow. You fall into poverty thinking—that "glass is half empty" thinking. Poverty thinking will not help you move toward any dream. Start out with gratitude instead. You'll quickly find yourself wallowing in abundance. That's a much better place to start from, when you go for your dreams.

What do you want to take action on? What's important to you? Get ready for some self-exploration exercises. It can be amazing to look back on these exercises later in life to see how much of what you dream about comes true.

Note: Just reading the exercises and not doing them isn't going to get you where you want to go! Write in the margins or get a journal to use for the exercises, and jot down thoughts as you read through the book.

Remember, we can't emphasize this enough: The research on happiness shows your overall satisfaction in life comes from identifying what you want and working toward it in some manner. Reaching your vision is not the definitive answer to overall happiness in life. It's the fact that you have figured out what you want, and you are taking action, even baby steps if need be, no matter where you are located, or what your circumstances. Happiness comes from engaging in life.

At a workshop, we heard a story that demonstrates this concept in action. As we set up our resource and props table for our workshop at Cannon Air Force Base in New Mexico, it was still early. The program manager and the club personnel were the only other people in the room. Just then, a young spouse walked in, glanced around, and headed over to Kathie.

"Are you one of the authors?" she asked. When Kathie answered yes, the young woman exuberantly put her arms around Kathie in a hug, saying, "Thank you for changing my life." We wish we could start every workshop that way. Talk about making our day.

Aneta Rude's story is unique and universal. Much of what she did illustrates many of the lessons we've learned and share in this book. Her story shows the importance of figuring out who you are and what you want, the key skill of possibility thinking, and the important concept of second and third right answers, all ideas we'll cover in depth.

"When I met my husband, I was a theatre major at a local university," she told us. "After our first PCS, I changed my major to psychology, thinking it would be easier than theatre to find academic programs, and later to find jobs as we moved. I was six months away from getting my degree, but realizing more and more it wasn't the career for me, and I was feeling hopeless and bitter. Then I stumbled on your book at the base library. Quite frankly, at first I thought your ideas could only work for spouses who were pursuing certain types of dreams, but couldn't possibly work for my dream. I decided to follow your method just to prove it wouldn't work for me."

Aneta sat down with the life exploration exercises and decided she really did want to be a high school theatre/drama teacher, not a psychologist. She opened herself up to possibilities along those lines. Many of the options she pursued were indeed not possible where they were stationed in England, but others were.

She connected with the base theatre troupe, found theatre classes at a local university, got herself and her children involved in children's theatre at a neighboring base. When they transferred to New Mexico and no theatre classes were available, she started on the education part of her dream, finding an online program that would give her a master's degree in education. During her observation hours with a local school, she was offered the chance to teach an acting class.

The last we heard from Aneta, she completed her master's in education degree and is teaching theatre at the local high school. During the summer months, she provides a theatre camp for children and teens through the local community college. "I fully believe this all came about because of your book," Aneta told us. "You showed me I didn't have to have my whole dream immediately, but I didn't have to wait on it, either. By finding little ways to put theatre back in my life with each move, I have an increased drive and purpose, and I am a much happier person. Thanks for the ideas and hope you give to those of us who sometimes feel trapped by our circumstances."

Aneta discovered what we did and what the research on happiness confirms. It's the journey that matters. It's being engaged in what you want to do in some manner, taking steps, taking action. It's looking at possibilities that do exist rather than focusing on what doesn't exist where you are.

Here's what many of us do. We have some idea of what we want and we have our one plan of action to get there. When that plan does not work because of where we are stationed, or because of constant moves and deployments, we give up. We have an "all or nothing" mentality. If we can't have it all right now, we do nothing. We get angry and bitter. We start to think we are sacrificing too much being married to the military.

However, the reality is rather than give up because your one plan doesn't work, you can open yourself to other plans, other approaches. That often means getting others to brainstorm with you to get past your own limited thinking and knowledge. We firmly believe no matter where you are, there is something you can do to move forward. And it's that movement, that engagement, that brings you joy. Even if you can only take baby steps because of your current situation, you don't give up on what you want.

The experiences of other military spouses support this positive, proactive approach to military life. Here's what other military spouses have to say.

"This life is not easy, but I wouldn't trade it for anything," says Tara Crooks, an Army spouse who has survived her husband deploying multiple times, giving birth to their second child during one of those deployments. "It is so rewarding to see spouses go from frustrated to empowered with the simple help of a battle buddy—someone who has been there, done that."

In an interview on *Navy Wife Talk Radio*, Navy wife Sarah Smiley, author of *Going Overboard: The Misadventures of a Military Wife*, said, "I was miserable during my husband's first two deployments, because I didn't have anything for myself. I was just waiting around for a call or an email. Later deployments were still hard, but I had my work to keep me occupied."

> *"When one door of happiness closes, another opens; but often we look so long at the closed door that we do not see the one which has been opened for us."—Helen Keller*

Angie was brand new to active Army life and had just arrived in Baumholder, Germany, with her husband, three children, and a brand new baby. A week later, her husband deployed. She was miserable the whole time he was gone, hanging out with other unhappy wives, complaining about life, gossiping, and generally stuck in negativity.

"I realize now, the reason I was so unhappy there was because I didn't have any dream or purpose of my own," Angie says. "Now I do." At the time, Angie was graduating from the Gene Juarez Academy nail school, going for advanced training and a guaranteed job at their Tacoma salon. "I have bigger dreams of owning my own day spa," she adds. "I've got my husband thinking of the future, too, so we are saving to buy property some day."

Amy J. Fetzer is a Marine spouse, mother of three children, and author of more than thirty novels and novellas. She's been involved with the military community, moved many times, lived overseas, and still managed to carve out something for herself. "The best way to have a happy life with the military is to have something you do for yourself," says Amy. "Establishing yourself and your work as an individual in an armed service, where individuality isn't the norm, means not just being a wife or mother. I was each of those things, still am, but I was always a writer, too. It gave me the separation as a person that I needed to be happy with who I was." When you have something for yourself, she adds, those times alone won't seem so lonely.

The key is to carve out pieces of your dream as you move with the military—and to fight for those pieces. That way, you'll be ready to grow them even further when you do stop moving. Do something that feeds your soul, starting now!

There are other important reasons to have something you do for yourself (just in case happiness and well-being aren't enough).

- It gives you an easy way to immediately connect with like-minded people as you move with the military, and after you leave military life.
- Having a passion for something in life, having a sense of your true self, has been shown to increase your self-esteem.
- As you move toward your dreams, you'll step out of your comfort zone, to try out and take on new things. That's the path to personal growth.
- It makes the alone times not so lonely. Many spouses told us it was that interest—whether it was a job they loved or a hobby, like scrapbooking or quilting, or a community project they were intensely involved in—that helped them through deployment. As one woman said, "It saved my sanity. For at least a few hours each day, I could manage to forget about Iraq. It kept the constant anxiety at bay."
- And, you might not be thinking of this now, but it makes the transition from military to civilian life easier, as you continue to develop and grow your passions in new and different ways.

In the next chapters, we'll share ways to clarify your dreams, to create a vision for your life, so you can then take steps to move toward what you want. First, let's point out some mindsets that are important to avoid.

Dump the "Shoulds" and Comparisons

As you create your vision of your life, here are two things best left out: shoulds and comparisons.

When Kathie first wrote a column for *Army Times*, one reader's letter stopped her short: "A year and a half ago, when I wanted to take a job, my husband casually mentioned it at work. His buddies said he shouldn't let me, because he works and goes to the field and busts his butt all day long, and why shouldn't he come home to a clean house and dinner on the table? It didn't stop there. For the next two weeks, practically every wife I knew was calling or stopping by to tell me how unfair it would be to my husband and children."

Kathie was reminded of an assertiveness training workshop she once took with a mix of military spouses and civilian employees in Germany. As they went around the room, explaining why they were there, one Army spouse said she was choosing to stay home with her kids rather than continue the career she had before marrying into the military. "I know it is the right choice for me. I just want to become more assertive in answering the question, 'What do you do?" and in dealing with the perception I'm a lesser person because I choose not to work outside the home right now."

> *"One of the most important questions you can ask yourself: Have I defined what success means to me, or am I working my butt off based on someone else's definition?" —Oprah*

The point isn't whether or not we should work, or go to school, or stay home with our kids. It isn't whether we should volunteer in our military community, or get involved with our church or civilian community. It isn't whether we should decorate our front door with each new season or create the perfect lawn. The point is, whatever we choose to do should be our own choice based on our needs and interests and situations. Our choice should be made based on discussions within our own family, not on "shoulds" we hear from other military spouses, from our military culture, or from society at large.

Here's the reality. We get a lot of "shoulds" thrown at us in life. First, our parents have ideas of who we should be, and how we should dress, and how we should act. Then our peers head us in different directions. Then our spouse has ideas for us. Even our kids, especially our teenagers, have ideas of how we should dress and act, and what we should say or not say. On top of all that, we have society's expectations—or at least how we interpret society's expectations. Finally, add the military community's expectations. Although things are changing in this military world, there are still many spoken and unspoken expectations of military spouses.

Here's the problem. When we have layers of shoulds thrust on us, it's often tough to sift through and answer the questions, "What are my priorities? What do I value? How do I want to live my life? Who is the real me?" Sometimes we think we want something and then realize we really don't want it at all. We just thought we did, because everyone else said we "should" want it. So, it's not an easy thing to do, ignoring the shoulds, but it's crucial. Learn to claim your own authenticity.

Holly's Story

I arrived in Germany pregnant with twins. No sooner did I come home from the hospital with our twins than my husband's unit deployed for a ten-month mine-clearing mission. Yes, we all know deployments are a possibility, but when they happen, we think "Why now—why us?" We had tried for twelve years to get pregnant. Finally, we have twins, and my husband is leaving! To top it off, one of the twins, Jack, was the classic nightmare baby, never sleeping more than forty-five to fifty minutes at a time, and screaming all the time. The poor darling had horrible reflux, and I literally wore a raincoat every time I fed him, because half of what I fed him landed all over me. The only way I could comfort him (and me) was to wear him in a sling for the first nine months. My other baby, Helen, was considered by my friends as a "high needs" baby. If Helen was a high-needs baby, Jack was an "insatiable needs" baby. I would go days without sleep. I felt so alone, even though I had other wonderful military spouses around me, willing to help. (It took me time to learn to accept help.)

How could I feel so alone with so much support around me? I didn't look at it as support—I saw all these other mothers, whose husbands were deployed, handling life much better than I was. I felt I should be able to handle things better than I was. I felt I should be able to take my new parenting role in stride like so many others seem to. I felt I should be able to help other spouses from the unit deal with the deployment challenges. I felt I should be able to keep my house clean. I should at least be able to comb my hair AND brush my teeth in the same day. I felt I should get regular letters and care packages off to my husband, like so many other spouses were doing. I was should-ing all over myself—no wonder I felt so down.

If you find yourself doing what Holly did, stop right now! Say these words out loud. "I am doing the best I can right now under the circumstances I am in, and I am proud of myself."

What you want to do is stop the negative thoughts that are beating you up. There is enough negativity in the world to beat us up. You certainly do not need to be your own worst enemy. During times of stress, you need as many allies surrounding you as possible. No better place to start than with yourself. Our should-ing problem doesn't take place only during deployments. We need to be aware of our self-talk every day.

Define your own vision of life, not someone else's vision for you. Leave out the shoulds!

Adopt an "As Is" Philosophy

There's a related challenge we all face. Many of us waste a lot of time and energy comparing ourselves to other people and coming up short in our own estimation.

We have noticed that most of us do not simply compare ourselves to one other individual. That might actually be realistic. No, we tend to do things just a little bit bigger than that. Here's what many of us do.

We look at one person and think, "She has her career all figured out. She knows what she wants and is taking steps and moving forward. I can't even find a job, and I feel stuck." And then we beat ourselves up. Then we look at another person and think, "What a great parent, doing all these fun, artistic, creative things with her kids. I have a hard time just doing the basics." And then we beat ourselves up. Then we look at someone else and think, "He is in such great shape, running regularly and working out with weights three times a week. I hardly do any exercise at all." And then we beat ourselves up. Then we look at someone totally different and think, "That house is so organized and spotless. They can even get their car in the garage. I don't even make my bed unless I know company is coming, and our car will never see the inside of our garage." And then we beat ourselves up.

Isn't that what we do? That is not one other person; those are four or five or more other people we are idealizing for comparison. We are comparing ourselves to a myth—to a super person—a creature that doesn't even exist. Of course we come up short! Then we wonder why we feel like failures. We wonder why we feel overloaded with all the things we feel we still have to do.

Here's the reality. Military spouses are incredible! But when we spend time comparing ourselves to others and trying to live up to everyone else's expectations, we often lose ourselves in the process—we lose our power and our true sense of self.

We end up trying to pretend to be someone we aren't. That's an impossible pretense to keep up over the long haul. A great passage in Rita Mae Brown's novel *Venus Envy* reads, "The trouble with conforming is that everyone likes you, except you." It's time we stop doing that. Let's adopt a different philosophy. The philosophy of "As Is."

Our favorite piece of jewelry is a pewter pin that says "As Is." Kathie's been wearing one for many years. Here's the interesting thing. Most people come up to her when they see that and say, "As is—I love that—great concept." Others come up and look confused. They sometimes ask hesitantly, "So who's ASIS (rhyming with basis)?"

Kathie readily admits she isn't quick on her feet. The first few times that happened, she went through a long convoluted explanation of what "As Is" means, about being accepted as is, faults and all. But now she's prepared. Whenever anyone says, "Who's ASIS?" she immediately replies, "Oh, ASIS is the Egyptian goddess of reality, and I'm one of her disciples. I believe in her philosophy, and I'm spreading that philosophy."

The artist who created that pin is Lena Guyot. She includes a card with each pin that explains her own concept of As Is. She gave us permission to include that here.

"As Is—On the journey of the self, there comes a time when we make peace with who we are, respecting our strengths and accepting our weaknesses. We cease to sit in judgment on ourselves or others and get on with life. 'As Is' is a proud declaration to the world and a reminder to ourselves that we are already quite wonderful, just the way we are." ©1994 Lena Guyot

Here's our interpretation:

As Is. Flaws and all. Take me or leave me—as is. Accept me despite my weaknesses. I'm great just as I am. I might be working toward my goals to make changes in things I'm not thrilled about. There is the conscious choice factor there. But I don't beat myself up over those things. I accept them lovingly as I work to make changes. Some of my weaknesses I simply accept and stop trying to change. I realize they aren't weaknesses at all—they are just areas that aren't my particular strong suits.

Our greatest happiness comes from using our strengths in life, applying those strengths for the greater good. That's a much better idea than focusing on our weaknesses.

Live from who you are, not from shoulds and comparisons. Authenticity is correlated to many aspects of psychological well-being, including vitality, self-esteem, and coping skills. Acting in accordance with one's core self, a trait called self-determination, is ranked by some experts as one of three basic psychological needs, along with competence, and a sense of relatedness.

As we step into this military world, we all want to find ways to maintain our sense of self as we connect with others and grow important skills.

The Myth of the Perfect Military Spouse

Ask any spouse who's been married to the military what preconceived notions they had about the typical military spouse or possibly the "good military spouse," and you'll often hear the myth.

The mythical creature described is a wife, has two children, and doesn't work outside the home; or if she does, she cheerfully puts her spouse's career first. She keeps a perfect house with seasonal decorations on the door, moves and settles into new quarters with curtains up in three weeks flat, easily keeps things running at home during deployments, and makes all food from scratch for unit gatherings.

How many of those mythical creatures do you know? In our many years of being married to the military, we can't say we've even met one, but the myth persists.

One thing that perpetuates this myth is the number of spouses, ourselves included, who try to fit themselves into some aspect of this myth, at least at first. We've both spent time trying to dress "right," fix our houses "right," entertain "right," say the "right" things. We tried to live up to everything we kept hearing in this military world. We often felt like we were black sheep who just didn't fit in. We beat ourselves up, comparing our less-than-stellar lives to this mythical ideal. It's certainly not a healthy way to go about your life.

The strength of the military community comes from the wide variety and diversity of its members. It's important to live from the place of your own authenticity and uniqueness rather than trying to fit yourself into some mold that isn't you. Besides, that myth developed in our military world many years ago, in a different society. That myth developed before most spouses pursued careers, before more women entered the military in larger numbers, before Don't Ask, Don't Tell was repealed. Our military world has changed. That mythical ideal is a very outdated myth!

We aren't saying, "Ignore all conventions!" Don't confuse authenticity with a license to blatantly disregard or disrespect common courtesies. You will encounter many formal occasions during your military life. Remember, we have already mentioned that military life is a lifestyle, not a job. We encourage you to find out about the military lifestyle by understanding military traditions. Ask questions and talk with your spouse and others. The formal occasions you are invited to are tied to long military traditions, traditions that feed into the pride and *esprit de corps* of the military. By learning more about the traditions in this lifestyle, you become more comfortable at formal functions and enjoy being part of tradition. Be your authentic self. But don't be stupid. A Change of Command ceremony for your spouse's unit is not the time to show off your new bellybutton ring by wearing short shorts and a halter top. You can show your own authenticity and still be appropriate to the occasion.

What about that mythical creature who shows up during deployments? Back-to-back-to-back deployments have raised the mythical creature again. Here's what we hear, and often what we read about in news articles and see in television interviews: "Military spouses are strong, self-reliant, courageous, independent…"—the descriptive list goes on. We are the first to stand up and say military spouses are amazing human beings who manage to handle more than most people will ever be asked to do. However, the key words are: human beings. Human beings get lonely, depressed, scared, and burned out during different times in their lives, especially during multiple deployments. That is reality.

One of the biggest responses to a topic on Military.com forums was to one titled "confessions." The moderator started with her own and added, "We won't judge you."

"I confess that in my husband's absence, I've been depressed and lazy. I confess that I don't do the very things that he didn't do and I nagged him for. Like, I don't put my dirty clothes in the hamper all the time. I don't make the bed. I confess I don't shower every day. I don't shave, either—who's going to see my legs?"

She struck a chord. More than 3,000 responses poured in.

- "I confess I've eaten an entire bag of popcorn for dinner on many occasions."
- "I confess I watch way too much TV and haven't set out to accomplish any of my goals for this deployment (i.e., lose weight, learn to sew, read more)."
- "I confess I have been lazy, and if it weren't for me having to get up and go to work I would probably never get out of bed."
- "I confess that I cry every night when I am alone in bed."
- "I confess that my son is getting himself ready for school in the mornings, and I get up in time to make his lunch and drive him to school in my pajamas and slippers."

It helps to know you aren't the only one who slips into this behavior during a deployment. It's not uncommon.

We've both been there. Holly remembers days when she really didn't manage to do more than brush her teeth. If she were able to brush her teeth AND comb her hair in the same day, it was indeed a wonderful day. Kathie can remember making little agreements with herself, such as, "Today, I'll finally leave the house and go to the store," but then she'd break that agreement, hiding out in the house and staying up way too late night after night watching videos or reading. Why shower when you can live in sweats with your hair pulled back and a baseball cap on your head? Why clean the house if you don't plan to have anyone visit?

We don't agree with people who criticize others for these actions and say, "Just snap out of it," or who put on a "better than thou" attitude because they are handling the deployment so much better. Deployments are difficult, period.

What happens, however, is that the longer you let the negative actions (or really, inactions) go on, the harder it is to break the inertia and get yourself showered, dressed, and out of the house. But getting up and going is essential to your energy and your sanity. It's important to be aware of that.

The only one who can make changes in your life is you. As one spouse added to the confessions, "I confess I have never felt so negative before. I confess I need to kick myself in the butt and get a move on!" She's right.

Sometimes we do need someone to kick us into action every now and then—to remind us to get out there and start living again—even in the midst of a deployment. The things we share in this book are exactly the things you can do to start making changes in your life and start living again. If you feel stuck, we hope this book will be what you need to pull up your bootstraps and get out there and start living your life. Engaging in life is key to your happiness, and you don't have to be a mythical creature to do so.

So, let's look at how you can identify what you want, and then, how to take steps to move toward that dream.

Key Points and Action Steps

> ▷ Think about all aspects of your life to create your whole-istic dream.
> ▷ Dump the shoulds and comparisons.
> ▷ Accept an As Is philosophy.
> ▷ Get yourself up and going!

Resources

Callings: Finding and Following an Authentic Life by Gregg Levoy (1998).

Chapter 4

Explore Who You Are and What You Are Passionate About

An Exercise to Help You Figure Out Your Priorities, Strengths, and a Vision for Your Life

A great starting point to figure out what you want, what your passions are, where your purpose lies, is the Ideal Life exercise. It's a chance to dream about many aspects of your life and what you ideally want.

Kathie's Story

I first did this exercise when I took a personal growth seminar offered by the Women's Resource Center at the University of Richmond when Greg was stationed at Fort Lee, Virginia. Since I'm a pack rat, I still have that description: "I get up in the morning when my body feels like getting up without an alarm clock going off. I walk out onto the deck overlooking the water with my mug of rich coffee in hand. I enjoy a breakfast of fruit and granola while I read a newspaper or a book, easing into my day. Then I start into my workday in my home office, reading, writing, talking with people on the phone." At the time, we lived in the city, and I started my day early, packing my car to get out on the road in my job as a pharmaceutical sales rep. My breakfast was usually a quick bacon biscuit and weak coffee at Roy Rogers while I planned my calls. A far cry from my ideal.

Now, many years later, I do wake without an alarm clock, walk out onto the deck with coffee in hand, and start my day with reading or journaling or writing, working from my home office at the Oregon Coast.

Since that day of awareness, doing the Ideal Life exercise in Richmond, my life has developed even closer to my dream of being a full-time writer. I've written regular columns, articles, the third edition of this book, a second book out recently, and have many more books planned, even a novel in the works. (And oh yes, other aspects of my whole-istic dream—regular yoga, gardening, spending time with family and friends—are all part of my current reality.) Did it happen by magic? No. But, I think clarifying the dream is the first important step toward making it a reality.

The key to doing this exercise is to unplug; take reflection time, time off by yourself with no distractions. Send everyone off to the movies, or get a sitter, or trade childcare with a neighbor. Go off to a café or the library (someplace where your laundry piles won't scream at you). Turn off your cell phone. Open yourself to possibilities. Don't limit yourself in any way. The Ideal Life exercise is an exercise in dreaming, so DREAM BIG! Pretend we can wave a magic wand and grant you whatever you want. If you had a perfect life, an ideal life, what would it look like? Write your description in first person and present tense as if it is already your world. Include as much detail as possible.

- What would you do, both for work and for play?
- What kinds of people would you interact with on a regular basis? Maybe they are artistic people, or children, or computer wizards, or dramatic people. What kinds of people energize you?
- What kinds of relationships would you have? What would your ideal relationships look like—with your spouse, children, extended family, coworkers, and neighbors?
- What would your family finances look like in your ideal life?
- What would your family life look like on a daily basis?
- What kind of spiritual practice would you have?
- What personal characteristics do you have? Describe who you are. Would you be powerful or self-confident or playful or childlike or dramatic or outrageous? Consider the characteristics you admire in others.
- What would your physical fitness look like? What kinds of physical activities would you engage in regularly?

- How about your appearance? For example, what clothes would you wear, and how would you wear your hair?
- Where are you living this perfect life? What's your environment? Is it a specific place in the world or a more general description of a place? Include your immediate environment—your bedroom, house, office, yard, or balcony.
- What pace would you like for your life on a daily basis?
- What might you be doing to give back to the greater community?

My Ideal Life

_____

_____

_____

_____

_____

_____

_____

_____

_____

_____

_____

_____

_____

_____

_____

No two people's ideal life descriptions are the same. Kathie's description runs three typed pages and changes as she discovers new things and changes her mind (you're allowed to change your mind). Her husband's is two-thirds of a page. Holly's is ten handwritten pages. Holly's Army engineer husband has his on index cards in bullet format! The format doesn't matter. Just get it in writing. Start with your notes here, and add to it in whatever way best fits your personality.

By the way, it's a really good idea to ask your spouse to do this exercise, too. You want to work toward mutual goals and dreams as a couple and as a family. The first step is to identify those goals and dreams, and, in the case of couples, look at areas you might need to work out some win/win compromises. The research on

> *Once others know your dreams, they'll help you in ways you would never have imagined possible.*

successful marriages conducted by John Gottman, PhD, over more than thirty years, indicates that working toward mutual goals and dreams is key to a good relationship.

Once you do your ideal life description, it's a great idea to ask a group of friends to do theirs, too. Read them out loud to each other. This accomplishes a couple of things. You will be amazed at what other people come up with as they truly dream big. You may find that although you try not to limit yourself, you may very well do so in your first attempt at writing your ideal life. Often your initial description is not your ideal life. It is your much smaller idea of what is possible for you, limited especially by moving with the military. Hearing others stretch will give you the courage to dream big for yourself. Reading your description aloud starts a magical process. Things start to happen. Resources and people show up in your life. Synchronicity and serendipity step in to help. Once others know your dreams, they'll help you in ways you would never have imagined possible.

Act on Your Description

Now that you have your ideal life description, what do you do with it?

Step One. Get a highlighter. Highlight everything in your description that is already in your life. First, be grateful that those things are in your life. Second, take steps to keep them in your life. Sometimes when we take wonderful things for granted, they go away. Whether it's our health or our good relationships, if we do nothing to sustain these, they can disappear. Write down two of the things you are grateful for and an action plan of what you will do to keep these fresh and vital.

1. _____

_____

2. _____

_____

Step Two. Figure out what's in your description that you can add into your current physical environment. We guarantee there are ways you can do that, no matter where you are stationed, no matter how dismal your current quarters might be.

For example, Kathie's ideal environment includes living on the water with a beautiful "secret" garden near the mountains with green all around. It includes wall-to-wall, floor-to-ceiling, built-in bookshelves, a wood-burning stove, a big overstuffed chair and ottoman, and a cat in her lap.

When she first wrote her ideal description, she and Greg lived on the top floor of an old building in downtown Richmond, Virginia, not near the water or mountains. There were no bookshelves, no wood-burning stove, no garden, no yard at all. She did have two cats. (And she was grateful for them and took good care of them; they lived to be twenty and twenty-one!) Since that time, she's lived in Washington State, Kansas, Germany, Oregon, back in Washington State, and now in Oregon. Until recently, she didn't live near the water. Until Oregon, she did not have a garden. But in all those places, she carried her ideal environment with her—big photos of the ocean and the mountains in her home office, a crystal box filled with sand and shells to remind her of the ocean, cards with beautiful flowers on her desk, and fresh flowers whenever she could afford them. All of those things brought her daily joy; they changed her daily experience of life. We don't know if it's the memory of things, or the anticipation of things, or just the beauty of these things. But they bring joy, especially if you are stuck in some of those quarters that were built as temporary dwellings in World War II!

Put more emphasis on changing what you can to make your environment work for you and your family as you move with the military. This exercise is a good start. This is a process, of course. You can create your own dream house binder and notebook or a garden notebook. Clip photos from magazines of rooms or furniture or colors or gardens that you love. Put them in the binder in plastic sleeves. Make notes of things that you notice in other peoples' homes and gardens that you like. Some of these will be long-term ideas for the future. Other things you can apply immediately.

Awaken your five senses to make your home warm and inviting. When your senses are stimulated in a positive way, any experience becomes more enjoyable. Look around you. What bits of your ideal environment can you add in right now? What can you do to create an environment that feeds your soul? List three things you can change about your current environment.

At Home:

1. _____

2. _____

3. _____

At Work:

1. _____

2. _____

3. _____

Schedule time in your planner to make these changes.

Step Three. Articulate the goals that are most important to you. Your ideal life description will reveal some of your bigger goals in life. Goal setting is one of the most important skills to master as you move toward your dreams. We'll spend a whole chapter on goal-achieving techniques.

This exercise is just one approach to bring awareness to yourself and how you truly want to live your life. By doing the Ideal Life exercise, you start the first part of the equation, figuring out how you want your life to be. Now let's look at identifying your strengths, so you can apply those to more effectively move toward the vision you've begun to clarify.

Key Points and Action Steps

▷   Do the Ideal Life exercise.

▷   Ask your spouse to do the Ideal Life exercise and discuss win/win compromises.

▷   Share your description and exchange ideas with friends. It will help you dream big, and you never know how someone else might be able to help you on the journey once they know what you want.

▷   Be grateful for what you already have, and take steps to keep those things in your life.

▷   Add dream items to your environment.

▷   Begin to articulate your most important goals.

Chapter 5

Identify and Celebrate Your Strengths

We often focus on the lack in ourselves—the things we need to improve or fix. Very often, we don't stop to recognize or even acknowledge what is already a strength.

A passage from *Meditations for Women Who Do Too Much* by Anne Wilson Schaef reads: "It is much easier to see what we haven't done rather than to see what we have done. Often, if we just stop and take stock, we really have accomplished quite a bit. In fact, we probably are a wee bit close to the edge of working wonders. Unfortunately, we miss the opportunity to marvel at our wonders, because we have so much set up still to do that what we have done pales into insignificance in relation to what is always yet to be done."

As military spouses, we are even guiltier of this. If we really thought about it, we often are working wonders, especially during times of deployments, moves, and other challenges of military life. But we don't give ourselves credit, partially because we can always point out someone who seems to have it harder than we do or seems to have it more together than we do.

What we need is an "I love me" wall like our spouses have. Only instead of having graduation certificates or unit awards, it would show things like:

- Packed up and moved the house by myself.
- Survived another deployment even with a car, toilet, and washing machine breaking down.
- Learned how to drive and get around in a foreign country.

- · Reestablished the kids and self once again in a new place with no immediate support.

Give yourself credit and a big pat on the back for these accomplishments.

When we've mentioned this in our workshops, we've had some spouses roll their eyes and say, "Well, of course, we've all had to do those things." That attitude negates the fact that those are accomplishments, a show of great strength, whether every other military spouse has managed to do the same or not. Our civilian friends are in awe of these accomplishments. Their comments: "Move nineteen times in twenty-five years? Oh, I could never do that! I struggled with just two moves so far in my lifetime!" "Deal with your spouse being gone for a year in a dangerous place? I can hardly cope when he's gone for a week-long business trip."

Military spouses are awesome. Give yourself accolades!

It is ironic that military spouses are designated as dependents by the Department of Defense, when most of them are the most independent people we've ever met.

Holly's Story

I don't want to say military spouses are better than other spouses, but I do believe there is a difference. Every military spouse I know has handled some major emergency on their own during deployments or TDYs, from car problems to plumbing problems to whatever. Military spouses just plain learn to handle things.

One of my favorite stories is of Sarah Selvidge, an Army spouse. While she was living overseas and her husband was deployed, her car engine gave out. She found a mechanic who was willing to fix her car if she could get another engine. Amazingly, the next thing I knew she was on her way to the junkyard to "pluck an engine" out of another car. It was something she had never done before in her life, but knew she had to do in order to have transportation. Not only did she "pluck" that engine, but she even assisted the mechanic in getting the car running again! She definitely wins the "I'm a military spouse hear me ROAR!" T-shirt.

We had to laugh when Marine spouse, Mickey Devers, shared her story at one of our workshops. She told us she was a champion spider killer. "When we moved into a civilian community," she said, "as soon as everyone found out we were military, they started coming to me with every problem." Whether it was a leaking faucet or a clogged drain or a big spider that needed killing, they came to her because she was a military spouse; so, they figured, she was strong and brave and could fix anything.

Holly's experience and training in the special education field taught her the importance of finding the gifts or strengths in each individual and then figuring out a way to build on those strengths. We all have been given gifts/strengths. Everyone—guaranteed! It's these gifts/strengths that help define our role in life.

The greatest gift you can give your children is to help them identify their strengths and help them nurture and build on those strengths. Teach them to listen within for guidance, and encourage them to use those strengths to help others in this world.

It's the greatest gift you can give yourself as well—identifying and using your strengths for the greater good. Doing this gives you a sense of purpose in life. Identifying your strengths is an important step so you can celebrate those strengths and work from them.

Ask Others to Help Identify Your Strengths

There are many different ways to recognize your own strengths and talents. It can be challenging to judge something too close to home. Often we simply take our strengths for granted.

Here's one idea. Photocopy the following list of positive characteristics. Give a copy to family members and friends and ask them to circle the strengths they see in you and to star your top ten strengths. Before you look at what they mark, do the same for yourself.

Your friends will likely identify strengths you simply take for granted, that you don't even recognize as strengths. So read them carefully, and pat yourself on the back for having developed and nourished those strengths!

There is another aspect to this exercise. If you circle characteristics on your sheet and no one else circles that same characteristic, it might be one of those blind spots we sometimes have about ourselves. It might actually be a weakness you aren't aware of. For example, if you circle "good listener" and not one other person who knows you well circles that quality, you might want to step back and pay attention to your listening skills and habits. And, of course, choose to work on that area only if you care to.

My Strengths

Please look through this list and circle any characteristics you think I have. Then star what you see as my top ten strengths.

friendly	funny	smart	organized
focused	confident	assertive	helpful
patient	outrageous	dramatic	artistic
caring	good listener	detail-oriented	disciplined
logical	proactive	balanced	decisive
mediator	creative	nurturing	enthusiastic
positive	optimistic	cooperative	objective
responsible	playful	leader	calm
problem-solver	studious	kind	honest
cheerful	persistent	energetic	risk-taker
steady	passionate	joyful	insightful
take charge	forgiving	aware	persuasive
professional	elegant	gracious	gentle
connector	powerful	modest	fun
present	peaceful	sharing	courageous
good parent	involved	independent	eccentric

Others:

_____ _____ _____ _____

_____ _____ _____ _____

_____ _____ _____ _____

_____ _____ _____ _____

Why Spend Time Identifying Your Strengths?

All this talk about living and working from your strengths is based on research. Donald O. Clifton is called the Father of Strengths-Based Psychology. In the mid-1960s, he noted how much the world of psychology focused on what is wrong with people, rather than what is right. He decided to buck that trend. In 1998, Clifton, along with Tom Rath and a team of scientists at Gallup, created an online StrengthsFinder assessment. Based on Gallup's forty-year study of human strengths, they created a language of the thirty-four most common talents and developed the Clifton StrengthsFinder to help people discover and describe those talents.

Why? Gallup studies show that people have several times more potential for growth when they invest energy in developing their strengths instead of correcting their deficiencies.

Gallup has had millions of people around the world take this test and has surveyed many of them. The studies indicate that people who have the opportunity to focus on their strengths every day are six times as likely to be engaged in their jobs and more than three times as likely to report having an excellent quality of life in general.

From Kathie's Journal

I recently read StrengthsFinder 2.0 *and took the online strengths test. You get an access code when you buy the book. They provide you with your unique results and an action plan.*

Here are a few of my results. I can see immediately how these strengths play out in this current work I love. I can also clearly see why so many other jobs I had earlier in life were never a good fit.

Strategic

People who are especially talented in the Strategic theme create alternative ways to proceed. Faced with any given scenario, they can quickly spot the relevant patterns and issues.

Learner

People who are especially talented in the Learner theme have a great desire to learn and want to continuously improve. In particular, the process of learning, rather than the outcome, excites them.

Ideation

People who are especially talented in the Ideation theme are fascinated by ideas. They are able to find connections between seemingly disparate phenomena.

No wonder I thrive on doing all this research into ideas and resources that can help military spouses and others. No wonder I love to constantly learn new ways to improve my writing and speaking skills. No wonder I'm naturally good at brainstorming and helping to connect people with ideas and resources and contacts. It's how my brain works. I'm happiest when I immerse myself in learning and brainstorming!

I can see why I was lucky to partner with Holly, who has strengths I don't have, and vice versa. Whereas she sometimes cringes when she hears me say once again, "Holly, I have an idea," it's often those wild ideas that move us forward. But they wouldn't move us forward without Holly's skill at taking action and putting things into place in a logical, planned way.

Does this mean we ignore our weaknesses altogether? We don't think so. We think it comes back to conscious choice. You decide what is important or not important for you.

As Kathie says, "It took me years to get it, but I finally let go of those things I'm not good at, like cooking. My friends know not to ask me to bring a dish. I happily bring wine or chocolate to potlucks." Does that mean she'll never choose to work on that weakness. No, just not at this time of life!

Kathie does have weaknesses she chooses to work on, such as using technology. She knows she needs to improve her technical abilities in order to streamline her life and her work. But she does it in her way, tapping into her strengths. Instead of quickly diving into new technology, she uses her learning strength to do in-depth research first.

She realizes she has used her strengths to compensate for her weaknesses all along. Neither she nor her husband is naturally organized. She constantly battled her tendency to have piles everywhere, especially of books, magazines, and papers. When she realized the clutter was causing her extreme stress and impacting her effectiveness at work, she tapped into her Learner strength.

"I read books on clutter control, watched the Clean Team's video on how to clean a house," she says, "and then I did the smartest thing. I bartered with naturally organized people for help, specifically with professional organizers." She got them to help her set up systems that work for her, and then she helped them with marketing ideas and business strategies, with articles about them and their business, using her strengths.

Choose Your Battles—Or Choose Your Weaknesses

Make a list of three weaknesses you know you have that you want to address. Make sure it's a priority of your own to strengthen these particular weaknesses. Then come up with one to two action steps you can take for each one. Discuss this with a friend for added accountability.

1. _____

Action steps: _____

_____

2. _____

Action steps: _____

_____

3. _____

Action steps: _____

_____

Then, make another list of three weaknesses you are willing to let go. They don't matter enough to you to spend your time and energy on them, considering the other things in life you do want to spend your time on. Write these "let-go weaknesses" on a slip of paper and burn it. Don't waste another minute worrying about those weaknesses! You might want to share this with your friend, too, so that person can remind you if you forget to let go and end up obsessing about those weaknesses again.

Imagine if everyone in your family, community, in the military, in the world, all had the same strengths. How boring would that be? Not to mention how dysfunctional. Our military community is so strong because we all bring different strengths to the table. Now that is something to celebrate!

Key Points and Action Steps

- ▷ You are more effective working from your strengths. So identify your strengths and celebrate them.
- ▷ Get input from family and friends to identify strengths you take for granted.
- ▷ Choose your battles. Identify the weaknesses you choose to work on. Let go of the others.

Resources

Meditations for Women Who Do Too Much, Revised Edition by Anne Wilson Schaef (2004).

StrengthsFinder 2.0 by Tom Rath (2007).

Chapter 6

Dive into Life Exploration Exercises

More Ways to Create
Your Unique Vision for Your Life

The Ideal Life exercise and identifying your strengths are great starting points. But no single exercise will help you create your dreams and visions. This chapter includes other exercises we've done over time that helped us clarify our own priorities and life visions. You don't have to do them all at once, but we wanted to put them all together so you can do them as you have time. You'll learn more about yourself and your life priorities each time you do one.

As Kathie's friend Claire says, "These are all tools to bring your awareness back to yourself and who you really are."

Create Your Life List

Lou Holtz, the famous football coach, was twenty-eight years old, had just lost his job, had no money in the bank, and his wife Beth was pregnant with their third child. He was so discouraged that Beth gave him the book *The Magic of Thinking Big* by David J. Schwartz to lift his spirits. The book suggested you write down all the goals you want to achieve before you die.

Holtz sat down and wrote down 107 impossible goals. His list included things like having dinner at the White House, being coach of the year, making a hole in one, jumping out of an airplane. More importantly, his list covered all areas of his life he wanted to improve, from professional to parenting to his spiritual life.

We've heard this described as making the future enticing enough to pull you toward it, to take steps, to take action. Of the 107 goals Holtz wrote down in 1966, he has achieved more than eighty. That's the power of identifying what you want!

Kathie's Story

When I first tried to write down 101 things I wanted in life—learn Italian, have a successful TV show, publish successful books, learn to garden, kayak in Alaska, hike in Utah—I ran out of ideas at about forty. I figured I could keep adding places I want to hike, kayak, and cross country ski, but even with that I ran out of wishes at sixty-four.

When I mentioned this to my success group in Heidelberg, Germany, Gail said, "Oh, I have one of those lists. I sat on a mountainside and made mine up after attending a seminar years ago." She found it and showed it to us. We were amazed at how many things on her list she had already achieved.

Seeing her list gave me a big ah-hah. I hadn't included many "to be" items. So I started adding them: be more self-confident and trust my instincts, be more spontaneous, become comfortable with technology. I started adding people I want to meet: SARK, Natalie Goldberg.

I read an article about making a list of the ways you want to make a difference in the world or in your community. So I started adding those: teach goal-setting to teenage girls; start an Author series or book club radio show. I got to 101.

So, why have this list? Won't it be discouraging if you don't get it all? We don't think so. It's a good exercise to stretch yourself to think of all the wonderful possibilities in this world. It is another way to identify goals, especially goals in more than one area of life. It opens you up to all kinds of opportunities.

Kathie admits she isn't the most organized person in the world, especially when it comes to files. She lost her 101 list for many years. When she found it as we started writing this book, we were impressed with how many things had already come true. She had only tried kayaking once through the Fort Lewis Recreation Center when she first wrote the list. Since then, she and her husband have indeed "kayaked in Alaska, kayaked in Baja, kayaked in the San Juan Islands," all items on that list. They even own their own kayaks. She had only just started writing a free column for a spouse club newsletter (after years of saying "someday I want to be a writer") but she wrote down "write a column for *Army Times*." Now where did that come from—talk about dreaming way outside the realm of the possible? Who knows where that came from, but she ended up writing a column for *Army Times* for one year, and we later spent four years cowriting a column for *Air Force Times*, *Army Times*, *Navy Times*, and *Marine Corps Times*.

This concept has become more widely known in recent years because of the movie *The Bucket List* with Jack Nicholson and Morgan Freeman. These two older men had a list of things they wanted to do before they "kicked the bucket." But we don't have to wait until we are old. In fact, each summer now, Holly asks her teenage twins to make out their "bucket list" for summer vacation, and they add in activities.

So call it your Life List or your Bucket List, but write it down (see pages 54-55). Shoot for 101. Who knows where it might lead!

Some good questions to ask yourself as you write your list:

- Who are your role models? What is it about their life that appeals to you?
- If you could apprentice with anyone, who would that be?
- Where would you like to go?
- What would you like to see?
- What would you like to share?
- How would you like to make a difference?

Start Your Heart's Desires File

If you don't currently feel ready to do any of these exercises, you can start in a quick simple way for now. Get a basket or file folder. For the next few months, as you read magazines or newspapers, tear out photos or articles or headlines that appeal to you. Include any visuals you love. They might be postcards or advertising mailers or photos from catalogs or travel magazines. They might be articles about what other people have done. Don't think about it too much—just tear them out and put them in your basket or file.

After a few months, sit down with a cup of tea and your favorite music playing, and browse through your file. See if there are any patterns, any themes. This can give you a good idea of what you want in your life, of goals you might want to work toward, of the kinds of work and activities or community projects you might want to get involved with, of the kind of person you'd like to be. Hang on to the file. It will come in handy if you decide to make a treasure map.

Create a Visual Treasure Map of Your Dreams

Kathie first learned about this tool from her friend Reba, who had created photo books of her dreams. Reba had some pretty amazing, almost magical results. For example, she was single but wanted to be in a relationship. She found photos of couples who looked like they were in love, mostly sitting on beaches at island resorts, and added those to her book. Reba looked at her photo book every night before she went to sleep and each morning when she first got up. A few years later, she met her husband, at a conference on an island!

Air Force spouse Dixie Schneider wanted to speak on cruise ships. She's a bit zany, so she used a different variation of treasure maps. She picked up cruise ship brochures from a travel agency, cut out the photos and put them all over her house. Open the refrigerator and there would be a photo of a cruise ship. Open the medicine cabinet door and there would be a cruise ship. Lift the toilet seat and there would be a cruise ship. Her Air Force engineer husband gave her a lot of grief, as you can imagine.

Well, Dixie has spoken on cruise ships all over the world. The first opportunity came by sheer serendipity. A former speech instructor of hers ran into her at the grocery store. He said, "I hear you are doing motivational speaking now. I was scheduled to speak on an upcoming cruise, but my mother is ill, and I can't do the cruise. Could you take my place?" Could she!

Now did those things happen by magic just because of the photos? No, of course not. Reba didn't just sit at home looking yearningly at the photo book. She was actively involved in interesting things, taking classes, taking action that happened to put her on the right island at the right time. Dixie didn't just look at the cruise ship photos and wait. She took steps, studying and learning how to be a speaker, doing free and then paid speaking, developing her platform and business skills, gaining visibility and a good reputation. She scoured thrift shops to buy evening gowns and cruise-type outfits. When the first opportunity to speak on a cruise ship appeared, she was ready to take advantage of the opportunity. And, she did a great job so she continued to get asked back.

What happens with treasure mapping is that by keeping the images of what you want clearly in front of you, you do not let yourself forget. You are pulled toward your dreams. Because the goal is so vivid in your mind, you make choices, you take action, and you take steps that move you toward that dream. Okay, we admit, we think there is a little bit of magic involved as well! The universe seems to step in to help.

You can do this by yourself or gather a group of friends for a fun night. You know all those magazines you've been meaning to read, those piles that add to your clutter guilt? Put them to good use and clear them out at the same time. Buy some poster board or foam core that is thicker and lasts longer as you move these in your military moves. Black or red make a more dramatic backing to the photos than white does. Put on fun music.

> *By keeping the images of what you want clearly in front of you, you make choices that move you toward your dream.*

Cut out photos of your dreams. Cut out images that "speak to you" even if you don't know why. Let your subconscious have some input here. Cut out headlines or make your own on the computer with large type and include those. Put a photo of yourself and your spouse and family in the center of the board and then surround yourself with your dreams. Show your friends your treasure map and describe what each visual means to you. Describing it to others helps you to clarify to yourself what you want to happen. Hang the treasure map in a place where you will see it every day...and watch the magic happen.

Tip: If you are looking for very specific items, you can use Pinterest to find photos. Print them out on photo paper to include on your board.

Encourage your children to make their own treasure maps. You can even make a family one. Holly found making treasure maps with her children to be a great rainy day activity. She had a craft box where she stashed her old magazines and added any pictures she thought the children would like. Once the box was full to the brim and one of those rainy days arrived, she set up the kitchen table with poster board, glue, scissors, and all the pictures and old magazines. The conversations that transpired during those "treasure map" days were priceless. Holly learned more about her children's dreams and desires just by talking about the pictures the children would cut out and glue on their poster board.

Another family makes placemat-size treasure maps each year. They laminate them and use them at meals during the year so they keep their goals right in front of them on a daily basis.

Kathie's friend Claire created what she calls her treasure map movie. It's a series of pages of photos and headings, one page for each key concept, for example, Financial Security, Retirement Home in France, Regular and Meaningful Connection with Friends. She scrolls through this PDF file every day with favorite music playing in the background, as if she is watching a movie of her future life. (By the way, as we write this update, we can report that Claire and her husband recently moved to France!)

Kathie's Story

I started out with a photo book. I was a little self-conscious about my dreams. They seemed a bit lofty and impossible for someone like me. Who was I to think I could do these things? I wasn't quite ready to have them out in the open for comments from my husband and anyone who came in my house. So I used the book and kept it to myself at first.

I included photos of myself with headlines cut from magazines—Successful Speaker, Successful Published Author. This was all before I ever started my writing, and at the same time as my very first free seminar at McChord Air Force Base. I included photos of women who looked confident and elegant and included the headlines: Confidence, Energy, Simply Elegant. I had a photo of a beautiful garden and the headline: A Lifelong Garden, Flowers All Year Long, even though I'd never gardened before.

I now proudly hang treasure maps around my house, mostly in my home office, where I spend much of my time. Six years after I did my first poster treasure map, I started a support group in Corvallis, Oregon. I suggested to them that we make treasure maps and showed them mine. My new friend Claire said, "I don't get it. This IS your life. These are mostly photos of what you already have. How does that move you forward?" She was right. Almost everything in that first treasure map had already happened in some way. That's the magic.

"That's just it," I told her, "I had none of those things in my life back when I put this together years ago. It did draw me forward, and now I want to make a new one for future possibilities."

And a side note about the "magic" of this. When we were editing the second edition of our book, I dug up my first photo book treasure map that I hadn't looked at in many years. I called Holly excitedly. "You won't believe this!" One photo showed a sailboat leaving a harbor in the Virgin Islands, with my headline "Sailing in the Virgin Islands," not something we'd taken any action on, since we saw that as a retirement dream. Well, that past year, our neighbors asked us if we'd fill in for a couple that couldn't join them in a long-planned sailing trip. We had enough frequent flyer miles to get there for free, and the trip itself was very inexpensive (with eight of us on a six-person boat). Here's the magic—we had done nothing to make this happen except be good neighbors. By chance, we sailed out of the exact small harbor that was in the photo in my treasure book! Now that's magic!

As we edited the third edition of this book, I pulled that photo book out again. More magic. I had put "speak on cruise ships" with a photo of a cruise ship departing out of New York Harbor. A few years ago, I did indeed speak on a cruise ship. Of the opportunities offered, the one that appealed the most was a cruise to Nova Scotia, a place my husband and I had never been. Guess where that cruise ship started out? Yep! New York Harbor.

By the way, we think the key part is identifying images that speak to you even if you don't know why. Even if you do the board or book and then put it away, you've given your subconscious something to work with. Whether or not you see these images regularly, you might just be surprised how they eventually manifest in your world in some way.

Identify a Passion to Help Others

Look back on your life. Have you overcome a major challenge? You can often use this experience and wisdom you've gained to help others who face the same challenge. Helping/serving others in need is a powerful way to connect to your passion and to increase your joy in life. Don't forget, the feeling that you are making a difference in someone else's life is one of the top routes to joy and may just be one of the central purposes for all of us in life.

By this point, you probably have some idea of your strengths and interests, possibly a good start on your whole-istic vision for your life. Let's look next at how you can proactively start taking steps toward your dream.

My Life List *(101 Things I Want to Do, Be, and Have in My Life)*

Date: _____

1. _____
2. _____
3. _____
4. _____
5. _____
6. _____
7. _____
8. _____
9. _____
10. _____
11. _____
12. _____
13. _____
14. _____
15. _____
16. _____
17. _____
18. _____
19. _____
20. _____
21. _____
22. _____
23. _____
24. _____
25. _____
26. _____
27. _____
28. _____
29. _____
30. _____
31. _____
32. _____
33. _____
34. _____
35. _____
36. _____
37. _____
38. _____
39. _____
40. _____
41. _____
42. _____
43. _____
44. _____
45. _____
46. _____
47. _____
48. _____
49. _____

50. _____   76. _____

51. _____   77. _____

52. _____   78. _____

53. _____   79. _____

54. _____   80. _____

55. _____   81. _____

56. _____   82. _____

57. _____   83. _____

58. _____   84. _____

59. _____   85. _____

60. _____   86. _____

61. _____   87. _____

62. _____   88. _____

63. _____   89. _____

64. _____   90. _____

65. _____   91. _____

66. _____   92. _____

67. _____   93. _____

68. _____   94. _____

69. _____   95. _____

70. _____   96. _____

71. _____   97. _____

72. _____   98. _____

73. _____   99. _____

74. _____   100. _____

75. _____   101. _____

Key Points and Action Steps

  ▷ Pick one of the exercises in this chapter to do this week. Share with a friend. Writing things down and speaking the words out loud starts a process.

  ▷ Schedule the other exercises over the next months. Write them into your calendar.

Resources

The Artist's Way: A Spiritual Path to Higher Creativity by Julia Cameron (1992). Great life exploration exercises whether or not you are an artist.

How to Think Like Leonardo da Vinci: Seven Steps to Genius Every Day by Michael J. Gelb (2000). Although this is about creativity, there is a lot about life and passion exploration in here.

Living Life on Purpose: A Guide to Creating a Life of Success and Significance by Greg Anderson (1997).

The Magic of Thinking Big (1987) and *The Magic of Getting What You Want* by David J. Schwartz (2007).

The Path: Creating a Mission Statement for Work and for Life by Laurie Beth Jones (2001).

Wishcraft: How to Get What You Really Want by Barbara Sher and Annie Gottlieb (2003), and Barbara's other books, *Live the Life You Love: In Ten Easy Step-by-Step Lessons* (1997); *I Could Do Anything if I Only Knew What It Was: How to Discover What You Really Want and How to Get It* coauthored with Barbara Smith (1995); and *It's Only Too Late if You Don't Start Now: How to Create Your Second Life at Any Age* (1999).

Women and the Blues: Passions That Hurt, Passions That Heal by Jennifer James (1990).

Chapter 7

Try These Effective and Fun Goal-Achieving Techniques

How to Move Toward Your Goals Even as You Move with the Military

Whatever your dreams and goals are—whether personal, family, community, career, business, or education—there are many ways to take action to achieve them.

Choose a Primary Focus for Each Stage of Life

Before we get into the how-to of achieving your goals, there is a key concept to consider—the concept of Primary Focus.

Kerry Vosler is a portrait artist who takes her art business seriously. She's also a mom and military spouse. She knew an upcoming deployment of her husband's unit would take up all of her time. As the brigade commander's wife with two children at home, she would have limited time for her art business during that time. To prepare for that circumstance, she took a few months ahead to focus almost exclusively on her art. As soon as her husband and kids were out of the house each morning, she put a sign on her door that read "Working on a project, please come back later," turned the music on, and painted with abandon until her youngest son got home from school.

When the deployment happened, and her life was consumed with acting as a single parent and helping the other families, she didn't resent the disruption. She had prepared for it by taking the time for her art first. She chose one primary focus for each of those times, rather than drive herself crazy trying to do everything at once.

When you dream big, you'll likely come up with some goals that seem to conflict. The truth is, if you try to approach every single one of your goals full-bore at the same time, you will only get frustrated.

Holly's Story

Kathie and I dreamed big, set goals, and made plans for our seminars when we lived in Germany. We started speaking all over Europe, having a blast, and making a difference in other people's lives. Then something else wonderful happened. I became pregnant with twins after twelve years of trying to conceive. I needed to make a hard decision. Speaking and traveling all over the place were not conducive to the goals I had set for myself as a mother. Yet, believe it or not, I felt torn. I loved speaking and helping other military spouses—it truly feeds my soul.

A passage from the book Care Packages for the Home by Barbara Glanz helped me at that time. "Choose a primary focus for each stage of life and be intensely committed to it! If you have decided what your PRIMARY focus is at this point in time, it will help you make hard choices a little easier. A primary focus gives you a frame for the way you approach the world. For example, if you have decided that your children are your primary focus at this point in time, then it will be easier to make decisions when you are offered a promotion in your job. One of the things I used in my 'self talk,' when I was confused and torn between a desire to be successful in my career and to stay at home with my children, was to remind myself that other jobs would always be out there if I kept my skills honed, while my children would be young only once. I was merely postponing one wonderful thing for another!"

I took Barbara's advice to heart. I chose to focus on my twins and still find small ways to keep my speaking skills alive. I created ways to speak occasionally without leaving town or leaving my kids. Because of my two master's degrees and teaching background in early childhood and special education, I found it easy to share my knowledge about child development and behavior modification in workshops for other mothers, in neighborhood playgroups, and church groups. I shared with other military spouses about deployments and how to get through them.

With my primary focus clearly in mind, saying no to speaking engagements that required travel became easier. My primary focus when my

> *children were little was to be with them. By keeping my skills honed, I was ready to start speaking again on occasion four years later. I still only travel for business when it works for my family.*

This concept is important to keep in mind during deployments. If you have children at home, they are going to need even more of your time and energy during a deployment than at other times. At the same time, you are taking on 100 percent of the household chores. Depending on your level of support, your finances, your own organizational skills, and energy level, this may well be one time where your primary focus is clearly spelled out.

Apply the Basics of Effective Goal Setting and Achieving

Follow this handy list of principles and steps to help you set effective goals and make real progress:

- Identify the goal and the benefits to you. Be sure the goal is in line with your values.
- Commit to it by writing it down. Research shows you are 25 percent more likely to achieve your goal simply by writing it down than if you have it just in your head.
- Set a deadline. Deadlines are often what we need to get ourselves moving forward. They give you a checkpoint to measure your progress. (Of course, we know things will happen in military life that will make many deadlines shift. Don't worry; deadlines aren't carved in stone. Just set one. It gives you a reason to get going!)
- Set a start date and schedule it in your calendar.
- Come up with a plan of action—the mini steps that will move you toward your goal.
- Take action.
- Build in accountability.
- Put rejection and failure into perspective. Not everything you try will work all the time. It's a process!
- Celebrate success!

Identify the Benefit to You

The first step in effective goal setting is to make sure the goal is truly your goal. Write down the goal, and then write down the benefits to you. What's in it for you? What's in it for your family? Why do you want to achieve this particular goal? How will you and your life be different by accomplishing this goal? What values does your goal support?

If you have trouble identifying the benefit to you and the values it supports, then it's probably not your goal. It's most likely someone else's goal for you. We don't know about you, but we have too many things we want to achieve in our lives to be wasting time on other people's goals for us.

Clearly identify the benefit to you to create a stronger magnet of a goal to pull you forward. Clear, compelling benefits can pull you around obstacles that show up in your way.

Clarify and Align Your Personal Values

Values are deeply held views of what we believe are important in life. Our values develop and evolve over time with experience. It's important to identify your values in order to make decisions and take actions in line with your values and to focus your time and energy.

From the list of values below, circle the ten that are most important to you as guides for how to behave or as elements of a life that works for you.

Achievement	Adaptability/Flexibility	Advancement
Adventure	Affection	Alone Time
Authority	Beauty	Career
Change/Variety	Comfort	Community
Competence	Control	Cooperation
Creativity	Decisiveness	Duty
Ecological Awareness	Education	Effectiveness
Ethics	Excellence	Excitement
Faith	Fame	Family
Financial Achievement	Fitness	Freedom/Independence
Friendships	Happiness	Health
Helping Others	Honesty/Truth	Honor
Influencing Others	Integrity	Intellectual Challenge
Intimate Relationship	Involvement	Job Security
Justice	Kindness	Leadership

Leisure Time	Lifelong Learning	Life Partner
Love	Loyalty	Meaningful Work
Merit/Recognition	Money	Optimism
Order/Predictability	Patriotism	Personal Development
Physical Activity	Physical Challenge	Pleasure
Power	Prestige/Status	Privacy
Quality of Work	Quality Relationships	Reputation/Image
Responsibility	Self-respect	Self-sufficiency
Service	Simplicity	Social Responsibility
Sophistication	Spirituality	Stability
Strength	Teamwork	Time in Nature
Tranquility/Serenity	Wisdom	Working Alone
Others:	_____	_____
_____	_____	_____
_____	_____	_____

Determine Your Outcome of Outcomes

Another way to look at the benefits of your goal comes from Henriette Anne Klauser, a former Navy spouse, mother of four (including one daughter in the Navy), and author of the terrific book *Write It Down and Make It Happen: Knowing What You Want and Getting It*.

Henriette asks you to determine your outcome of outcomes. "Instead of just writing your goal, consider why you want the goal in the first place, how attaining it will enrich your life or others' lives," she suggests. This takes it even deeper than that benefit to you. What will your life be like if you go for that goal?

There are so many goals we might not be able to go for fully at the moment because of where we are located or what our life is currently like due to our military circumstances. But there may be a way to still get at least part of the "outcome of outcomes."

For example, Susan is a Navy spouse and mother of two. One of her goals is to go for her Master of Fine Arts (MFA) degree in creative writing. That isn't possible right now, time-wise, location-wise, and finances-wise. But the "outcome of outcome" for her is, she wants to immerse herself more fully in the writing world, to become a more creative writer, to build her confidence and credibility to sell more of her writing, to get books published, and to eventually make a living with her writing.

Okay, so what can she do right now—without the MFA program— to achieve that?

- Read books and magazines about the writing craft.
- Start or join a writer's group.
- Attend local writing workshops.
- Join a professional writer's association for information and networking.
- Write, write, write!

Most importantly, she can do all of that right now, right here, while she builds up her savings for the MFA for when her life situation allows for that total immersion. Who knows? She may decide later she doesn't even need the MFA. She might discover a different route to her goal.

Develop a Plan of Action and Get Moving

Okay, so you know what you want to take action on, regardless of where you are stationed. How do you move forward?

First, come up with an action plan. Here's one great way to do so. Start with a blank sheet of paper. Put your goal in the center of it. First, write the benefits to you. Then simply brainstorm with yourself. Think of all the things you could do that can move you toward the goal. Think of the people and organizations you need to work with, the skills you need, the resources you need to tap into. Write them all over the page. Don't worry about order or priority right now. You can even draw pictures of what you need. Adding color and sketches activates your creative right brain.

Then set it aside for a few days or a week. Give your subconscious a chance to work on this. Come back to your page with a fresh mind to see what you can add. Then prioritize the steps, break big steps into smaller steps, and schedule these smaller steps into your calendar.

To make this even more effective, once you have the basic brainstorm down, gather a group of friends. Four to six is good. Put what you've come up with on a big piece of flip chart paper on the wall. Tell them what your goal is and ask if they have any other ideas, resources, or contacts to add to your action plan. The ideas will fly, synergy will step in, and you'll come up with a much more complete plan of action.

As an added bonus, you now have all these other folks who know your dream and will help you and keep you accountable. Why would they do this for you? Hey, they are your friends! Plus, once they see the power of this, you can return the favor and do the same for them. Remember, it isn't achieving the goal that brings the joy; it's the process of working toward the goal, the fact that you are moving toward what you want. It's the journey, not the destination. Don't agonize over the plan of action itself. Just come up with one and start moving forward. Your plan will change as you step out to take action. You'll discover new things. (Plus, neurology researchers have found that diving into a new experience triggers the production of dopamine, one of the body's feel-good chemicals, so you'll immediately bump up your happiness by taking on the new.) Jot down a few thoughts to come back to later:

Write down one goal: _____

_____

What are the benefits to you of achieving this goal?_____

_____

_____

What are some resources, skills, people, etc. you can tap into to move toward this goal? _____

_____

_____

_____

Write down a few small steps can you take right here, right now.

_____

_____

_____

Schedule Appointments with Yourself

One great way to move forward is to schedule appointments with yourself in your calendar or day planner, in ink, or set a reminder alert in your smart phone or computer to work toward your goal, to take the mini steps one at a time. Hey, you hold your appointments with other people sacred. It's time to start making appointments with yourself, and holding those appointments sacred, to move you toward your dreams.

Set Short-term and Long-term Goals, Big and Small

Kerry, the military spouse artist, suggests you set a really long-term high level "in the clouds" goal. Her long-term goal is to become known as an American master painter, recognized by her peers and the country.

We've heard these bigger goals described as BHAGs—Big Hairy Audacious Goals! Doesn't that make it sound like more fun? But as Kerry adds, "Set some flexible realistic short-term goals for yourself as well." With this military life, you will face challenges, and you won't be able to follow a straight-line path forward. By having some smaller goals you can achieve more quickly, you'll see and feel success. Once you experience success in one goal, you'll be encouraged to go for your next one.

As Kerry says, "The reality of this military lifestyle is that you have to keep your expectations in check a bit; otherwise you can feel like a failure." That is especially true if you constantly compare your level of success in whatever you do with your peers who are not moving every three years, who are not dealing with deployments and other military challenges. "For me," Kerry says, "as long as I continue to see progress, I feel successful."

Remember what the research shows. The joy is in the journey, in the fact you are doing something for you that you are interested in, that you are engaged in life. You aren't always putting your needs and interests on the back burner, waiting for retirement or some other distant future. Write down your big goals, but start by working toward one smaller short-term goal. Make it a little bigger than what you think is realistic, so you have to stretch yourself.

Spend Five to Ten Minutes

One of the problems with our goals is they seem too big sometimes. And our lives seem too full. That's where baby steps come in. Think of one thing you can do toward your goal that will only take five to ten minutes. Then set a timer and do that one thing, today.

Research book titles that have information for your dream. Call to schedule an appointment with a counselor at the education center or spouse employment office. Contact your professional association for an information packet. Make a list of people you could do information interviews with, and then call at least one to schedule a time. Clean out one drawer. Get your quilting project pieces organized in one place. Set up your easel and art supplies. Take a quick walk around the house.

Kathie learned the magic of ten minutes a number of years ago. It's a good tool to beat procrastination, to get you moving forward. After years of saying she wanted to start a yoga practice, she made a commitment to herself. She would do yoga at least ten minutes a day, even if those ten minutes were split into three different time periods doing just one yoga posture each time. That seemed manageable, whereas finding time to get to and take a one-hour class seemed impossible. Ten minutes was manageable. Often, those ten minutes went longer. Years later, she does yoga almost every day, for twenty to forty minutes each time. And yes, sometimes it's still only ten minutes divided up into three time periods. Daily yoga became a true practice, ten minutes at a time.

Here's another example. Overwhelmed by your clutter, or possibly that one drawer or closet that is overfull? Dream of having a clean, organized house? Well, set the timer and spend five minutes starting on one area. When the timer buzzes, stop with a clear conscience. The key is you took the first step; you got started. And, once you see even baby successes, it will spur you to keep going. You'll take the next baby step, and the next, and the next. Before you know it, you will accomplish your goal.

Finance Your Dream

One important step in goal achieving, no matter what your dream, is to take control of your finances.

If we had our lives to do over, that is one big thing we'd do first. Kathie admits, "If I were a young spouse new to the military now, I know I could do a whole lot more for our family's long-term financial situation if I spent some of my time learning about finances and investments rather than spending the kind of extreme time I used to spend on running or job-hunting, or watching television, or shopping for the best curtains for our house with each move." We both wish we had started reading about finances much sooner. Just take a look at compound interest tables, and you'll see how much better off you will be with even small-level investments early in life!

When it comes to finances and your dreams, it's crucial to take your family finances into consideration as you make decisions. Budgets really are crucial, as is making clear decisions on any purchases. (For one thing, studies show that material items don't ever bring the kind of long-term satisfaction experiences do.) Learn to think carefully about purchases, learn the fun in living frugally in order to have funds for what matters most to you and your family, learn the magic of compound interest! Take advantage of the free financial counseling the military provides. Check out your family service center to find what is available, and get your family on track early on.

Reap the Rewards of Risk Taking

As you move toward your dreams, you end up stepping outside your comfort zone. "A ship in a harbor is safe, but that's not what ships are built for" is a quote that has helped Holly many times over the years when she was scared to take a risk. Yes, there are times when it seems a lot easier to just stay doing the same thing, but sometimes you have to get out of the harbor (your comfort zone) and set sail. You've heard the old saying, "If you always do what you've always done, you'll always get what you've always got." If you want things to change, you have to change. Often, that means doing something scary. As Kerry, the artist, said, "I never turned down a commission, even when they were scary as hell!"

Kathie's Story

I did it! I faced a big fear and lived through it. I know it's good to step outside your comfort zone every now and then, but that's easier said than done—especially if you are like me and have that tendency to be able to visualize the worst possible outcome. I'm such a worrier, and I have to work hard to turn those negative pictures around and visualize positive outcomes. But I am learning to do it.

I've found it helps to write down the expected positive outcome in my calendar for the day. So on November 22, I wrote down: "Enjoy successful radio show. Have fun!" For good measure, I added a Fantastic sticker to it.

As we were driving to AFN (Armed Forces Network) in Frankfurt, I told Karen this was going to be fun. (I don't think she believed me. I don't think I believed it, either.) Karen is another military spouse I convinced to join me in this scary enterprise—a three-hour call-in radio show about careers. Neither of us had ever been on the radio, and here we were committed to three hours! The listening audience would include people we live and work around, including our spouses.

In thinking back over the ways I've forced myself to face fears in the past, I realize I use a trick. Whether it was giving a seminar, doing my first keynote, going on a four-day hike, trying out rock climbing and rappelling, tackling the Team Tower, trying whitewater kayaking, or doing this radio show—in each case, I scheduled it way in advance.

Somehow, the fear isn't that big when it is so far away. And when you have so many other things going on, you sort of forget about this fear until the time comes. Where I probably wouldn't be able to say yes to something fearful if it was happening tomorrow, somehow it doesn't seem real when it is a long way off.

The other thing that helps me is reminding myself of all those fears that are no longer fears. Certainly, in some cases, the activities I tackled, like whitewater kayaking and rock climbing, might be things that go into the "once is enough" category for me. But I'm glad I had the experience. It did increase my overall self-confidence. The ones I remind myself of most when facing a new fear are those that are no longer fears. I remind myself that I now really enjoy doing seminars and keynotes. I remind myself that I loved the Hut-to-Hut hike, even with a twenty-pound pack on my back.

And, yes, I really did have fun doing the call-in talk show. As Karen said afterward, "The last thing I thought this would be was fun, but it really was!"

Tricks to help you take risks:

- Tell everyone you know that you are going to do something. As one person told us, "That way there is no backing out. You have to go through with it to save face." And many friends won't let you forget. When Navy spouse Sarah kept saying she wanted to try inline skating, for example, her mother and sister called her on it and bought her inline skates for her birthday. When they sat in

Sarah's closet for five months, her sister came and made her try them out.

- One possible exception to the "tell everyone you know" technique is to not tell the naysayers in your life. Instead, tell positive, supportive people who will encourage you to take action. We say that because we both have enough self-doubt that a naysayer fuels our doubts and keeps us from taking action. However, we've had other spouses tell us they have the opposite reaction. If someone tells them, "You can't do that," they dive into action to prove that person wrong. So know yourself. If you have self-doubts, avoid naysayers. If naysayers motivate you, then seek them out!

- Visualize success. Close your eyes, relax, and start visualizing yourself successfully doing what you want to do. Include all your senses. Do this frequently, and when you actually do the activity, you'll feel like you've already done it, and it will be easier to do. Really! There are many studies that prove this is true.

- Take someone along. It's easier to do something challenging when you do it with a friend. That radio show didn't seem quite as overwhelming with a friend along.

- Be courageous and make mistakes. If we don't make mistakes, how do we ever learn? As Sophia Loren said, "Making mistakes is part of the dues one pays for a full life." Success doesn't come from making the fewest mistakes. It comes from getting results. You can't get results without first taking action.

- Accept that not every risk will turn into what you thought it might, but every risk you overcome will help you grow. Your courage muscle grows each time you stretch outside your comfort zone, which means you have a little more courage and confidence to take on that next risk.

- Flex your risk-taking muscle with small things. Look for daily opportunities to flex that muscle. Order a new food on a menu; take a different route to work; talk to a stranger; listen to a new kind of music. With each risk, you build your ability to take on larger ones. You expand your world experience and get out of your rut at the same time!

Tara Crooks tells us how each new thing she takes on with *Army Wife Talk Radio* and *Army Wife Network* has been scary. She just keeps reminding herself of the scary things she's already done that worked out just fine.

We kill our fears by tackling them, by taking action. Taking action builds our self-confidence and allows us to live more fully in life.

From Holly's Journal

Kathie and I have a mantra we use when something doesn't quite go the way we wanted it to when we try something new. "Weelll, that didn't work!" It makes us laugh and pick ourselves up and try a different approach the next time.

It resulted from our first keynote together at a spouse conference at Ramstein Air Force Base in Germany. Rather than having to say, "Now Holly will..., now Kathie will...," we had decided on transition lines between our parts. There was one crucial one. However, we failed to realize Kathie said that line at least two times before the time I needed to step in. So Kathie's sailing along, and I'm leaning against a table, practicing things in my head. Suddenly, my subconscious hears the line, long before expected. The ultimate professional, I jumped in and started. Kathie, in the meantime, is standing there, her mouth open in shock, wondering what the heck I'm doing. It meant we left out a huge chunk of material, but, of course, the audience didn't know that.

At first we beat ourselves up about it, but then I couldn't help but laugh. "Listen to us, putting ourselves down, focusing on the negative. Let's look at the good part of what we did today. That's what we teach after all, focus on the good. For the other, let's just say 'Weelll, that didn't work' and move on."

Know that Failure Isn't Always Failure

One key thing to realize is that your goals aren't set in stone; they may very well change along the way. Sometimes what happens is you move forward toward a goal, start to achieve it, and then realize it isn't something you want after all.

After years of changing jobs and sometimes careers with each military move, Kathie decided to try a business instead, as an image consultant. She spent a lot of time and money in research and setting things up, only to discover that particular business wasn't for her. Now, should she consider that a failure, a total loss? She doesn't.

"It got me into the idea of having my own business," she says. "And by doing workshops to get clients and by writing articles to get my name out there for visibility, I learned what I really love to do." That "failure" led her to speaking and writing as a career path. She now considers that first experience just one important stepping stone on the path to her dreams.

We hear that from so many people as they pursue goals. Many goals lead them to other things they weren't even aware of when they got started. Choosing to give up on a goal, once you learn it really isn't for you, isn't failure. It's conscious choice. Plus, even if you do fail, remember this. Failing at something is still better in the long run than always wondering and regretting something you never even tried.

From Kathie's Journal

By the way, share your failure stories. So often we look at other people who have succeeded at something and all we see is their success. We don't know the failures it took to get there. Or as my friend Claire says, "We compare our inners to their outers." We know all about our own struggles. We so often don't have a clue about the struggles "successful" people went through in their process.

I recently got an email from a military spouse friend who "got fired" from a column she was writing. She was devastated, feeling like a failure. So I shared with her a number of my own journal entries, from two different times I got fired from columns, in one case because "my writing was flat." And yes, I cried over those events. But then I picked myself up. I thought, first off, other editors have liked my writing. Second, I'll use these events as catalysts to learn more about creative writing, to improve.

My friend said my email and sharing helped her put her current failure into perspective, to realize it was all part of the process, the journey.

I collect stories of "failures" to inspire me. One favorite: when Katie Couric first graduated with a degree in journalism, she got a grunt job at CNN, and submitted her demo video because she wanted to be on camera. Reese Schonfeld, the president of CNN at the time, said, "Don't ever let that woman on TV." She didn't let him stop her dreams. Look at her now!

The key to goal achieving is to make a plan of some sort and take action. Start with one small step. Once you make a commitment and start moving forward, things will happen that you could never have planned. You may find you reach your goal in a completely different way than you expected. It will happen because you are out trying to make things happen. It won't happen if you just sit at home and watch TV, or complain about your situation.

Key Points and Action Steps
- ▷ Choose a primary focus for each stage of life.
- ▷ Apply the basics of effective goal setting and achieving.
- ▷ Determine the outcome of your outcomes.
- ▷ Develop a plan of action and get moving.
- ▷ Schedule appointments with yourself.
- ▷ Set short-term and long-term goals, big and small.
- ▷ Reap the rewards of risk taking.
- ▷ Know that failure isn't always failure.

Resources
Care Packages for the Home by Barbara A. Glanz (1998). Kathie bought eleven of these books for friends—full of great ideas for your families. We love all of Barbara's books, including *Care Packages for the Workplace: Dozens of Little Things You Can Do To Regenerate Spirit At Work* (1996) and *Balancing Acts: More Than 250 Guiltfree, Creative Ideas to Blend Your Work and Your Life* (2003). www.BarbaraGlanz.com.

Feel the Fear…and Do It Anyway: Dynamic Techniques for Turning Fear, Indecision, and Anger into Power, Action, and Love by Susan Jeffers, PhD (2006).

Write It Down, Make It Happen: Knowing What You Want—and Getting It! by Henriette Anne Klauser (2001). We highly recommend all of Henriette's books, especially *Writing on Both Sides of the Brain: Breakthrough Techniques for People Who Write* (in its 27th printing!), and *With Pen in Hand: The Healing Power of Writing* (2003). www.HenrietteKlauser.com.

Financial Resources

To understand the military pay system and learn how to read a Leave and Earnings statement, there is great information offered through programs like Army Family Team Building and the equivalent Military 101 programs. Check with your family support center to find out what is available.

How to Save Money Every Day (2000); *Money Doesn't Grow on Trees: Teaching Your Kids the Value of a Buck* (2005); *Shop, Save, and Share* (2004); and *Living Rich for Less: Create the Lifestyle You Want by Giving, Saving, and Spending Smart* (2008) by Air Force wife and mother of seven, Ellie Kay. Read her column in *Military Spouse* magazine. www.EllieKay.com.

Military Money Might, a blog on finances for military members by Hank Coleman, an Army soldier and financial education enthusiast. www.MilitaryMoneyMight.com.

Military Money online magazine. Full of good articles geared specifically to military life. Check out the spouse section and education section for tips, ideas, and resources. www.MilitaryMoney.com.

MilitarySaves.org. Started in 2003, the Military Saves campaign is part of the Department of Defense's Financial Readiness Campaign.

SaveAndInvest.org. Provides tools to educate military members.

Chapter 8

Discover the Possibilities and Ways Around the Obstacles

I f we were to say there was one chapter that was the most important chapter of this book, this one would be it. To create a life that works for you within this military life, you have to open yourself up to the possibilities. You have to find new approaches to your dream when the approach you have isn't working or isn't possible due to a specific assignment or due to military life. It's important to learn to automatically ask the questions, "What is possible here? What can I do here to work toward my dream? What is available here that might not be available in other places?" Be open, and access the many possibilities that do exist. Learn the magic of second and third right answers.

Brainstorm Second and Third Right Answers

In our workshops, we give participants an opportunity to share dreams and brainstorm with the group to find those second and third right answers.

Charmin's dream was to own and run a bed and breakfast (B&B) in Tennessee. When asked at a Fort Stewart, Georgia, workshop for her plan of action, she started with, "We hope to get stationed at" and "As soon as he retires, I'll…" Notice how those are actions outside her own control and focused on future events. When we pushed for things she could do right now, she added a few: read books on running B&Bs, search the Internet for information, and test breakfast recipes.

We then asked the other workshop attendees for help. Ideas flew. Join the B&B Association for information and contacts. Intern at a B&B to learn the ropes, or "babysit" one while the owners take a vacation. Take a class on how to run a small business: taxes, accounting, marketing, and so on.

By the time we finished brainstorming, her eyes were shining as she saw possibilities, all things she could do right here, right now, not waiting. Imagine the fun and excitement Charmin can now create in her life anywhere they are stationed, moving toward her dream.

The key is realizing there are paths you can try out, rather than simply seeing a dead end in front of you. Brainstorming with others is the first open gate on the road to possibilities.

A reality of military life is the fact that some things you want to do aren't possible, at least not exactly the way you envision them. Your career won't proceed in a straight-line fashion. You can't build your business the same effective consistent way your peers who stay put can. You won't have that dream house you keep working on year in and year out to get it just the way you want. You won't have a garden that matures and evolves over time.

Many of your dreams may seem impossible where you happen to be assigned at the moment. Does that mean you have to give up your dream? No. It just means the approach you are thinking of—your first right answer—won't work right here.

That's where second, third, and higher right answers come into play.

Too many of us stop with the first solution to our situation. If that solution isn't possible, we often give up and end up frustrated and angry with the military—for moving us in the first place or for sticking us in this godforsaken place. (We know from experience, since we each did that in early assignments.)

> *The key is realizing there are paths you can try out, rather than simply seeing a dead end in front of you. If your first right answer isn't possible, look for the second right answer, or as many as you need until you find one that will work right now, right where you are.*

By looking for, and finding, the right answer that does work right where you are, you keep moving toward your dream. You continue to engage in activities that matter to you. You can be quite content wherever they send you as you take advantage of the possibilities of each new assignment.

The theatre major Aneta Rude, mentioned earlier in the book, is a good example of someone who chose to look for the possibilities that do exist, rather than what doesn't exist. When she couldn't work on the theatre aspect of her dream with one assignment, her husband suggested a second right answer for that location. "Why don't you work on the education part of your dream?" he asked. To be a drama teacher, after all, she needed both theatre training and education training. Bingo. That second approach was possible at that assignment, and she kept moving toward her dream.

Let's look at other examples of how this works:

Janie, a Navy spouse, worked as a secretary for many years and had been able to move that career as she moved with the military. Then she moved with her husband to a small military community in Japan. There were no secretarial jobs at her level and, in fact, there weren't any secretarial jobs of any level open at the time.

Janie could have stopped there, frustrated and angry for three years. Instead, she decided to look at the situation differently. "Although I've always worked as a secretary because I'm good at it and the pay was good," she says, "my dream has always been to open a bakery." She decided to see this move as a forced golden opportunity to move toward her dream. She took a job at a submarine sandwich shop operating off base.

"I couldn't have justified doing that in the States where the secretarial pay is so much higher than the minimum wage I earn here," she says. "I don't see myself as a minimum wage worker at a sub shop, however. I see myself as getting paid to take a hands-on course in small business management." She approached her job differently from the other minimum wage workers, asking questions, taking notes. She learned everything she could about the ins and outs of a small business, in preparation for her own future business. Now that's a second right answer!

And by the way, had secretarial work been her dream, she could have created a virtual assistant business, even in a remote location, if there were no local secretarial jobs available.

Diana McCarthy is an Army spouse who wanted to go to law school but that wasn't available where they lived in Germany. She figured she'd have to wait until they returned to the United States and just hoped to be stationed near a law school. When she shared that dream and first right answer with our workshop group, she listened to the other ideas shared.

We received this email from her a few weeks later. "I just wanted to let you know you have motivated me and made a difference in my life. I have volunteered for the local Judge Advocate General (JAG) office and signed up for distance-learning law classes as I go to the library and check out books all the time to help me with my law career." She paid attention to the second and third right answers that came out of the brainstorming session, and took action to start moving toward her dream—without any change of assignment or circumstances.

What if the next assignment was a rural location in the United States with no law school close by? She could continue online courses. She could volunteer for CASA (Court Appointed Special Advocates for children), where she would gain valuable court experience that would benefit her when she gets her law degree.

Alicia Kunz graduated with her bachelor's degree in nursing and was working at her dream job at the Mayo Clinic and starting on her master's studies when she met her husband. Then he enlisted in the Army, and they ended up in Germany. She couldn't find a job in nursing and was miserable at first. Until she expanded her thinking.

She ended up working as a wellness counselor and supervisor of the WIC (Women, Infants, Children) program overseas. It was great experience and great hours, providing her with continuing education money and time that allowed her to work on her master's degree to become a nurse educator.

"I'm halfway through my program," she says proudly, "and I haven't had to pay a dime yet, all because of the military and my job's continuing education money."

Kathie's Story

I started doing seminars when my husband was assigned to Fort Lewis, Washington. I landed an audition with one of the national seminar companies to do programs for them all over the United States. My new business was on its way!

Then we got orders to Germany. The national seminar company had no work for me overseas. In order to market my seminars to corporations in Germany, I would have to pay German taxes. My business wasn't large enough or advanced enough to justify that. I thought I'd have to give up seminar work for three years. My first right answer wasn't possible in Germany.

At a newcomer welcome luncheon, I happened to talk with a spouse who told me about the American Women's Activities Germany conference held every year. The proposals for workshops were due that week. Talk about serendipity. Another new acquaintance told me about the Office of Personnel Management and how they provide training workshops to US government offices all through Europe. Their headquarters happened to be a two-hour drive from where we lived.

I spent the next three years doing seminars for military spouse groups and for military offices throughout Europe. I was able to build my skills, material, and reputation, and continue in this field I had almost given up on during that assignment. And, I was now able to market myself as an "international speaker," something it might have taken me years longer to achieve living in the United States. Not to mention the fact that I got to travel to wonderful places like Garmisch, Germany, and Venice, Italy, to speak. And it all happened because other spouses opened me up to second and third right answers to what I wanted to do.

At one of our workshops, as we described the concept of second right answers, a military spouse challenged us. "That still sounds like you are making a sacrifice, since you can't go after what you want, the way you want," she said. Well, yes, the reality is that we are making sacrifices as military spouses—just as our spouses are making sacrifices by serving in the military. There is no question, life might be much easier and more straightforward if we weren't married to the military. But, the fact remains that we are.

So, choosing to look for the second, third, and higher right answer makes sense. Your other option is to simply give up when the first way doesn't work and to wallow in frustration and bitterness. Instead, doesn't it make sense to be creative, and to get the help of other creative people to find an answer that does work? The interesting thing is, often that second, third, or higher right answer ends up being a better route in the long run.

The most important thing is that it keeps you making forward progress and not giving up on your dream. Sacrifice or innovation? Whatever it is, it keeps you moving toward your dreams, fully engaged in life!

No Yes Buts

When we brainstorm in our workshops, we make the spouse whose dream we are working on wear a button that says "Yes, But" with a red line through the words. No "Yes Buts!" It's human nature. When people give us ideas, we often start saying, "Yes, but I don't have the money"; "Yes, but I don't have the education"; "Yes, but I'm too young"; "Yes but I'm too old"; "Yes, but…" "Yes, buts" don't move you forward!

We don't want editing when we brainstorm. We want lots of ideas, wild and crazy, even impossible ideas. Even the most impossible idea might have a nugget of a possible idea inside of it. Those second and third right answers will show up, if you let the ideas flow.

We read an interview with Vicki Johnson that made us smile. Vicki is a clinical social worker, Army spouse, and mother. She's been called the Dear Abby of the military world. Her column "Dear Ms. Vicki" appears in several military newspapers and *The Washington Times*. She is also a DoD contracted counselor.

"You have to find a way to make your own opportunities," she says, "I hear from so many people I call 'Yes, but-ers.' You don't get anywhere saying that. You have to make this military life work for you."

Are you stuck on that first right answer for your dream? You say it's just not possible where you are living right now? Well, start looking for that second and third right answer. Enlist your friends to brainstorm ideas. Email us. We mean it. We love to brainstorm possibilities. Try us. We'd love to share your success story with others.

Open Yourself Up to Serendipity

Kerry Vosler, the artist, does not have an art degree. "I pieced my career together over time as we moved, by working with artists one on one, by going to workshops, by self study and doing art," she says. She has taught art in schools and one on one in her home. She has painted many portraits on commission.

At one point, when they moved to Missouri, she got discouraged. "It was pretty dry for artists," she explains. She volunteered some time with a Chautauqua festival there, creating their advertising poster. A contact from that organization led her to an interview with and a commission to do the portrait of Ike Skelton.

"Just when I thought my art career was over," she says, "I got asked to do a portrait of the leading Democrat at the time." That led to more work. You'll notice, she wasn't sitting at home doing nothing, bemoaning her fate, when the opportunity came up. She was actively out in the community, moving forward, doing something with her art, even when it seemed like limited forward movement.

We've experienced serendipity ourselves many times over. We had been volunteering our seminars for military spouses all over Germany for three years. Newly returned to the States, we heard they were sending soldiers to Bosnia for a year—the longest deployment for the Army at that time since Vietnam. We thought, "We want to present seminars for those spouses." But we didn't think the Army would pay to bring us back to Germany, so we brainstormed ways to make it happen.

We decided to find a corporate sponsor. To create the best proposal possible, we needed testimonials from spouses who had participated in our workshop. We sent out letters to them. All of a sudden, we got an email from the spouse of the Army's commander in chief of troops in Europe (CINC-USAREUR) saying our letter had been passed on to her from one of the women we sent it to. They had been discussing the need for something like this. There

Chinese proverb: "A peasant must stand a long time on a hillside with his mouth open before a roast duck flies in."

were family support funds available. The seminars happened—not the way our goal plan said—but serendipitously in a quicker way, because we'd been taking action and moving forward.

The key is that you aren't sitting back just waiting for something to happen, just waiting for someone else to step in, just waiting for the perfect assignment or circumstance. That would be like the Chinese proverb: "A peasant must stand a long time on a hillside with his mouth open before a roast duck flies in." You need to be out there taking steps, starting the momentum. And then, things happen! Who knows? That roast duck might even show up.

Key Points and Action Steps
- ▷ Brainstorm second and third right answers.
- ▷ Enlist your friends to help you see the possibilities.
- ▷ Open yourself to serendipity.

Chapter 9

Get Help for Your Dreams and Your Life

How to Effectively Ask For and Create the Support You Need

S o many of us think we have to do everything by ourselves—that we have to be totally self-motivated and self-disciplined—that we shouldn't need to ask others for any help. We've found it's much more effective and fun to create the support that can help you—and help others— go for your dreams. Here are some ways to do that.

Consider Being on a Team

Kathie's Story

When we moved to Fort Lewis, Washington, I decided to take a leap and start my own business—very scary! Someone heard what I was doing and said, "You should meet Reba—it sounds like you two have a lot in common." We met for a lunch that turned into one of those amazing connections. We talked nonstop for hours and came out of the restaurant full of ideas, energy, and motivation. I told Reba, "We need to keep meeting."

That is how my first support team was born. We found four other women with dreams of their own and started meeting weekly to help each other with ideas. We nudged each other along, providing the support we each needed to keep going toward what we wanted. In many cases, the group first helped us figure out exactly what it was we wanted!

Since then, with each move, I've created a new team. Once you've been part of one, you will always want to be part of one.

One reason groups are so important to me is that I'm a recovering procrastinator. I'm one of those people who is slow to action. I plan, research, reflect, and talk about things long before I ever act on what I want to do. I really have to trick and push myself to take action and move forward. The group helps a lot.

So, what are these groups? And why would you want to be part of one? You'll hear them called all sorts of things: success teams, mastermind groups, boards of directors, life makeover groups. We call them Dare to Dream Teams. The basic concept is the same—the group helps each member go for his or her dreams.

We could go on and on with examples of what such groups have helped people accomplish. And these are all military spouses like you. Stephanie, an Army spouse, wanted to learn how to work a computer. Within a few years, she'd built a computer-based service company she then sold to another firm. Army spouse Mary Styron got her resume together just because everyone else in the group was doing their resumes, and she decided to tap into those resources. Within days of arriving at their next assignment, as she signed her kids up for school, she dropped off the resume to see if she could at least substitute teach. She walked out with a full-time position. Army spouse Cara had never spent time with young children. When she had her baby, her group helped her with important parenting ideas and resources.

There's more, of course. Groups help you figure out how you want to live your life, what's really important to you, and they help keep you from getting off track.

Recently, we heard a woman talking about her husband deploying once again. "I gain twenty pounds every time he deploys," she said, "I guess I eat out of boredom and for comfort." We immediately thought, "This woman needs a team!" Especially during deployments, your team can help you stick to good health patterns and more importantly, help you get excited about a project or goal, so there's less space for the boredom and anxiety that can lead to negative habits.

These groups work so well for a number of reasons. The accountability factor is key. You report each meeting whether or not you accomplished the minigoals you set the meeting before, which everyone wrote down. It's easier to justify procrastination when you are only accountable to yourself. It is much harder to face four or five other people and say, "I didn't do it—again!"

The group expands your resources, contacts, and ideas. You are only one person, with one set of experiences and way of thinking. Your group not only brings in their ideas to add to yours, but the synergy of the group in brainstorming creates completely new ideas. You might see only one way to accomplish what you want—and it may not be feasible based on your location, finances, or experience level. The group will come up with alternate paths that are feasible right now, wherever you are stationed.

Your team members bring strengths to the table you don't have and vice versa. That's why we recommend shooting for differences in team members. Don't just start a team with a group of friends who are just like you. Besides, close friends sometimes have limited ideas of what you are capable of, while strangers don't have any preconceived notions. And in a group like this, you won't be strangers for long.

You gain courage from the group. The group members provide a sounding board for your doubts and fears and support you in pushing past them, in both practical and concrete ways, and on an emotional level. Sometimes group members go along physically to provide moral support during a challenging task. As author and speaker Cheryl Richardson says, "Groups are like Jell-O molds. They hold you up until you can stand on your own."

The group acts as your own personal cheering squad. When you succeed at something, your group helps you celebrate. When you feel down, it helps to be around "up" people who can remind you that you won't always feel this way. As one woman said, "The reason groups work so well is because not everyone is depressed at the same time."

The group helps you learn to live in the magical world of "possibility thinking."

Your group provides additional antennae. Since your group members all know your dream, they bring in articles, contacts, and information for you that they run across—information you might never have discovered yourself.

The group helps you learn to live in the magical world of "possibility thinking." As you see others move toward what they want, and succeed, you get inspired and motivated to take action yourself.

Is this type of team only for people trying to run their own business? Not at all! It doesn't matter what your dreams or goals are—personal, parenting, spiritual, physical, financial, educational, whatever! They can be small or large, short term or long term. The group is just a means to get—and keep—you moving toward something you want. The best part is you have a lot of fun, laughter, and great conversation in the process!

So many of us as military spouses feel our dreams have to stay on the back burner as long as we move with the military—or as long as the kids are still growing—or until we become more motivated. But that isn't true. We can all move toward what we want, with help.

As Army spouse Monica Dixon says, "My mastermind group saved my life. We focused on Problem—Solution, Problem—Solution, No Whining!"

Mary Styron's Story

One Thursday morning, I found myself driving over German hills, looking for a town I couldn't even pronounce. I was apprehensive. I just met Kathie sitting at an AWAG conference. She called a few days ago, caught me at a moment of weakness, and asked me if I wanted to attend a meeting of her "success group." Yeah, right.

So there I was, driving to this 11:00 a.m. meeting, picturing group hugs and the word "empowerment" hanging in the air like a battle cry. My husband admonished me that morning, "The first hint of man-bashing or feminazism—run like the wind."

I arrived at Kathie's house and was greeted ominously by whole-kernel bran muffins and tea. Tea. I am strictly coffee, black, lotsa caffeine. Those little hairs on the back of my neck stood up and wiggled. I braced myself for crystals and incense.

The clock struck 11:00; the polite chatter ceased. A kitchen timer was placed in the center of the table with reverence. Kathie explained the process. Each of us had ten minutes to talk about ourselves—our goals, our frustrations, and our needs. The next ten minutes were to be spent in discussion and feedback. I was getting a little confused. She sounded so businesslike, not "new-agey" at all.

Gail was first. I imagined she would bare her soul, bash her man, and blame society or the military. She began talking about the business she had started here in Germany. Business was so good she had to rent a stall at the PX. I was agog. This woman was telling me about positive things. She went on to talk about the books she was writing!

Kathie's turn. This woman is a one-person enterprise. Neither woman ever said "empowerment." They both adore their husbands. They both took charge of their lives.

My first "success group" meeting ended, I bounced back to my car and raced home, listing dreams, formulating plans, and discovering possibilities. I was challenged to determine what I really wanted to do with my life. I have rarely missed a meeting of my success group since that first one, almost two years ago. The group has changed from a few timid women, quite unsure of their direction, into a bunch of well-focused individuals. We are housewives, mothers, single professionals, and Army officers. We have little in common but much to learn from each other.

The group I so reluctantly joined has done wonders for me, the most important of which is accountability. I could resolutely tell my husband "Tomorrow I will do X" and never make a move to make that resolution come true. I could stare at my dimpled thighs all day long and swear the Nordic Track to be my best friend, and never walk those two blocks to the gym. I could envision my dream vocation at every pause and not open a book to find out "how." But, tell a group of tenacious women "I'm going to get it done before the next meeting" . . . and I'll do it or die trying!

This group has taught me the power of networking, the beauty of friendship, the strength of dreams, and the satisfaction of getting things done.

Note from Kathie: *When Mary first said yes to the group, she said to her husband, "What am I thinking? I already have too much on my plate." With three active boys, involvement in their activities, and being president of the spouse club on post, she did have a lot going. Her husband said, "If you take anything off your plate, don't take this off. It's the only thing you do for YOU." Now that is spouse support.*

Interested? Do you want to start your own group? We would love to help you start a support group, Dare to Dream Team, whatever you choose to call it. (Kathie's group in Corvallis called themselves the Big Group because they wanted to learn to live Big!) Here's what we can do to help.

- We have a detailed Dare to Dream Team handout spelling out what these groups are and how to start and run a meeting, at MilitarySpouseJourney.com.
- We are happy to answer your questions as you get going with your group, to give you ideas of exercises, to brainstorm resources and contacts for whatever dreams your group members have (we are really good at that and love to do it.)
- We want to hear your stories as your groups develop. They might just be things we can include in an article or a future book to inspire other military spouses.

Get Your Spouse's Support

Heidi is an Army spouse pursuing a freelance writing business. To get started, she sent letters to editors and directed them to her web site for further samples. "My husband helped me get all the letters out, and he created the web site," she adds.

Kerry, the artist, tells us, "Whenever I went to a workshop, my husband supported that—he took care of our two kids."

Monica Dixon, an Army spouse with two boys, managed to get her doctorate despite many moves and one unaccompanied tour. Her research on body image and women's sexuality resulted in speaking engagements, a television interview, and a book deal. "In order to write the book," she says, "I had to physically leave home every three to four months for a weeklong period. My husband took care of the children, and an amazing thing happened—he became a dad!" She couldn't have written the book without her husband's help.

Just as we make adjustments and compromises to support their work, they do the same for us, for this work we love.

We could not do the work we do without the support and encouragement of our spouses. Just as we make adjustments and compromises to support their work, they do the same for us, for this work we love.

Everyone we interviewed who was involved in interests of their own mentioned the support of their spouse. Their service member supported their interests just as they supported their spouse's military career. It's a partnership—a win/win situation.

Invest Time in Information Interviews

Before you dive into your particular dream, do a little more research on the activities you think you are most interested in. Conduct information interviews. These are commonly thought of in the career world, but they are useful for anything you want to do in life. Talk to people who have done what you want to do.

The idea is that, rather than judging a job or any activity as appropriate for you just based on what you imagine, talk to people doing that activity to see if your perceptions match reality. Gather information, see how your skills fit in, make contacts, and determine your energy and enthusiasm for that endeavor—before you dive in.

Why would someone grant you an information interview? People love to talk about what they do. Most people will say yes.

This powerful tool helps with life decisions. For example, if you are thinking about homeschooling your children, or taking on a volunteer position, or creating a new program in your community to fill a need you see and care about, use the information interview format. Talk to others who are doing the same thing you want to do. Then make the decision with facts instead of an imaginary image of what you think it might be like.

From Kathie's Journal

I had a dream of starting an Author Series when we settled down. So I searched online and found a program that had been in place for a number of years in another town. I called the founder of that program. She spent hours on the telephone with me, telling me what had worked and what didn't. She gave me sample forms she used. She gave me a list of great authors to contact, along with mentioning one or two who had been a bit "high maintenance." Why did she do all that? She loves what she is doing and likes sharing with like-minded people.

I was able to start the program in my town in a much quicker, smoother way, because I'd done the information interview. Two years later, another woman contacted me because she wanted to start a similar program where she lives. I happily gave her all of my information, my program plan, the forms we use, and authors to contact, glad to help someone else with her dream.

Learn from Books and the Internet

Another way to research is to read books about the activities you are interested in. We are convinced you can find how-to books for whatever you want to do in life. Want to run a Bed and Breakfast? Read *The Complete Idiot's Guide to Running a Bed and Breakfast*, or one of about twenty other similar books. Want to homeschool your children? Read *Homeschooling: The Early Years: Your Complete Guide to Successfully Homeschooling the 3- to 8-Year-Old Child*, or one of many other similar books.

If you are pursuing your education and need additional funding, check out *Scholarships, Grants and Prizes: Millions of Awards Worth Billions of Dollars* (Peterson's Scholarships, Grants & Prizes), updated regularly.

Check out the list of *For Dummies* books or the *Complete Idiot's Guide* books. Penguin's web site says, "Smart people read *Idiot Guides*." It's true. Why not learn from the experts, people who have done what you want to do. It gives you a good base, a good starting point. You don't have to reinvent every wheel.

And, there are many helpful web sites and blogs. For career field information, check out the Department of Labor's Occupational Outlook handbook and other resources where you can search by career field to find out about the field, salary potential, and career growth potential by state and nationally. www.BLS.gov.

Intern to Learn

One in-depth way to research a dream before undertaking it is to find an intern opportunity working for someone who does what you think you want to do. Check out Internships.com, Experience.com, Idealist.org (for non-profits) and MediaBistro.com (for media internships). Or try PivotPlanet to see if you can try out your dream job before diving in more fully.

Kathie wishes she'd thought of this earlier in life. "If I were starting out in the speaking world today," she says, "I'd find a speaker I admired and ask to work with him or her for free, to learn. Most speakers are on a shoestring budget and can use help. I'd learn the ropes and make contacts without spending my own time and money. I would have eventually started my business much more effectively than I did."

One friend worked for a chef for six months, for free, before applying to culinary school. The experience taught her that cooking, as a job, really wasn't for her after all. It was nice to discover this before spending her time and money on a career field it turned out wasn't a fit.

Take a Class

Great resources are available at extended learning centers, offered through universities or community colleges and organizations like the Learning Annex. You can take concentrated one-evening courses on just about anything. For example, here are a few courses listed in one catalog: "eBay 101: Selling/Buying Skills and Tips"; "Secrets of Unshakable Self-Confidence"; "Improve Your Speaking Voice"; "Break into the Import/Export Business"; and "How to Start a Greeting Card Business." We can point to valuable information we've received in classes, such as "How to Find an Agent for Your Book" and "The Secrets to Self-Publishing." Plus, these classes are another great place to meet like-minded people.

Many of these classes are now offered as teleclasses online, archived so you can attend on your own schedule.

Tap into the Knowledge and Connections of Professional Associations

Army spouse Lynn built a career as a meeting planner over many military moves. She has always been involved with Meeting Professionals International and Society of Association Executives. "Your professional associations are key," she advises, "especially moving internationally. The dues may seem high, especially at first, but membership is worth its weight in gold."

Other spouses echo this idea. Amy Fetzer, Marine spouse and romance author, belongs to The Authors Guild and the Romance Writers of America. "Both organizations provided me with information I might not have found," says Amy, "especially since my writing took off when we lived in Okinawa."

Cydnee, an educator, belongs to the National Education Association and National Association for the Education of Young Children. "My memberships have helped with resources and referrals," she says.

Artist Kerry belongs to the Portrait Society of America and she joins art clubs in each area as she moves. "Your peers shorten your learning curve; they can save you a lot of time and money," says Kerry. "And with your association," she adds, "you have access to the famous people in your field; you get to talk to them at conferences."

Kathie credits the National Speakers Association with shortening her learning curve as she built her speaking business.

Associations are not just for careers or businesses. Check out *Gale's Encyclopedia of Associations*, usually available at your library. You'll find associations like The Knitting Guild Association, United States Equestrian Federation, and American Homeschool Association. Browse through *Gales* and you might be reminded of interests you have! Or simply search online for any interest you have and include "+ association." There is probably a web site for that association. There's even a US Lawn Mower Racing Association. See what we mean? Who would have guessed? There are other people who do what you want to do, and they are ready to help with information and resources.

Associations often have regular publications, interactive search engines on their web site, job posting systems, and mentoring programs. You can often choose to be an associate member of an association for a reduced fee when you are just starting out in that field.

Another great thing about belonging to your professional association is that you keep running into your peers at events even as you move nationally and internationally. Where you won't be able to keep your actual office mates in a job as you move, you can stay in touch with the larger "family" of your profession or interest. With members all over the world, you always have someone to connect with when you move to a new location, and it's an easy connection to make.

Ask for What You Want

When Gail coordinated a trip to Nepal, Kris, an Army spouse, really wanted to go. However, she had just started a new job and knew her boss wouldn't let her take a two-week leave so soon.

"Why does it all have to come at once?" she complained to her husband. "Why couldn't the job be starting after the trip instead of right now?" At some point, he got tired of listening to her and passed on these words of wisdom. "Here you are complaining because your boss won't let you go," he said, "and you haven't even asked him. Why don't you ask him before you complain?" She did ask her boss, and he happily granted her leave without pay. She got to start the job and go to Nepal. Because she asked.

We keep Kris in mind whenever we really want something and assume the answer will be no. It's amazing how often we decide what the other person's response will be without ever giving them the chance to speak. We'll never know how many opportunities we miss out on simply because we don't ask.

There are important things to consider in asking for what you want.

- Be specific. If you tell someone you are looking for a job, it would be hard for that person to help out. But if you specifically say, "I'm looking for contacts in the hospitality industry in the Washington area," they just might be able to give you the contacts you need.

- Be persistent. "No" often doesn't mean "No." It often just means "Not now." Caroline, an Air Force spouse, learned this in marketing her writing. She sent one query to a military magazine every year for four years in a row. She knew it was a good article idea specifically targeted to the audience of that publication. The responses indicated the timing just wasn't right, not that the idea was wrong for them. On the fourth try, the editor bought it. In the sales world, they say it takes eight sales calls to make the sale. Keep asking.

- Get support to help you ask. This is why the Dare to Dream Team concept works so well. When you have a hard time asking for what you want, your team can help you clarify it, help you practice asking, and sometimes even go along to lend moral support when you ask. They can provide the extra "kick in the pants" you need to ask. Whenever you keep putting off asking for something you want, your group will call you on it.

- Ask as if you expect to get it. Expect a yes rather than a no, and you likely will manifest one. It certainly changes the way you ask— your word use and tone of voice and body language. These factors impact the way you are perceived by the other person, which might just impact the decision.

For anyone who has trouble asking, we recommend the book, *The Aladdin Factor* by Jack Canfield and Mark Victor Hansen. It's full of inspirational examples, tips, and techniques. The book reminded us of things we've wanted to ask for but hadn't had the guts to do so. Reading the amazing results others have had gives you motivation to try for yourself.

Can we tell you that you will always get what you ask for? Of course not. But we can predict what you will get if you fail to ask. As Patricia Fripp, a speaker and writer, says, "Everything in life is a sales situation…and the answer is no if you don't ask."

Tap into Resources Available to You Because You Are a Military Spouse

There are so many resources available to us as military spouses, because we are military spouses. And those resources change all the time. If we tried to list them all here, the book would be too long and it would be out of date too quickly.

The key is to ask. And ask again. Ask your family service center. Ask other military spouses. Ask organizations like the National Military Family Association and Military OneSource. Keep asking. Research further, even if you think you know what is available.

For example, early on, Kathie went to the spouse employment office on one base. The person running the program was effectively "retired in place." Kathie knew more about job finding than he did. She got the impression from that experience that the spouse employment offices weren't worth her time. Well, she was wrong. Like any office, the quality will often depend on the individuals working there. And new programs and services are added all the time. Here are examples of programs:

- Want to become a financial advisor/financial educator? Check into NMFA's partnership with the Association for Financial Counseling and Planning Education. Since the program began in 2006, more than 1200 spouses have received funding to become Accredited Financial Counselors.

- Want to get a degree? Thanks to the Higher Education Opportunity Act of 2008, spouses of active duty service members who are attending public schools are eligible for in-state tuition rates in the state of the military member's permanent duty station. Additionally, spouses who maintain continuous enrollment retain in-state tuition eligibility even if the service member is transferred out of state.

One great way to keep up with new programs and services available to you as a military spouse is to use Google Alerts with key words to get news. Or sign up for Twitter feeds from key agencies or informational resources such as www.ArmyWifeNetwork.com and www.MilitaryFamily.org.

Key Points and Action Steps

▷ Download the Dare to Dream Team handout.

▷ Start talking to people about the team concept to get your own team going.

▷ Ask for your spouse's support.

▷ Learn more about your dream field through information interviews, books, searching online, or taking a class.

▷ Find out about military spouse resources available to you.

▷ Write us with any questions.

Resources

Dare to Dream Team information at www.MilitarySpouseJourney.com.

Girls' Night Out: Celebrating Women's Groups Across America by Tamara Kreinin and Barbara Camens (2002).

National Military Family Association, Inc. 2500 North Van Dorn St, Ste 102, Alexandria, VA 22302-1601; 703-931-6632, fax 703-931-4600; www.MilitaryFamily.org.

Teamworks! by Barbara Sher and Annie Gottlieb (1991). This is out of print, however you may find it at the library. Their book *Wishcraft: How to Get What You Really Want* (2003) also has information on the success team concept.

The Aladdin Factor by Jack Canfield and Mark Victor Hansen (1995).

Chapter 10

Take Action in Career Dreams

Finding Meaningful Work as You Move

I s it really possible to have a mobile career? Yes, although it isn't easy! Some career fields lend themselves more readily to this mobile lifestyle than others. But even in those fields, there are challenges with moving state to state and out of country. The move itself and the time involved finding, starting, and learning a new position all affect your career path.

Sometimes a straight-line career path is possible. Army spouse Karen Ridley managed to move her career specialist role as an Army contractor for nineteen years. She progressively moved up without facing job searches or breaks in service with each move. She worked on the same Army contract, providing job search counseling through the Army Career and Alumni Program (ACAP) offices, first with Right Associates Government Services at Ft. Bragg and then in Germany and DC. Although her actual employer switched from Right Associates to Resource Consultants Inc. (RCI) and later to Serco Inc. (who purchased RCI), Ridley continued on in her job in a relatively seamless manner.

Another example is Coast Guard spouse Elaine Wilhelm-Hass. Elaine works in nursing and nursing administration, career fields with jobs more readily available just about anyplace. With our aging population, the need for nurses keeps growing. During her twenty-five years of being married to the military, Elaine moved more than fifteen times and was able to find a job with each move, each one generally paying better than the one before.

Cydnee Gentry is a Marine Corps spouse who moved ten times in fifteen years. She found jobs in her field of education with each move. "Education is a great field and I've never had a problem finding a teaching job or a job working with kids," she says.

Navy spouse Doreen Griffith, a certified public accountant (CPA) with a bachelor's degree in accounting and a specialty in taxation, managed to work as a tax professional doing tax planning and compliance for corporations and high net worth individuals throughout sixteen years and seven moves with the military. Even changing companies with each move, she was promoted to partner for Grant Thornton, one of the largest accounting firms in the United States.

But what if your chosen career field isn't easily mobile? Plus, even the mobile career fields have challenges because of this life. Here are the basic difficult realities of this mobile life for most of us considering careers:

- You lose time with each move due to the logistics of the move and unpacking itself, and to the time spent in a job search.
- You sometimes have to start at lower income levels with a move, having to prove yourself all over again with a new employer.
- You may not find available work that fits your career field in some places, especially in overseas assignments.
- You may not be able to take promotions or other opportunities with a company you work for if those opportunities mean moving yourself to do so (unless you choose to have a distance marriage for a time as some military couples do).
- You may find it difficult to give your job your all when you are acting as a single parent during a long deployment, responsible for all house and childcare activities during a time when children need even more of your energy and attention than usual. We know spouses who have chosen to quit work during those times. Even though they know it was the right decision for them, that decision adds additional holes to their resumes.
- You might have to spend time and money to recertify in each new state as you move, depending on the requirements for your career field.

Trying to pursue your spouse's military career and your own at an equal level as you move is tough. Hopefully, that will change as military moves become less frequent and as virtual positions and telecommuting make distance work more acceptable and available to spouses. For many of us, we make the choice that the military career is the lead, and we manage to do what we can with our own careers as we move. In some situations, the couple chooses to ask for military assignments in locations that will benefit the civilian career as well. These decisions can limit the military member's long-term promotion potential. It's important to make these as conscious, joint decisions.

Other couples choose to have commuting marriages at certain times in order to allow the civilian spouse to continue in a great job or to accept a promotion that requires a move. Some couples make these commuting marriage decisions at times because of children's schooling considerations as well. We've talked with many spouses who have chosen the commuting life for a year or more. Most have said that,

> *There are ways to pursue meaningful work that allow you to grow your skills with each move.*

although they know it was the right thing for them to do at the time, it's a tough decision to make, especially considering the many separations already built into military life. They wouldn't recommend that choice if you can avoid it.

The good news is there are ways to pursue meaningful work that allow you to grow your skills with each move. And it's crucial that you do that if work is one of your priorities. Once again, remember the research. It isn't achieving your career goal that brings the joy—it's the fact that you identify what interests you and you work toward achieving it in some manner. In many cases, the end result is more enriching than that straight-line path you can't take, even if it doesn't feel like it at the time.

Kathie's Story

As a brand-new military wife at Fort Rucker, Alabama, I got my resume together and started clipping want ads every day. There weren't many in rural Alabama. After months of searching, the best job opportunity I could find was selling vacuum cleaners door to door, hardly what I'd gone to college for and not something I wanted to do. (Mind you, this was at Ft. Rucker in earlier years when it was a small, sleepy post and community.)

My second plan was to go for my MBA or law degree, only neither one was offered anywhere nearby.

I saw that assignment, that particular location, as empty of possibilities, a dead-end to my dreams.

That was early in my married life. Knowing what I know now, I realize that even that location was full of possibilities and opportunities. I just didn't know where to look or how to go about finding them. No one had ever taught me anything about job finding or goal setting or possibility thinking. Plus, I was trying to do the job search all by myself, the least effective way to do one.

In fact, many military spouses pursue their career they way Kathie did—the least-effective way. With each new duty station, Kathie found jobs based on the suggestions of others (without any further research into that field) or based on newspaper want ads. With no career plan in place, Kathie hopped from career field to career field, from human resources to pharmaceutical sales, to advertising sales, to advertising agency work.

So what's wrong with career hopping? Sure, it is one way to try out different things to find out what you like and don't like, but it's the least effective and most costly way. More important, when you keep changing career fields, you don't build up credentials and a reputation in any one field, you don't build connections that can help you as you move, and you are constantly in the beginner mode of the learning curve. It's hard to move up progressively position- and salary-wise when you continually start over in a new field.

After interviewing military spouses from all services, we've found many spouses are much more strategic in their career path. Lynn, an Army spouse, is a great example. We'll use her story as one example of this strategic path along with examples from other spouses. As you read this, consider how the strategies that worked for them might work for you, no matter what career field you want to pursue.

Follow Mobile Career Strategies

- Know what you want. Complete the assessment/interest inventories and pay attention to them.
- Join and stay active in your professional association.

- Complete informational interviews with more than one individual already working in the field in which you want to work.
- Obtain professional certification. Be proactive about continuing education.
- Look for mentors, negotiate career-building opportunities, and be proactive in developing cross training.
- Start early in your job search before you move to the next assignment, while you are still employed.
- Tap into the many (and growing) resources geared to help military spouses find employment.
- Learn to promote yourself and the unique set of skills and experiences you bring to an employer. Turn your transient lifestyle into an advantage in interviews.
- Build networking skills to make and keep great connections. As Army spouse Lynn says, "It's who you know who knows how well you work."
- Create your own visibility. Learn the art of personal PR and marketing yourself.
- If no job in your career field exists in a particular location, figure out what skills you need to gain or improve that you can work on at that location, either in a paid position, or by telecommuting, or as a volunteer.
- Adopt a mindset that opens opportunities for a richer career experience in the long run.

First Know What You Want

Many of us skip the first and most important step in any effective job search. That is taking the time—and, yes, doing the work—to really figure out what it is we want to do. Many of us simply fall into careers based on others' suggestions, based on the money involved, or the jobs we find listed in newspapers or online.

If, instead, you factor in your values, skills, preferred work characteristics, and those you know you don't want, you're more likely to find a lasting fit. Besides, knowing what you want makes for a more focused and effective job search as you move.

Lynn did the interest and values analysis to find a career field that fit her.

"I'd always been about fun," she says. "I loved being involved with planning the prom, helping create school fundraisers, coordinating silent auctions. I've always been the one to plan get togethers for my group of friends." She took a Recreation 101 course in college. As the professor described the ideal recreation professional (outgoing, organized)—as well as the types of jobs available, Lynn thought to herself, "This is me!" She graduated with a degree in leisure studies. When she ended up married to the military, it turned out that working in the hospitality industry was one of the best career fields she could have chosen for this new lifestyle.

As she points out, no matter where you move with the military, there are hotels, tour companies, convention centers, resorts, event facilities, golf courses that do large events, and (of course) military Morale, Welfare, and Recreation (MWR) opportunities.

Complete the Interest Inventories and Pay Attention to Them

Many of the resources and assessment tools you would have to pay to access in the civilian world are available for free or at a lower cost through the military. But you have to take action to access them, and then be sure to pay attention to the results as you consider jobs. How does each career field or job fit your interests and skills? Currently, the best place to start is at the Spouse Education and Career Opportunities (SECO) at Military OneSource. SECO offers all military spouses comprehensive education and career opportunities to support the pursuit of portable careers.

SECO consultants are bachelor's- and master's-level advisors and counselors who promote and provide self-directed solutions to empower military spouses with knowledge and skills necessary to become self-reliant in their educational and career development.

- Career exploration: SECO consultants help spouses explore all options, with tools like career assessments, interest and skills inventories, portable career statistics, and earning potential metrics.
- Education and training: Spouses work with SECO consultants to create a plan of action that considers financial aid options, education and training program resources, credential/license information, and, for eligible spouses, the Military Spouse Career Advancement Accounts program (MyCAA).

- Employment readiness: SECO consultants help spouses perfect their resumes and hone their interviewing skills. They also cover job search techniques, relocation planning, and flex-work options.
- Career connections: SECO consultants help spouses get the right job in the right career by leveraging existing relationships and resources, such as the Military Spouse Employment Partnership (MSEP), USAJOBS.gov, and CareerOneStop.org.

SECO provides high quality education and career services, resources, guidance, and consultations accessible through the convenience of a telephone call to 1-800-342-9647.

The reality of our military life is that you most likely won't move in a straight line upward in your career as you move with the military. You can, however, craft a rich career by being proactive, creative, and adopting a mindset that opens you to possibilities.

With each move, Lynn had a different kind of job within the industry. "Be open to that," she advises, "it deepens your experience and value." She's done unpaid internships in hotel sales. She's held jobs in recreation planning for MWR Korea, marketing for Sheraton Savannah Resort, sales for a historic inn, management for Yakima Valley Visitors and Convention Bureau, convention sales for Ocean Shores Convention Center, and now does contract meeting planning, coordinating large events for clients like Microsoft and the Invitational World Golf Championships.

Consider Opportunities in Military-Affiliated Organizations

A recent job placement ad included one line not often seen in a career ad: "Military spouses may work remotely from a home office." After so many years of military spouses trying to hide the fact that they were military spouses in interviews with potential employers, finding the term "military spouse" highlighted in a job ad is encouraging!

This ad happened to be from Victory Media Inc., a national media company that publishes military-niche magazines and web sites, including *G.I. Jobs, Vetrepreneur,* and *Military Spouse* magazine. *Military Spouse* magazine was started by two military spouses, and with its readership being primarily military spouses, it makes sense to hire military spouses to the staff.

Another organization with military members or military families as their core client base is the military exchange system.

Army spouse Tina Lovitt is the Army and Air Force Exchange Service (AAFES) western region area manager. She's been with AAFES for more than twenty years. "The retail aspect of working for AAFES turns out to be the perfect fit with a military lifestyle, since the AAFES motto 'We Go Where You Go' is so true," she says.

AAFES promotes its Military Spouse Preference program, which allows priority consideration for posted jobs when a spouse transfers with the military member. Its Spouse Continuity program allows for priority placement into a position of similar category to retain benefits, as well.

Of course, the biggest organization with military ties is the federal government. There is good news for spouses looking to enter federal employment. The US Office of Personnel Management (OPM) is facing what has been called a "retirement tsunami" as baby boomer workers reach retirement eligibility. 2011 saw a 24 percent increase in retirements over 2010 and the rise continued in 2012. That means a lot of job openings.

You can find out about federal job opportunities at www.USAJobs.gov or check the web sites of specific agencies for position vacancies. Check guidelines on military spouse federal employment at www.FedsHireVets.gov.

Another great resource was created by In Gear Career, one of the premier networking organizations geared specifically to military spouses. The organization developed a Federal Employment Toolkit for Military Spouses. The toolkit gives a detailed overview of government service, how to apply for federal jobs, and considerations specific to military spouses. Their goal is to give military spouses the information they need to determine whether or not government service is the right choice for them, and if so, the information they need to pursue that career path. www.InGearCareer.org.

Companies that have long-standing contracts with the military are another option to consider as you conduct a job search. Your military tie is an immediate plus.

Throughout fifteen years and ten relocations, Marine Corps spouse Deborah Mayberry worked as a government employee and a contractor. Her contract positions included career counselor, Exceptional Family Member Program coordinator, project manager, and program manager for contractors such as ESI and Zeiders Enterprises. She then opened her own consulting firm, DMI, providing project management and strategic planning services to prime contractors.

"Contracting is not the same as government employment," Deborah says. "Contractors typically hail from the corporate sector where employment law applies and is different from government HR policies. Whereas, government usually has set compensation schedules, contractors may not, and a military spouse must be prepared to negotiate pay and benefits."

Navy spouse Marcia DeFalco worked as military strategic communications director for Ceridian, working primarily on the Military OneSource and Military Severely Injured Center programs. She came to this job from a position with another military contractor, Axiom Resource Management, working on their TRICARE contract.

"Some contract positions will offer more vacation more quickly than with the government," Marcia says. "Some offer lucrative bonus programs and flexibilities, such as telecommuting opportunities."

Marcia points out another benefit to contract work. "If you choose, you can do some moving around based on your skills and interests, often more than on a GS track."

Jessica Kujat, a Navy spouse of seven years, has her MBA with a specialization in human resources. She found her current job with Booz Allen Hamilton via a job posting on the Blue Star Families Network Group on LinkedIn. She has been with the contractor one year as an employee referral recruiter for the Employee Referral Program and Alumni Program.

"I should be able to take my job with me whenever I have to move due to military orders," says Jessica. "I've had this discussion with my supervisors, and the great thing about my position is that I telecommute 100 percent of the time. Essentially, I can perform my current role from anywhere, as long as I have an Internet connection and some type of phone (VoIP, cellphone, landline, etc.). Working overseas (if it were to ever come to that) may present more of a challenge due to time differences. However, I believe it would be doable with some creativity."

In 2012, Booz Allen Hamilton received the Military Spouse Employment and Mentoring Award from the US Chamber of Commerce. Finalists for the award were nominated by nonprofits and service agencies working in veteran and military spouse unemployment, and a peer committee of veterans and military spouses selected the winner.

Booz Allen is proud of its concerted effort to recruit and retain military spouses, including participating in the Hiring Our Heroes Military Spouse

Career Forums. The firm offers flexible work schedules and the opportunity to work remotely to accommodate spouses who may be required to move during their employment with the firm. The contractor supports military spouses employed at the firm with resource groups, mentoring circles, and education and leadership programs. In addition, Booz Allen helped launch the MilSpouse online mentoring program with Academy Women, which offers military spouses personalized career guidance, advice, support, and inspiration from more experienced military spouses, career mentors, and military spouse-friendly employers.

A Google search for "top Department of Defense contractors" turns up a list of the top 100 contractors, such as Lockheed Martin, SAIC, and CSC, with a breakdown by service. Most contractor web sites include job listings searchable by location and by job type.

CSC, for example, is located on almost every military installation around the world and employs more than 98,000 people worldwide. They ask you to include "military spouse" in your resume because they actively recruit military spouses! As part of their military spouse employment program, the company offers assistance in employment transfers, working virtually, and career portability.

One great place to look for potential employers is Military Spouse *magazine's annual Top 20 Military Spouse-Friendly Employers list, compiled each year since 2007.*

USAA is another good example of a military-affiliated company. They've ranked number one in *Military Spouse* magazine's Top 20 Military Spouse-Friendly Employers list.

"We know military spouses sometimes feel corporate America prefers not to hire them because of their transient lifestyle. Well, we're different," said USAA CEO Maj. Gen. Joe Robles, USA (Ret.) in an interview with *Military Spouse* magazine. "USAA was founded by military personnel who were experiencing the same discrimination from insurance companies that thought their transient lifestyles made for a bad risk. That kind of corporate thinking was wrong in 1922 and it's wrong today, because military service members and spouses are great employees as well as great customers."

USAA is one of the companies proactively looking for ways to employ military spouses in virtual work, so they can continue working for the company as they move with the military.

Target Companies with Locations Nationwide or Worldwide

Army spouse Emmy Oliva started in human resources with Target while living in Texas. With a move to Washington State, she was able to continue with the company and hopes to do so with future moves.

A recent search for "retail management" at Military.com resulted in 5000 listings. Many companies have chosen to list themselves as "military spouse-friendly employers." Companies such as Ann Taylor, Best Buy, Brookstone, Home Depot, Radio Shack, Sears, and Starbucks have locations around the country and many have great benefits.

Starbucks, for example, has more than 20,000 locations in sixty-two countries. The announcement for baristas and store supervisors in San Antonio, Texas, for example, noted a comprehensive benefits plan for partners working more than twenty hours per week. Benefits include medical, dental, vision, stock options, tuition reimbursement, and night pay differential (and, ah yes, one free pound of coffee each week). Other companies have vacation and sick leave, flex time, and store discounts.

Corporate opportunities are increasing due to efforts of Joining Forces and the Military Spouse Employment Partnership (MSEP), formerly the Army Spouse Employment Program. MSEP has more than 160 partners who have hired more than 36,000 military spouses. Partners include companies like 3M, Microsoft, Lockheed Martin, and Humana. These are companies who have committed to hire military spouses!

Get Your Professional Certification

"I looked at the jobs I wanted five years down the road and asked what those folks did to get there," Lynn says. "In my world, it's the certified meeting planner or CMP. It gives you instant credibility." Most of us as military spouses feel we have to reestablish our credibility and professionalism with each move and each job, but professional certification helps cut through that.

Elaine, the nurse, echoes that. "I see myself as competing again after every move, and I position my skills and knowledge to help that competition." She chose to get a master's degree in business and a quality certification to make her more competitive. She took courses to keep her computer skills up to date, something necessary in today's healthcare world, and something many nurses don't do. "You have to go beyond the minimum required for your state re-licensure if you want to position yourself to compete."

Educator Cydnee agrees. "You have to have a lot of flexibility and multiple certifications," she says. "As the Marines say, Semper Gumby, Always Flexible."

Look for Mentors, Negotiate Career-Building Opportunities, and Proactively Cross Train

"You have to create your own opportunities," says Lynn. "Speak up and take on things." When she worked at the Yakima Valley Visitors and Convention Bureau, for example, she said to her boss, "I'm not interested in your job since we'll be moving, but I want to learn." He let her sit in on board meetings and city council meetings. When her boss told her they couldn't afford to give her the raise she deserved, she negotiated time off and the entry fee to pursue her CMP training.

Start early in your job search and be persistent. When she found out they were moving to Savannah, Lynn got the event facilities list from the Convention and Visitors Bureau (CVB) and sent a cover letter and resume to every business listed there before she moved. Then she called those businesses, asking for informational interviews and an opportunity to discuss the industry in that community. Once they arrived in Savannah, she went to CVB luncheons and stood up to say, "I'm new here and bring a wide skill set," handing out lots of cards. Even though she was frustrated that she didn't find something immediately, she says, "I did stuff every day—calls, meetings that forced me to get dressed, and I toured Savannah to get the lay of the land."

Some other ways to get started before the move:

- Update your resume and gather letters of recommendation. Put together a portfolio of successful projects and performance appraisals. This is much easier to do before you move and preparing ahead pays off. (By the way, Elaine recommends you keep a running list of all employers with contact information. "One place checked my references ten jobs back," she reports.)
- Create a professional web presence and check your web presence by searching yourself online every now and then. You want to know what employers will find if they check you out that way. Be aware and strategic as you use Facebook and other online social networking sites.

- Search the local Chamber of Commerce web site for information on local businesses. Most membership directories can be searched by type of company.

- Start a subscription to local business publications to read and clip files on companies that interest you (or read these online). You'll find information on contracts, problems, and new projects. This is part of the research you should do for any interview anyway.

- Search web sites like CareerBuilder.com, your local Craig's List, and Monster.com for jobs in your field and city. For nonprofit sector jobs, go to Idealist.org.

- Take advantage of job aggregators, such as Indeed.com and SimplyHired.com, to search the major job sites, company sites, associations, and other online job sites by keyword and location.

- Use LinkedIn and Facebook to network for job opportunities. Tap into LinkedIn groups like Military Spouses Connected, Blue Star Families, and your alma mater's group for job leads and information. Hyperlink your resume to LinkedIn.

- Make use of web sites specific to military spouses. MSEP (part of SECO) at MilitaryOneSource.mil includes listings from a growing list of partner companies specific to military spouses, along with career information and hiring fairs. Military.com/Spouse lists jobs specific for military spouses from more than a hundred employers, including Ann Taylor, Bell South, and Procter & Gamble. At Military Spouse Corporate Career Network, MSCCN.org, you'll find job listings from companies such as Boeing and Trammel Crowe Company. All of these are free to you and searchable by location and specialty, and they provide one-on-one employment recruiter assistance.

- If you belong to a professional association, contact the chapter in the new city. Ask to receive their newsletters and meeting announcements ahead of the move to start collecting names to contact (many of these will be available on a web site or Facebook). Ask if they have a job bank you can tap into.

- If you are a college graduate, contact your alumni association and ask if there is a chapter in the new city. Or use your alumni directory to identify individuals in the city or make contacts through their LinkedIn group. Alumni like to help fellow alumni.

- Most important, tell everyone you know where you are moving to, and ask them if they know people there. It doesn't have to be someone in a hiring position or even someone who works in your line of work. You just need contacts. Those contacts may know the person you need to talk with. Plus, you just might make new friends in the new location in the process. Networking and following up with leads is key.

Be willing to take a pay cut for new experience or just to continue in your field in a smaller community. In Savannah, Lynn accepted a pay cut to work in sales at a high-end facility. Six months later, she was promoted to director of sales. It may feel like one step forward and two steps back at times, but continuing to work in your chosen career path, continuing to make contacts and connections, might just be worth it in the long run.

Be Prepared to Think of Your Work Differently

Some jobs in the hospitality industry, for example, do not allow family flexibility. But some do. When Lynn had her second child, she chose Convention and Visitors Bureau work that was 8:00 a.m. to 5:00 p.m. and negotiated three days a week of work instead of five. Later, wanting even more flexibility, she started her own consulting firm.

As Peggy Frede, Air Force spouse and long-time educator says, "Accept jobs that stretch you professionally. Take the opportunity of a forced move to learn and try new techniques and methods." Peggy kept her mind open about opportunities in her career field. "I am an educator," she says. "Notice I didn't say teacher." It's a mindset that opened her to opportunities outside traditional schools when jobs weren't available there. Peggy has done traditional teaching in schools, managed a retraining program at a computer learning center, and taught technology at a law firm.

Elaine Wilhelm-Hass, the nurse, took advantage of the many moves to provide her with a wider range of experience, adding to her resume and marketability as she moved. She has worked in many different aspects of nursing, from staff RN to operating room manager, to director of surgical and parent/child services at a hospital, to quality improvement director for a TRICARE region, to healthcare consulting work.

Air Force spouse Leslie Boone is an occupational therapist, one of the big growth career fields due to our aging population. She is a certified hand therapist, but had to be flexible as they moved. Positions in her specialty are mostly only available in areas with large populations, not always the case near military bases. "If you keep your OT 'hat' on and don't worry about specializing," she says, "there is always a job."

She's had to switch focus several times, from teaching at a voc-tech for the certified occupational therapy assistant program, to working in and taking on managerial duties in acute care. "That managerial experience helped me get a job at our next assignment," she says, "where I managed five outpatient centers for a large health care organization."

Consider Project Work for Flexibility

Navy spouse Heidi Evans speaks for many military spouses when she explains why she chooses to do project type work rather than pursue a full-time career.

"I have three young children at home," says Evans. "When my husband was in submarines, his hours were long when he was home at all. When one parent is so tied to this career and frequently unreliable to help with parenting, it becomes more critical for the other parent to be available when you can for everything from baseball games to a case of the flu. Taking contracts and working from home ensures that at least one of us can be there when the children need a parent."

As families continue to endure back-to-back deployments, many military spouses face this single parent challenge. How do you keep a career going and be available for your children? Other military spouses without children are looking for short-term work that can supplement income while they develop a business or complete their education.

Many spouses turn to project work as one solution.

In Heidi's case, she is a freelance writer. From a regular local column at one location to writing assignments with Military OneSource and *Military Spouse* magazine, she takes on projects that work with her family and life schedule. Freelance writing is one of the more obvious examples of project work. There are many others that get overlooked.

Market research analysis, market research, marketing communications writing and editing, special event planning, grant writing, contract recruiting, merchandising, training, translating, tutoring, background investigations, and web design are just some examples of project work.

Temporary agencies like Adecco Group and Kelly Services (both on the Top 20 Military Spouse-Friendly Employers list) are a great resource for anyone looking for short-term work. They find the assignments for you. Some agencies even provide limited benefits along with your hourly pay. And realize, these temp jobs are not only administrative jobs. They include engineering, medical, science, industrial, creative, marketing, and other fields.

USIS, a private company, is the largest supplier of security background investigations for the federal government. The company also does preemployment screening for retail, transportation, medical, and financial fields.

"I would see it as a potential career opportunity for military spouses," says Michael John, USIS spokesperson. "Our contract investigators, especially, have some control on the amount of hours and can schedule their work around other activities." As a contractor, you can choose to accept or reject specific assignments based on your availability.

Some project work opportunities are very military-life specific. One example is Military OneSource, which contracts with individuals (many military spouses) to be project assistants, traveling regionally to present information about Military OneSource to military family members at conferences and other events.

Learn to Sell What You Bring to an Employer

"I'd basically say, 'Lucky you, I bring a unique set of skills to town,'" says Lynn. After all, as a military spouse, you bring a wide experience of seeing how other companies run things, often bringing in new ideas that can help an operation. You bring the strength of flexibility and being able to deal with change, not a common skill but a necessary one in the business world. You've most likely learned to work with individuals from all levels of society and from different states and countries. People skills like that are key to any position. Recognize and sell the value you bring.

Angela Toda is an Army spouse and public relations professional who managed to successfully move her PR career during eight moves in thirteen years of married military life.

"I have progressed, but not in the traditional trajectory," Angela says. "I'd likely be more focused within my first love, high-tech, versus being more of a generalist, or 'jack of all trades.' That said, our travels have brought me opportunities and valuable international experience. The world of business is undeniably global. Business people with proven international skills are very much in demand. Military spouses who can build a career that leverages their international experiences can make themselves very marketable."

As Elaine, the nurse, says, "At first, I lamented that I'd always be the 'new RN,' working all the weekends and holidays—but here's a secret! The new kid from out of state is often perceived as more clever or desirable than existing employees. I capitalized on that."

Cydnee carries a portfolio with performance appraisals and letters of recommendation from previous duty stations, including any certificates of recognition or accomplishment for volunteer positions.

By the way, don't underestimate the skills and experience you've gained from your volunteer positions. Kathie heard one friend say disparagingly of herself, "I haven't had a paid job in so long, I don't know how marketable I am." This came from a woman who is as professionally polished and organized as any paid professional Kathie's ever worked with, and who has successfully run large programs and organizations of volunteers. But that attitude of "lesser than" can hurt you in an interview. As

Don't underestimate the skills and experience you've gained from your volunteer positions.

Kathie points out from her years as a corporate personnel manager, "It's essential to appear enthusiastic and self-confident in an interview." Recognize the value of your skills and practice to sell them effectively in an interview.

Peggy, the educator, says, "In interviews, be up front about your transient lifestyle. Turn it into a plus. I emphasize the wide range of subjects I've taught as well as the range of ages. I point out the varied perspectives and input I can provide from that wide experience at other locations."

As Richard Bolles, author of the classic *What Color is Your Parachute?*, says, "When people change jobs frequently, their learning curve accelerates. They get the chance to learn more—and in less time. If I have one job for two years, and I get bounced out of it, or I decide to leave and go to a new place, I have to start learning new stuff—a whole new set of skills that I didn't need in my last job. This makes me a more valuable employee, wherever I go." Based on that, military spouses have to be some of the most valuable employees anywhere! Be aware of that and sell yourself accordingly.

Here's a partial list of the benefits military spouses bring to employers:
- Ability to deal with change/flexibility.
- Ability to learn quickly.
- Ability to work with people from all walks of life.
- Ideas, experience, and best practices from many other companies and organizations.
- Strong people skills.
- Global experience and familiarity with international customs.

Build Networking Skills to Make and Keep Great Connections

We can't emphasize enough the importance of networking! "My industry is very incestual," says Lynn. "The management and sales jobs rarely make it into an ad. It's always through networking. It's who you know who knows how well you work!"

If you are not a natural networker, check out the books by Anne Baber and Lynne Waymon in our resource list. It is a skill anyone can learn.

Create your own visibility—learn the art of personal PR and marketing yourself. Lynn volunteers to speak and teach classes on the leisure industry for community colleges, universities, and at conferences. She has volunteered time on the boards of the state chapters of her professional associations.

All of these strategies work with any industry.

And finally, for all military spouses pursuing careers, tap into the huge network of military spouses. One resource that goes underutilized is other military spouses. Think about this. With 74 percent of military spouses working, and all of us moving frequently, there seems a great possibility of referring each other for positions and providing a service to our current employers at the same time. Each time you leave a good job because of a military move, you have left an open position that could be filled by another competent military spouse. Kathie used to work as a corporate personnel manager. She loved to get recommendations from good employees who already knew the organization and corporate culture. The Internet has opened up the possibility of networking virtually all over the world. Tap into that opportunity.

Two great military spouse career networking groups are In Gear Career and National Military Spouse Network. Both offer tips and career fairs, along with other professional development and networking opportunities.

Tap into Military.com's network, where you can search for veteran or military spouse mentors and connections by location, career field, or industry.

Think about it. We network with others to find out where to have our hair cut or our car fixed. If we more effectively tap into the network of more than one million military spouses, we can help each other find good jobs and help our employers find good workers.

Appreciate the Gift in the Challenge

What if you do the skills and interest inventories, and still don't know what you really want to do? Well, then, look at this military life as a true gift as you get the opportunity to try new jobs/careers on for size with each move. We both know plenty of civilian friends who continue unhappily in jobs they've been at for twenty years just because they are too afraid to make a change. Sometimes forced change is good.

Use Service Partnerships

The services know that mobile careers for spouses are a key factor in keeping us happy, which means better retention rates for service members. It costs money to constantly recruit and retrain new military members. One way for the military to keep active members is to keep their spouses happy. That's why they put new programs in place to help us. For example:

- The Department of Defense partnered with Military.com and Monster.com to create online resources where military spouses can look for job openings and apply online, with the services free to military spouses.
- The Navy and Marines created the Adecco Career Accelerator, www.Adecco.com.
- The Air Force pioneered the Virtual Assistant Training program, which expanded to all services, www.Staffcentrix.com.
- The Army partnered with corporations to promote the value of Army spouses for traditional, telework, and virtual positions. That successful program expanded into the Military Spouse Employment Partnership (MSEP), with a growing number of Fortune 500 companies and other partners.

We're excited to hear about new programs. Tap into them all. Realize, however, that successfully transferring your career or business and finding work at each location still comes down to a lot of personal initiative, creativity, and flexibility.

Janet Farley, author of *The Military Spouse's Employment Guide*, says, "Use the services available to you on the military installation, but also take advantage of those services offered within the civilian community outside the front gate. For example, register with the Department of Labor (DoL) and inquire about the availability of unemployment benefits. Laws are always changing in this area and if you are eligible for this benefit, use it. Aside from that, the DoL is well plugged into the community and will refer you, free of charge, to employers."

Forty states and the District of Columbia offer some level of unemployment benefits to military spouses who have to leave jobs because of a military move, so check that out. In some states, workforce-training dollars are available for spouse education and training. Ask!

If There's No Job in Your Career Field with this Move, Go to Plan B

It happens. You move with the military, and what you want to do is simply not available at that location. What do you do? Give up? Settle for a career field you aren't excited about? Take a job, any job? Unfortunately, that is what many of us do. Yes, sometimes, financially, you have no choice but to do so.

When you can't find a job in your specific career field, at least be selective in what is available. Rather than just taking any job, look for a job that allows you to learn or improve on skills you need in your chosen career. On the job, ask for opportunities to take on projects or training to enhance those skills.

If you can manage without a paycheck for a time, see if you can find or create the job you want via volunteer work. Identify the skills you need for your dream job—be it computer, marketing, managing others, fundraising, PR—and find volunteer work to teach you those skills.

If you do volunteer work to gain or maintain skills important to your career, there is a resource that helps you take your volunteer experience and the skills that you gained and turn them into career skills on a resume. Blue Star Families, www.BlueStarFam.org, developed a Military Spouse Resume Toolkit that explains how to translate volunteer work and military life experiences into effective resume points. It also outlines strategies for overcoming gaps in employment on resumes, and how to talk about gaps in job interviews. It includes military spouse-specific career advice and sample resumes tailored for different types of employment, including corporate, public sector, and nonprofit jobs.

And if none of these are possible, look at that assignment as a time to spend more energy and hours on other aspects of your whole-istic life vision. Engage more fully in another aspect of your life that matters to you.

As Janet Farley, military spouse and author, adds, "If you can't find the job of your dreams at your next duty station, use the opportunity for what it is…an opportunity to try something new. You never know, you just might latch onto your true calling, compliments of a set of orders you weren't too thrilled with in the first place."

Why It's Crucial to Your Well-being Not to Simply Give Up

Long-term studies reported in the book Wellbeing *by Rath and Harter emphasize how important it is to engage in something we enjoy doing. The authors reference a study reported in* The Economic Journal *that revealed that unemployment might be the only major life event from which people do not recover within five years. This study followed 130,000 people for several decades. It found that our well-being actually recovers more rapidly from the death of a spouse than it does from a sustained period of unemployment.*

According to the research, you don't need to earn a paycheck. Whether working in an office, volunteering, raising your children, or starting your own business, what matters most is being engaged in the career or activity you choose.

Sarah Selvidge, an Army spouse, wanted to work in marketing, so she volunteered at the Bamberg, Germany, community marketing office to learn the ropes. She later worked as a marketing manager for World Vision in Seattle.

Samantha wanted to own her own pet resort. She first volunteered at her community's vet clinic and was eventually hired at the vet clinic at her next location, giving her the opportunity to learn the ropes and build her credibility before she puts her own money and time into her pet resort.

The bottom-line reality is that you probably won't have the steady, straight-line career path your nonmilitary peers may be able to manage. And that may be the best thing that ever happened to you!

Army spouse Berkeley McHugh has had some fabulous opportunities because of moving around and teaching at different schools. "I went back to Texas ten years after I first taught there," she says, "and many of my former coworkers were still there, teaching the same subject in the same room. I feel that I had additional opportunities to grow and be challenged because of my new environments."

As Air Force spouse and educator Peggy Frede says, "I have a variety of great experiences I wouldn't trade for a thirty-year career in any school district!" We hope you end up saying the same, whatever career you pursue.

Key Points and Action Steps

 ▷ Adopt mobile career strategies to help you stay flexible and open to opportunities.
 ▷ Complete interest inventories and explore expanded nationwide career options.
 ▷ Complete your professional certification.
 ▷ Join associations that support your profession.
 ▷ Create a list of key networking contacts and schedule time on your calendar to nurture those relationships.

Resources

Federal Employment Toolkit for Military Spouses, www.InGearCareer.org.

Impact Publications. One of the most comprehensive lists of job search/ career fields books, www.ImpactPublications.com.

In Gear Career. Networking for career-minded military spouses, www.InGearCareer.org.

Make Your Contacts Count: Networking Know-How for Business and Career Success by Anne Baber and Lynne Waymon (2007). Great information and tips, tools and techniques on networking. www.ContactsCount.com.

Military.com and Monster.com. Information and job search tools specifically for military spouses.

Military Spouse Corporate Career Network, www.MSCCN.org.

The Military Spouse's Employment Guide: Smart Job Choices for Mobile Lifestyles by Janet I. Farley (2012).

Military Spouse Employment Partnership, www.MilitaryOneSource.mil.

The Military Spouse's Employment Pocket Guide by Ron Krannich, PhD (2010).

Military Spouse Resume Toolkit, www.BlueStarFam.org.

National Military Spouse Network (NMSN), www.NationalMilitarySpouseNetwork.org.

PivotPlanet, www.PivotPlanet.com.

Spouse employment services on your installation:
    Army Employment Readiness Program
    Air Force Career Focus Program
    Marine Family Member Employment Assistance Program
    Navy and Coast Guard Spouse Employment Assistance Program

Ten Steps to a Federal Job, Third Edition with CD by Kathryn Troutman (2011).

What Color is Your Parachute?: A Practical Manual for Job-Hunters and Career-Changers by Richard N. Bolles (2014), www.JobHuntersBible.com.

Work Worldwide: International Career Strategies for the Adventurous Job Seeker by Nancy Mueller (2000).

Chapter 11

Pursue Your Dream Business

Moving a Business as You Move

Some military spouses choose to create their own business. It's something you can move with you, rather than constantly conducting a job search with each move. A business is something you can continue to build as you move, with an eye to expanding it even more once you stop moving.

Is a business right for you? There are many things to consider in setting up any business. Establishing a business you have to move every few years raises additional considerations.

This is a huge topic to try to cover in one chapter. But we want to give you things to think about and resources to refer to if you are considering owning and running a business.

The Realistic News

Statistics aren't promising. Data from the US Small Business Administration shows that regardless of the year when they are founded, the majority of start-ups go out of business within five years, and two-thirds no longer operate ten years after being formed.

According to Sharon Barber, assistant district director for Tacoma's Small Business Administration office, there are two key reasons why small businesses fail. The first is under capitalization, not having enough working funds. This is often caused by not doing a business plan ahead of time. A business plan helps you have realistic expectations for what your business will require in funding and what is possible. The second reason is poor management. "Many people have the skills to do the creative or production part of their business," she says. Where they fall down is in the accounting and management side every business requires.

We don't know statistics for businesses run by military spouses, but we know those businesses face added challenges when you factor in frequent moves, deployments, and other aspects of military life.

Can You Make Money Right Away?

Many of us who start businesses have the misguided idea we can make money right away. That might be true in some cases. For example, if you work for a corporation and they agree to contract with you to do that same work as an independent contractor, you probably can make money immediately. Some virtual assistant businesses show profits from the start. For most start-up businesses, that isn't the case.

Many of the spouses we've talked to, ourselves included, will tell you they've had mixed experiences with the financial side of their businesses. As one woman describes her experience only half-jokingly, "When I took this business on, I didn't realize I was taking on a major volunteer position in a nonprofit endeavor." One woman's husband calls her business her "most expensive hobby." Many admit they would not have the guts to try their own business if they didn't have their spouse's income and benefits as the stable base to allow them to take time to grow the business.

There are a lot of start-up costs for any business, from business equipment and supplies to business stationery to Internet connection. Even the simplest of businesses has expenses. Realize many of those costs reoccur with each move, as you have to file your business in the new state and pay for new Internet connections and new business cards.

When you have your own business, you have monthly overhead costs, expenses that recur whether or not you are bringing in income. For example, your monthly telephone bill, Internet service provider, and web hosting fees must be paid each month.

If starting your own business is about money, and not about passion, or at least about the flexibility, you might want to think again. As Barry Moltz says in *You Need to Be a Little Crazy: The Truth About Starting and Growing*

Your Business, "Make no mistake; it is easier and in the long run more profitable to get a job than to start your own business." (Unless you turn out to be the next Steve Jobs or Bill Gates or Martha Stewart.)

Where Will You Get Your Customers or Clients?

Successful businesses are built on client relationships and referrals. One consideration for us as military spouses in looking at a business is whether or not those referrals will work across the country and the world.

For someone in a direct selling business such as The Pampered Chef, Avon, or Silpada Designs, referrals and repeat business can move with you. For a speaker or trainer, your referrals and repeat business can also

> *One important thing to consider before starting any business is how moving might impact your current and future client base.*

move, as long as you have access to the Internet, a major airport, and clients willing to pay travel expenses. For a writer or virtual assistant, all you need is a telephone, computer, and Internet connection. Some writers get by with an iPad and cell service. One important thing to consider before starting any business is how moving might impact your current and future client base.

Are You Ready to Do It All?

Many of us start businesses that allow us to do things we love and in areas where we can excel. The challenge is that as a small business owner, you also undertake many other tasks just to stay in business. These may not be things you love to do or do well. Activities such as accounting, tax preparation, marketing, sales, data entry, pricing, proposal preparation, invoicing, customer service, record keeping, understanding and abiding by government regulations, purchasing, order fulfillment, and calling for overdue payments all have to be taken care of. If you don't do them, you have to pay someone else to do them. Most small business owners don't start out with enough money to pay anyone else.

As Michael Gerber says in *The E-Myth Revisited: Why Most Small Businesses Don't Work and What to Do About It*, "The business that was supposed to free him from the limitations of working for somebody else actually enslaves him. Suddenly the job he knew how to do so well becomes one job he knows how to do plus a dozen others he doesn't know how to do at all."

Are You Cut Out for Entrepreneurship?

It's a good idea to approach a new business the way you would a new career field. Do the research. Conduct informational interviews with those who have successful businesses to find out what it takes and what the possibilities are. If you don't do the research and apply solid business practices, you may end up with the situation described by Gerber, a situation many small business owners find themselves in after a few years.

"You one day realize," Gerber says, "you don't own a business, you own a job! What's more, it's the worst job in the world! You can't close it when you want to, because if it's closed you don't get paid. You can't leave it when you want to, because when you leave, there is nobody there to do the work. You can't sell it when you want to, because who wants to buy a job?"

It's important to be honest with yourself as to your work habits and skills and how those might translate into business management. Are you organized, detail-oriented, good with follow through, and self-directed?

Probably the two most important attributes are the ability to connect with others and the ability to sell. As Moltz says, "Only sales will build your business…if you are afraid to sell, you have two choices: You can get over it or get a job."

How Will This Affect Your Family?

There is the time and family balance issue. If you aren't careful, a business can take over your life. Air Force spouse Janelle Davis says, "The key advantage to a virtual business is staying home with my daughter and setting my own hours…and the main challenge of this business is working at home with my daughter." Other home-based business owners echo this. Virtual assistant and Air Force spouse Charlotte Lingard-Young says, "My biggest challenge is being able to balance my time so my work does not take over all of my time with my kids…the main reason I decided to stay home."

Home-based businesses do provide flexibility, but they also require lots of organization skills, self-discipline, and family understanding.

Direct Selling Companies

Many spouses turn to direct selling companies such as Thirty-One Gifts or Mary Kay to start a business. These companies provide a ready-made product, training, and assistance to help you succeed. You don't have to figure things out and create everything from scratch. Although you are still a one-person operation, you have the support and camaraderie of other distributors and the specific help of your director.

Is a network marketing/direct sales business for everyone? Of course not. So much of it depends on how you work it. We've heard of spouses making more in their network marketing business than their military spouses made in salary and benefits. We can also share stories of spouses who spent more money than they ever made in a network marketing business. The median income from direct selling is $2,400 annually, according to the Direct Selling Association, but those who work the business full time and recruit and manage others can earn significantly more.

The Virtual Advantage

The Internet has opened up incredible opportunities for military spouses who want to own a business. The Internet allows you to have a web site and email address that stays the same as you move from place to place, so your customers and prospects can easily find you. That wasn't the case in the past, as business owners had to change contact information with each move.

As Army spouse, mother, and freelance writer Regina told us after one move, "I have enough work lined up in advance, I can keep the momentum going with this upcoming move—as long as I have my laptop with me."

Virtual Businesses Today Can Cover a Wide Range of Specialties

Air Force spouse Charlotte Lingard-Young's business, C.Y. Virtual Solutions, puts her background in healthcare and master's degree in applied psychology to work for her clients doing Internet research and general and psychiatric transcription, among other services.

Army spouse Jeri Winkler combines a computer science degree with real estate experience in her virtual business called The Secret Assistant. She provides realtors with everything from database management to prospecting to web site maintenance. Her familiarity with popular real estate software programs allows her to handle time-consuming office tasks from a distance.

Air Force spouse Janelle Davis combines a law degree and experience in commercial litigation and appeals to provide motion and brief preparations for her clients.

Chris Durst, who is credited with founding the Virtual Assistant (VA) industry in 1995, points out, VAs are home-based entrepreneurs who run their own shows, offering business support services to other businesses via email, phone, and fax. Durst and Michael Haaren, cofounders of Staffcentrix, have trained, taught, or mentored more than 3,800 VAs internationally. In their book, *The 2-Second Commute: Join the Exploding Ranks of Freelance Virtual Assistants*, they identify more than eighty varieties of expertise, ranging from basic word processing to high-end corporate consulting.

Many specialties listed in their book seem tailor-made for the background and experience of military spouses: event planning, expertise in foreign markets, interpreting, import/export support, nonprofit support services, government procurement expertise, resume writing, fundraising.

Staffcentrix's Portable Career & Virtual Assistant Training Program, geared specifically to military spouses, kicked off with a pilot at Cannon Air Force Base in 2002. Since then, Staffcentrix has provided programs to many other military sites. Their train-the-trainer program certifies spouse employment professionals from all services.

If you think about it, any business that a military spouse runs and moves from location to location is a virtual business.

Businesses by Chance, Serendipity, or Because of Military Life

Some spouses fall into business opportunities, due to adversity, or seeing a need to fill, or simply from experiences they have because of military life.

Ellie Kay is married to a former stealth fighter pilot and is mother of seven. She weathered eleven moves in thirteen years and dealt with deployments. Ellie wanted to stay home with her children and get rid of their family's $40,000 debt, so she had no choice but to draw on her business background and learn how to handle her family finances in a masterful way. She became so good at it, she started giving volunteer "Shop, Save, and Share" seminars to other military families at their local base. Her seminars came to the attention of Lenn Furrow, director of the Airmen and Family Readiness Center at Holloman Air Force Base. Lenn approached the Air Force Aid Society to fund a film project based on the seminars. That became a video distributed to Air Force bases worldwide.

Serendipity stepped in and the seminar came to the attention of a literary agent, who took it to Bethany House Publishers, which resulted in Ellie's first book *Shop, Save, and Share*. The success of that book quickly led to others. She later wrote *Heroes at Home* for military families, now in its third edition. Her business has grown with fourteen books published and appearances on or in over 600 media outlets, including a regular slot on *ABC News Now* as well as *Nightline, CNBC, Fox News, MSNBC*, and *The Today Show*.

Ellie is a consumer finance consultant with Fortune 100 companies, such as Walmart and Procter & Gamble, where she gives advice on how consumers can make the most of every dollar. And all that started by living through and sharing a military life experience.

Army spouse Tara Crooks switched from her customer service job in retail management to Mary Kay cosmetic sales because she "wanted her own thing." In the process, she taught herself web design and opened a candle business, which she later sold for a profit. As she started focusing on marketing and advertising for moms in business, she happened to be interviewed numerous times on *Work At Home Moms Talk Radio*. The host suggested she should have her own talk show. That triggered *Army Wife Talk Radio*, which Tara started at home while her husband was deployed to Iraq.

It's important to be honest with yourself as to your work habits and skills and how those might translate into business management.

Seven years and more than 400 shows later, she's found her passion and in the process met her battle buddy, Army spouse Star Henderson. The pair cofounded *Army Wife Network*, www.ArmyWifeNetwork.com, in 2009. The web site holds true to its tagline "Interactive Empowerment for Army Wives" by featuring field exercise events, *AWTR* podcasts, live chat features, featured columns, *Loving A Soldier* blog, message boards, military shopping links, resource database, post directory, and social media galore.

Krista Wells is a Marine Corps Reserve spouse with a PhD in psychology and ten years' experience in business consulting and career counseling. She is a certified coach through the International Coaching Federation, writer, and public speaker. In her case, she chose to specialize in working with military spouses, and is known as The Military Spouse Coach.

"I coach in person two days a week in my office as well as over the phone with spouses from around the US who are looking to find a career, transition to a new career, or be mentored as they start their own business," she says. She writes for various military sites such as MilitarySpouse.com, MilitaryMoney.com, and OperationHomefront.net, and presents workshops and motivational keynotes at military spouse events.

Lorna Dupuoy spent ten years as a Marine herself (including work in protocol at high levels), and then married into the Navy. As a Navy spouse for eighteen years, she held a variety of positions, including high school teacher and general manager for a family theme park in Virginia Beach. Since her husband had three commands over that time, she spent a lot of time organizing functions and entertaining. "I always loved people and parties and events," she says, "Now I'm doing the same thing and getting paid for it." When her husband retired, she pursued her dream business. They invested in a big, old house behind a long stonewall fence in the resort area of Saratoga Springs, New York, where Lorna grew up. She's created two businesses at that location: an event/retreat center named Villeroy, along with The Etiquette School of New York. She not only teaches etiquette to children, teens, and adults, but to military members as well, especially those stepping into protocol positions.

"I've always had a passion and talent for decorating and organizing," says Army spouse Sandee Payne, author of the books *That Military House: Move it, Organize it & Decorate it* and *Move Your House: Plan it, Organize it & Decorate it*. "No one else, in my extensive research, was catering to the military, so I took the opportunity and am so happy I did. My business and book have proven to be so beneficial to our lifestyle."

We could go on and on with examples of military spouses who've developed a business inspired by military life: Navy spouse Babette Maxwell, who cofounded *Military Spouse* magazine; Air Force spouse Terri Barnes, who writes the "Spouse Calls" column and blog for *Stars & Stripes*; Navy spouse Beth Wilson, columnist and founder of *Enlisted Spouse Talk Radio* and Enlisted Spouse Community; Air Force spouse Julie Negron, a cartoonist who created the Jenny cartoons published worldwide by *Stars & Stripes* and in fifty-plus military publications; Navy spouse Wendy Poling, who founded *Navy Wife Talk Radio* and expanded to MyMilitaryLife.com. They each found a passion in sharing this military life and helping other military spouses with ideas, resources, and support.

Military Spouse Business Mentoring and Networking

One prime example any budding military spouse entrepreneur should know about is Roxanne Reed. This proud military brat, military spouse, and mother of two is the CEO and founder of Jane Wayne LLC. Her brands include Jane Wayne Gear and the All Fired Up Candle Company, to name a few. She pioneered the trend of "designed by military wives," which shows in every brand she and her teams develop. She's known for painting the world pink camouflage.

Although Roxanne's passion is in design, she loves to share her experiences with other spouses and founded a mentoring program called Building a Business Military Spouse Style. Her program and business consulting has helped a number of military spouse start ups around the country and is now part of the Military Spouse Foundation, MilitarySpouseFoundation.org, cofounded with Celeste Beaupre.

Many military spouse businesses are thriving and growing.

Navy spouse Lanette Lepper, Army spouse Rebecca Poynter, and Navy spouse Joanna Williamson, all of whom are entrepreneurs, joined together to found the Military Spouse Business Association, MilSpouseBiz.org. The association provides information, networking, forums, and a directory of military spouse businesses.

The Bottom Line

Many military spouse businesses are thriving and growing. Other spouses told us they learned by doing that running a business was not for them. However, as they all pointed out, if they hadn't tried, they would always have wondered and probably lived with regrets.

Some businesses have done well in some locations and faltered during other moves and economic upheavals. Many business owners we talked with are simply happy to see forward progress with each move and fully expect the profit situation to improve dramatically only when they stop moving and can stabilize the business. However, many of these spouses still say they are happy they've been moving a business rather than searching for a job with each move. They are doing work they love, building something for the future, enjoying more flexibility than they might otherwise, and have tax write-offs for much of what they do.

Staffcentrix tracked the outcome of the military spouse virtual assistant training through quarterly reports from all military spouses who attended training. Eighty-nine percent of spouses who launched a VA business reported improved quality of life. Isn't that what our life choices are all about?

Key Points and Action Steps

▷ Talk with other business owners to help figure out if the entrepreneurial route is for you.

▷ Create a business plan to include projected expenses and income, how you would service your clients when you have to move your business, and where you can get support for your endeavor.

▷ Get your family's buy-in to your business ideas and how it might affect them.

▷ Look to other military spouse business owners for mentoring, networking, and lessons learned.

Resources

The E-Myth Revisited: Why Most Small Businesses Don't Work and What to Do About It by Michael Gerber (2001).

Make Your Contacts Count: Networking Know-How for Business and Career Success by Anne Baber and Lynne Waymon (2007), and additional resources at www.ContactsCount.com.

Making a Living Without a Job: Winning Ways for Creating Work that You Love, Revised Edition by Barbara Winter (2009). Full of great stories and inspiration for those of us looking to have a small one-person business. We find her ideas of having "multiple profit centers" key to what we do. www.BarbaraWinter.com or www.JoyfullyJobless.com.

Military Spouse Foundation, www.MilitarySpouseFoundation.org.

Military Spouse Business Association, www.MilSpouseBiz.org.

Working from Home: Everything You Need to Know About Living and Working Under the Same Roof, Fifth Edition by Paul and Sarah Edwards (1999), and their book *Home-Based Business for Dummies*, coauthored with Peter Economy (2010).

Working Solo: The Real Guide to Freedom and Financial Success with Your Own Business, Second Edition by Terri Lonier (1998).

You Need to Be a Little Crazy: The Truth About Starting and Growing Your Business by Barry J. Moltz (2008). From a "serial entrepreneur" with both failures and successes in various businesses, full of lots of quotes and stories from the trenches showcasing the realities rather than the fantasies of owning your own business.

Resources for Virtual Assistants

International Virtual Assistants Association, www.IVAA.org.

REVA Network (Real Estate Virtual Assistants), www.REVAnetwork.com.

Staffcentrix, www.Staffcentrix.com. Designed the first virtual-work training programs for the US Department of State and Armed Forces.

The 2-Second Commute: Join the Exploding Ranks of Freelance Virtual Assistants by Christine Durst and Michael Haaren (2005). Also, their book, *Work at Home Now: The No-Nonsense Guide to Finding Your Perfect Home-Based Job, Avoiding Scams, and Making a Great Living* (2010).

Examples of Military Spouses with Businesses

Tara Crooks and Star Henderson: www.ArmyWifeNetwork.com.

Lorna Dupuoy: www.EtiquetteSchoolofNewYork.com.

Ellie Kay: www.EllieKay.com.

Charlotte Lingard-Young: www.CYVirtualSolutions.com.

Sandee Payne: www.ThatMilitaryHouse.com.

Wendy Poling: www.NavyWifeRadio.com and www.MyMilitaryLife.com.

Roxanne Reed: JaneWayneInc.sitegidget.com.

Krista Wells: www.MilitarySpouseCoach.com.

Jeri Winkler: www.SecretAssistant.com.

Chapter 12

Make a Difference as a Volunteer

Giving Your Time has Benefits and Challenges

Jenna arrived at Fort Hood, Texas, as a new bride, moving to the United States from Canada. She was entering a new country and a whole new world. "When I first got here, I knew nothing about the military," she said. "I knew nobody, and nobody knew me." It's an apt description for most new military spouses. We know nothing about the military, we know nobody, and nobody knows us.

Another military spouse told Jenna about the free Army Family Team Building (AFTB) program, a series of classes to teach spouses everything they need to know about military life. After one class, Jenna wanted to get involved. She started teaching classes, volunteering as briefing manager, and creating the monthly newsletter, spending from five to thirty hours a week volunteering. She became involved in other volunteer projects in activities that interested her, from helping create the family readiness group for her husband's unit to helping with duathlon and triathlon competitions on post.

Jenna talks about the sense of satisfaction she gets out of volunteering. She describes the deep friendships she's developed. She no longer feels alone. She's now part of a community going through what she's going through.

Volunteer to Connect to the Military Community

Our military communities and our quality of life are deeply dependent on volunteers. Volunteering can be a win/win opportunity. You make a difference, increase your own self-esteem and happiness, develop new skills, and connect with others. But volunteering has its challenges and sometimes can have a negative effect.

We have each experienced both ends of the spectrum with volunteering. We hear the same from many military spouses we talk to. We both started out in the "not involved and choosing not to be involved" group of military spouses. We were busy with careers and resented the expectation all military spouses should volunteer. We especially resented the fact that in earlier years, spouse involvement (or noninvolvement) was actually included on our husbands' military efficiency reports. Really! That is no longer allowed, thank goodness.

That change came about through the actions of military spouses. Twenty-seven years ago, military wives were expected to volunteer, but not to work for pay. In 1985, two Air Force colonels' wives spoke out, creating lots of adverse publicity. As a result, a subcommittee of the House Armed Services Committee interviewed wives in the US and overseas and confirmed that wives had been told not to work. In 1987, the Department of Defense issued Directive 1400.33, "Employment and Volunteer Work of Spouses of Military Personnel." It stated, "no DOD official, individual commanding officer, or supervisor shall directly or indirectly, impede or otherwise interfere with the right of every military spouse to decide whether to pursue or hold a job, attend school, or perform voluntary services on or off a military installation." Secretary of Defense Caspar W. Weinberger signed a letter on October 22, 1987, addressed to the secretaries of the military departments. The letter emphasized, "Spouses ...have a right to seek employment, to be homemakers, or to volunteer for command-sponsored activities." He further stated, "no military member will be adversely rated or suffer any adverse consequences from the decision of the member's spouse to seek employment."

That may sound like ancient history to you, but we know ourselves and hear from many spouses that, even though things have changed since the 1980s, in some cases expectations remain. It's the expectation that they "have to" volunteer that spouses resent. They resent the judgment of others if they don't choose to volunteer.

In our cases, we weren't interested in many of the things we were asked to do, especially those during the workday when we couldn't participate even if we wanted to. The thing we didn't realize at the time was that, by avoiding all opportunities to volunteer, we kept ourselves apart from the military community. When we had to go to unit functions, we didn't know people. We felt awkward and uncomfortable at those functions. We were living a life separate from the lives of our spouses.

Eventually, we each chose to volunteer when we had the time and saw a need that matched our skills and interests. It was our choice, not a requirement from anyone. The interesting thing for us was that those volunteer activities changed our experience of military life. We went from living on the outside to feeling connected and enriched. We also felt more of a partnership with our spouses.

Is volunteering the only way to feel connected to this military world? Of course not. We know military spouses who are fully connected with their neighbors on post or base, or through their work in a civil service position or teaching at a school on the military installation. Some of them do no volunteering in the military community. They choose instead to be involved with

> *When we started volunteering, we went from living on the outside to feeling connected and enriched.*

programs outside the military community, in their churches, or in national programs. Some have full lives without any volunteering at all. We just know that volunteering in the military community has been one avenue for many of us to connect quickly. As with everything else, there is no one model of community involvement that works for everyone. You have to find what works best for you.

We also know many spouses who live rich full lives without any real connection to the military world. They don't feel a need for any further connection. They've created their own support system outside the military. Keep in mind, though, when you are dealing with a deployment, you often have an easier time if you live on the military installation or at least connect regularly with other spouses dealing with deployment. There is a sense of camaraderie and the knowledge that so many others around you are dealing with the same thing. Off the military installation, you often feel as if the country has all but forgotten that your spouse is deployed and in danger. You can feel truly alone.

Kathie's Story

I volunteered first to write a regular column for the Fort Lewis wives' club newsletter about fun things to do around Fort Lewis, Washington. It was a way to get connected, to help the editor out, to help other spouses explore this area, and to force myself to finally start writing, as I kept saying I wanted to do.

I took over as editor of our family support group newsletter as a way to force myself to learn desktop publishing, something that has helped tremendously in my business.

I spoke for free at military spouse groups at Fort Lewis and McChord Air Force Base for two years and then all over Europe for three years. That allowed me to provide a service and build my speaking skills and material while I connected to the community.

I now spend a lot of time one on one with other military spouses by email and telephone, brainstorming ways they can move toward what they want in life, sharing ideas, resources, and contacts.

As you can tell, for the most part I choose to do things I can do at home and on my own schedule. I knew I wanted to build a business and didn't want to be tied to meetings and other people's schedules. My choice of volunteer projects allows me to fill a need, connect with others, be part of the community, and keep the flexibility I want. It also gives me the chance to learn things I want to learn.

Holly's Story

From the day I started planning my wedding to Jack, I assumed I'd be going to Germany. I couldn't wait to go, in fact! Ten years later, when we finally got to Bamberg, Germany, the reality was totally different from what I'd visualized.

I found myself living on a military installation in a foreign country, and not wanting to venture outside the gates because of the unknowns and language barrier. Kathie had just moved to Heidelberg. She could tell how frustrated I was, so we got permission for me to attend Heidelberg's FLAG (Families Learning About Germany) orientation program, something the Bamberg community did not offer at the time. It made all the difference.

I didn't want other spouses to go through what I'd gone through at first. So I joined forces with Bamberg's Family Advocacy Program manager, Heather Reekie, to create an orientation program for Bamberg. I volunteered forty to sixty hours a week to co-create and market the new program called PEP: People Encouraging People. It was so successful, we ended up with waiting lists of people. We even presented briefings to other communities on how they could create a similar welcome program in their community. I was having a ball and getting fully connected with this community. I was energized by what I was doing.

The best thing was that it made a difference. At the end of one session, we had a spouse come up and say to us, "Two weeks ago I had asked for a divorce just so I could leave Germany. I just couldn't survive here. Now I know I can. I have friends, I know my child is okay in daycare, I have activities I'm interested in—and I even know how to use the bus to go downtown and order items in stores." Talk about a sense of satisfaction!

The irony is that after two years, I was hired to do the program for pay as a contractor, something I hadn't even envisioned. The greater irony is two years later, we returned to Bamberg, where I had my twins and ended up being a single mom and head of our family readiness group when my husband's unit deployed for ten months. I would not have survived that deployment and time as well as I did without that deep knowledge of Bamberg, the military community, and its resources. I would not have had that knowledge without my involvement with PEP.

Look around your military community. So many of the programs that make this challenging life easier or richer came about because someone, often another military spouse, saw a need and set out to fill it. Volunteers make it possible to have programs such as Army Family Team Building, Marine Corps L.I.N.K.S., Navy COMPASS, Air Force Heart Link. We have children's sports programs and other youth enrichment programs. There are new spouse orientation programs and amazing spouse conferences held in Germany, Hawaii, Fort Lewis, Fort Benning, and other locations. There are many important programs outside our military installations that can use our help. It's another way to connect to local communities.

Volunteer to Increase Your Energy and Happiness

When you are truly generous without thought of gaining something back in return, you get a warm, fuzzy feeling inside—an actual biochemical response—that has been called a "helper's high." Not only do you make a difference in someone else's life by your volunteer efforts, you make a difference in your own. Volunteering increases your psychological and physical well-being. It can even add extra years to your life, according to research at both Cornell University and the University of Michigan. The Cornell Study showed that actively involved women have high self-esteem, enjoy greater total well-being, and are more likely to live longer than those women who aren't involved. The Michigan study showed people live longer because they volunteer, rather than that people volunteer because they're healthier and, hence, likely to live longer.

Volunteering can increase your energy. When Holly co-created the PEP orientation program in Bamberg, Germany, she worked well over forty hours a week. She was full of energy and enthusiasm and excited to get going every day. That's what happens when you volunteer for a project you are excited about. When you do something challenging, that you care deeply about, you can easily lose sense of time. You are in psychological flow, which can be one of the happiest states in life.

Volunteering can help combat depression. According to Richard O'Connor, PhD, psychologist and author of *Undoing Depression: What Therapy Doesn't Teach You and Medication Can't Give You*, one way to pull yourself out of depression is to connect with others. Doing a good deed for others is particularly powerful, he adds. By volunteering, you do both. You connect with others and do good deeds.

Army spouse Natalie Finley wrote a letter to *Army Times* in response to another spouse's letter titled "Alone at Home,": "I encourage all you lonely spouses out there to get involved. Loneliness is a choice you make by doing nothing. Once you get involved and meet people, your life will be richer for it, and the time during deployments will be much more bearable."

Susan Agustin, an Army spouse, discovered Huggee Miss You dolls when relatives sent one to her three-year-old daughter, Maddie, with photos of her cousins to keep in front of her. These simple cloth stuffed dolls have a plastic sleeve instead of a face, a spot to place the photo of a loved one. "When my husband, Gene, deployed to Qatar, Daddy's photo replaced the cousins," says Susan. The daddy doll went everywhere with Maddie. Gene would call and ask, "Where did we go, and what did we do today?" The teachers at her daughter's school told her that every child dealing with deployments or any parental absence needs one of those dolls. Susan finally started selling them on post and through a web site. She created a way to allow family support groups and other military spouse groups to sell the dolls as fundraisers.

Susan realized quickly, a business wasn't what she was about. "I just wanted to get these dolls into the hands of children who needed them, children affected by deployment," she says. She chose to close her business and start a volunteer program called Operation Give a Hug, www.OGAH.org, where she collected donations from businesses to get these dolls into the hands of as many children of deployed military as possible. Since its inception in 2004, Operation Give a Hug has given out more than half a million dolls to children who have parents serving our nation

Volunteering can increase your energy and help combat depression.

in all service branches, distributed through family readiness groups, family liaison officers, family programs coordinators, casualty assistance officers, and Tragedy Assistance Program for Survivors (TAPS). The dolls are also being used by pediatric psychologists and school counselors to help children cope with deployment.

"If you'd ever told me I'd be speaking in front of large groups of business people," Susan adds, "I wouldn't have believed you. But when you are passionate about something, you step outside your comfort zone."

Susan's story is just one of many. The military has always run on volunteerism, with military members and family members making a difference on post/base and off, and in foreign lands. They end up making a difference to themselves, too. Research shows that giving altruistically is one key way to experience lasting happiness. It turns out making a difference is contagious as well.

Research by Jonathan Haidt, PhD, associate professor of psychology at the University of Virginia, suggests that seeing or even reading about others' generosity can not only make us better people but increases the likelihood we'll do good works of our own. What he terms "elevation" is what happens when we witness acts of moral beauty (e.g., compassion, courage, loyalty, generosity). Elevation elicits a physical sensation of warmth or openness in the chest and motivates people to help others or to become better people themselves. As Haidt says, "Recognize that your own actions often have a ripple effect you don't realize."

Volunteering really is a win/win situation. You fill a need in the community. You increase your own happiness and sense of satisfaction in life. You connect more deeply to the community you live in. You might even trigger generosity in others around you. And, you can learn key skills.

Volunteer to Develop Skills

Think of a skill you want to cultivate. Where could you apply that skill? What volunteer organization or project holds meaning for you, and gives you the chance to learn or improve a skill that is important to you?

Interested in volunteering on post/base? The volunteer coordinator at your family service center will know what is available at that location and can help you find the best fit for you.

Spouse Janet Farley credits her volunteer work with Army Community Service for getting her the job as a career counselor with Resource Consultants, Inc. (RCI) "The job required actual teaching experience," she says. "They accepted my Army Community Service training experience in lieu of paid teaching experience." The job with RCI eventually led her to write her books, columns, and many articles.

You can build the skills you need through volunteer opportunities. Kathie did that with writing and speaking and desktop publishing. Jenna and Holly did that with learning about the military and their communities and sharing that knowledge with other spouses.

Listen to how Marine spouse Lori describes her experience. "I am currently a career counselor at Camp Pendleton. What I find with many military spouses is they don't have the skills to compete in the workforce or they lack direction in their career search. I was one of them when I first married my Marine. I assumed my degree would guarantee me work. However, when I went on job interviews, they didn't ask about my degree; they asked about my skills and experience, what I had to offer. Having been only a full-time student, I had no skills except how to study.

"After six months of job searching, I was still unemployed, bored out of my mind, and clinging to my husband, because he was the only person I could talk to. I finally started volunteering out of desperation. From working at the thrift shop, to acting as key volunteer coordinator for my husband's unit, to becoming publicity chair for L.I.N.K.S. and other programs, I started developing skills. With our move to Okinawa, I volunteered as publicity chair for Navy/Marine Corps Relief Society, continuing to hone my public speaking skills and building my resume.

"When I started job interviews again, I had skills to sell. I got the first job I tried for as outreach coordinator for the University of Maryland. With my next move, I once again got the first job I applied for, now that my two-page resume is filled with skills and experience (the bulk of it gained in volunteerism). Through volunteering, I gained experience and skills, I've met lots of great people who helped me grow, and I've discovered who I am."

Volunteering helps you develop life skills. We've watched people blossom through volunteering. One extremely shy friend started volunteering with Army Family Team Building, went through the train-the-trainer program, and ended up as a master trainer. You should see her now: poised, self-confident, well spoken.

Volunteering often pays back later in ways you don't anticipate, in new passions or career paths, in contacts that bring you jobs or friends later, in skills that are exactly what you need down the road for another important project or for your business or career.

Blue Star Families developed a tool to help you take your volunteer experience and the skills you gained and turn them into career skills on a resume. The Military Spouse Resume Toolkit explains how to translate volunteer work and military life experiences into effective resume points. It also outlines strategies for overcoming gaps in employment on resumes and how to talk about gaps in job interviews, and includes military spouse-specific career advice and sample resumes tailored for different types of employment, including corporate, public sector, and nonprofit jobs.

Be Aware! Volunteering Can Also Cause Problems

You know the saying, "You can have too much of a good thing." Well, it applies to volunteering, too. Just because there is a need to be filled doesn't mean you are the best person to fill it at this time. You've heard, "If you want something done, give it to the busy person." Well, that may be true to a point. Sometimes that person becomes too busy, because they just don't know how to say no to requests.

We have both been in situations ourselves and watched many friends get into situations of taking on too much. The result can include extreme stress or even illness for the individual, and a neglected family. It can mean an important volunteer task doesn't get done as effectively as it might. That does not fit into the win/win formula of healthy volunteerism.

It's important to make conscious choices in volunteering, just as it is important to do so in the rest of your life. Those choices should be made based on a number of factors: the importance of the task, your own family priorities and schedules, your interest in the project, and possibly the opportunity to learn something new you want to learn.

Stress is what happens when your gut says "No" and your mouth says "Sure, I'd be glad to."

Vivian Rhodes, an active volunteer and highly-esteemed Army spouse, offered Holly countless tips and tools for dealing with the challenges of military life. Vivian always encouraged Holly to take care of herself and her family first before thinking of delving into a new volunteer project. When in a leadership position especially, take on what you think is important, and delegate what you can. If no one else wants to do it, then let it go. You may have to ask yourself, "What does it really matter in the light of eternity?" Recognize you can't do it all.

When faced with a decision to volunteer for something or not, Vivian recommends asking yourself the simple question, "What part of this activity will energize me?" If you are energized by the thought of getting involved, then say yes. If just the thought of it drains and depresses you, don't do it. Trust your gut. If it energizes you, go for it. If you don't have the emotional, physical, or spiritual energy for the task, don't take it on.

We've both been in the position of asking for volunteers. We don't want someone to do a task begrudgingly with a bad attitude, or simply not enough time or energy, just because they weren't able to say no to us. The last thing we want is to cause someone family or health problems because of time spent volunteering for our project.

Saying no can take practice. We saw a button once that said, "Stress is what happens when your gut says 'No' and your mouth says 'Sure, I'd be glad to.'" Give yourself time to listen to your gut. One good first step is to give yourself space to make a conscious decision by saying, "Let me check my calendar and get back with you." It's also key that you know what you are committing yourself to do before you make your decision. Holly always asks the question: "What does that entail?"

Often the problem isn't that you *want* to say no; it's the reality that your current life situation *needs* you to say no. Here are some good questions to ask yourself when you are asked to do something you'd like to say yes to, but you know will make your life crazy if you do say yes.

- Is it necessary? Does it fit in with my values and priorities?
- Will this opportunity come around again?
- Can I shift something else, cut anything, or delegate something to make space?
- Are my family and I willing to take on a time period of craziness in order to say yes to this? If so, no whining allowed!

It's important that we all learn to say no graciously when no is the right answer for us at the time. It's important we role model that healthy practice for other military spouses and for our kids.

It's also important we are clear whether a volunteer task is a necessary and useful task, and whether we should ask someone else to take it on or we should take it on ourselves. We can probably all share examples of things we've been asked to do that didn't make sense and didn't serve a real purpose. In some cases, the tasks were a result of outdated practices and "the way we've always done it" thinking. It's up to all of us to work toward useful, meaningful, and conscious volunteering. We really can make it win/win by making conscious choices.

Volunteering can change your life and connect you with an amazing community. As Army spouse Theresa Donahoe says, "Volunteering gives me a group of people outside my home and my neighborhood to fill my mind and perhaps become my newest 'family' in the absence of my own."

Key Points and Action Steps

▷ Weigh the pros and cons of volunteer opportunities you encounter. Will it bring you energy and joy?

▷ Check your local community and base/post contact for volunteer opportunities that fit your time and talents or that provide a chance to learn skills that support your dreams.

▷ Say no when you need to.

Resources

How to Say No Without Feeling Guilty: And Say Yes to More Time, More Joy, and What Matters Most to You by Patti Breitman and Connie Hatch (2001).

Military Spouse Resume Toolkit provided by Blue Star Families. www.BlueStarFam.org/Policy/MilSpouse_Resume_Builder

Chapter 13

Know What Research Says About Relationships

Ask any military spouse who has been through a deployment or other challenge of military life, "What helped you get through that time?" and you will probably hear the answer, "My friends." Spouses who have the hardest time with military life are those isolated by circumstances or who choose to isolate themselves.

Relationships are key to our happiness in life, during deployments and otherwise. A study conducted at University of Illinois ("Very Happy People" Diener and Seligman, 2002) found that the most common characteristic shared by those who have the highest levels of happiness and the fewest signs of depression are those who have strong ties to friends and family and a commitment to spending time with them. All the research we found concluded that the happiest people are those who have strong relationships and strong positive support structures. That can be your spouse, your family, your friends, a church group, or other kinds of groups.

Here's another interesting study: the 2006 Friendship study at Duke University. Okay, it wasn't called that. It's called "Social Isolation in America." The study found that one-fourth of all Americans report they have nobody to talk to about important matters. Another quarter has only one such close friend. And for the average American? In the twenty years since a duplicate study was done, the number of confidants of the average American has dropped from three down to two.

We started making lists of the many deep friendships we enjoy, even if our friends are spread around the world. These are friends we regularly have deep discussions with, even if many are by telephone or email to allow for different times zones and life schedules. Our lists both have way more than three! (And yes, these lists only include the friends we really could call up in the middle of the night, knowing they would take our call without hesitation.) The large numbers on our lists aren't that common with many of our civilian acquaintances.

Hanging out with your girlfriends in times of stress is a necessity. It is a scientific fact.

One big reason shows like *Friends* and *Sex in the City* became so popular is that, for many people, the characters portrayed on the show became surrogate friends. Many civilian friends tell us they have had no time to get together with their friends since high school or college (or at least since their children were born). One woman said, "To me, tuning into *Sex in the City* was like getting together with my girlfriends, only I didn't have to get dressed and go out."

In talking with thousands of military spouses over the years, one comment arises frequently: deep friendships tend to occur more frequently with military life. Why? For one thing, you are often involved with a community during deeply challenging times like deployments, where your experiences and your connections are more intense than normal. And when you are new to a place, without extended family and old friends around, you are forced to reach out and make connections just to get things done in life.

Extensive studies by Gallup, reported on in the book *Wellbeing*, show that "people who have at least three to four very close friendships are healthier, have higher well-being, and are more engaged in their jobs. The absence of any close friendships can lead to boredom, loneliness, and depression."

Gather and communicate with your positive friends to reduce your stress and increase your happiness. One word of caution. Don't just surround yourself with people only to be around people. Look for positive people. If you are someone like Holly who is very empathetic, she finds that negative people drain her energy. When you live this challenging military lifestyle, you need all the energy you can muster. Sure, we all need the opportunity to vent frustrations, but the last thing we need is to be surrounded by negative, constantly complaining people who can pull us into their negative spirals and cause added stress.

Friendships during stressful times might be even more important for women. A landmark UCLA study ("Biobehavioral Responses to Stress in Females" Taylor, Klein, et al., 2000) suggests women respond to stress with a cascade of brain chemicals, an increase in oxytocin. The study showed that the hormone oxytocin buffers the fight or flight stress response and encourages women to tend their children and gather with other women instead. These "tend and befriend" activities counter stress and produce a calming effect. This doesn't occur for men, because their higher levels of testosterone counter the effect of oxytocin in their systems. Men tend instead to respond to stress in true "fight or flight" behavior—by becoming aggressive or withdrawing.

So what does that mean to military wives? Hanging out with your girlfriends is not a luxury in times of stress. It's a necessity. It's a scientific fact! So if you've been putting friendships on the back burner while you focus all your time and energy on everyday demands of life, think again.

Our friends are important parts of our lives. As Marla Paul, author of *The Friendship Crisis: Finding, Making, and Keeping Friends When You're Not a Kid Anymore* says: "Friends assuage our guilt, ease our stress, make us laugh, recharge our energy, carry our grief, and celebrate our successes."

Let's look at ways to develop that strong positive support structure. We'll look at three important aspects:

1. How to make and maintain friendships and keep important connections with friends and extended family as you move.

2. How to strengthen one of the most important support structures: your relationship with your spouse.

3. How to incorporate the help of others in challenging times.

Key Points and Action Steps

▷ Relationships are key to our happiness in life, and deep friendships tend to occur more frequently with military life.

▷ In this military life, you need all the energy you can muster, so gather and communicate with your positive friends to reduce your stress and increase your happiness.

▷ Hanging out with friends is especially critical for women in times of stress, so make that girls' night out a priority.

Resources

"Biobehavioral Responses to Stress in Females: Tend-and-Befriend, not Fight-or-Flight." *Psychological Review*, 107, 411–429, by S.E. Taylor, L.C. Klein, B.P. Lewis, T.L. Gruenewald, R.A.R. Gurung, and J.A. Updegraff (2000).

The Friendship Crisis: Finding, Making, and Keeping Friends When You're Not a Kid Anymore by Marla Paul (2005).

"Social Isolation in America: Changes in Core Discussion Networks over Two Decades." *American Sociological Review,* 71 (3), 353-375, by Miller McPherson, Lynn Smith-Lovin, and Matthew E. Brashears (2006).

"Very Happy People." *Psychological Science,* 13 (1), 81-84, by Edward Diener and Martin E.P. Seligman (2002).

Chapter 14

Make Friends and
Stay Connected as You Move

During the question-and-answer period at a Fort Lewis, Washington, library meet the author event, Army spouse Shequita Gatlin stood up and asked Kathie, "How do you make friends when you are new, other than knocking on doors and looking weird?"

Her question prompted us to add this chapter to our book. Since the research shows that positive social relationships, friendships, are a key ingredient to human happiness, we need to know how to make friends. And as military spouses, we can't just do that once. In our mobile lifestyle, even more than for most people, we have to do what our old Girl Scout song taught us, to "make new friends and keep the old." The fact is military spouses who are isolated by circumstances, or who choose to isolate themselves, will have the most difficult time with this lifestyle. And the reality is that some of those who are isolated are often isolated because they are introverts and don't know how to go about making friends.

Making friends really is a skill you can learn. As a military spouse, you get a lot of opportunity to practice. Let's look at some ways.

Ask Your Friends for Contacts

With Facebook and other social media, it's easy to ask your friends who might know someone in your new location. That's a much easier call to make with a common friend connecting you.

Find Other Newcomers

Most posts/bases have newcomer orientation programs. These are helpful ways to quickly discover what resources and facilities are available in your new community. Overseas, they also help you learn the new customs and logistics of life in a foreign land. And they are an easy place to make new friends since everyone there is new and likely looking to connect.

Another place to connect is with newcomers groups. Check out the Newcomers Club Worldwide Directory at www.NewcomersClub.com for listings by state and by country.

Army spouse Martha Klinck says, "Ten years and eight moves later, I have found the easiest way for me to make friends is with those people arriving at post at the same time. In the US, it is especially difficult to break into established 'circles.' Overseas it tends to be much easier to make friends—we are all in the same boat together."

Don't Limit Yourself

Let's celebrate the fact we have the great opportunity to interact with such a diverse group of people. Army spouse Theresa Donahoe says, "One thing I've learned in this lifestyle is to expand my definition of 'friend' in the military spouse arena. I had to learn that just because my initial impression of someone might be they were 'not my type,' I often found that my 'type' was changing, and I enjoy a much larger variety of friends than I ever had growing up. People I may never have given myself a chance to know in my old life turned out to become some of my closest and dearest friends." Those diverse friends help you stretch and grow as you move through this life. We've found there is a strong bond among military spouses—or at least there can be if you are open to it. We have all entered a life that is different and often difficult for all of us.

Attend Activities that Interest You, and Talk with People

We looked back on how we met our many military and civilian friends, and we asked many other spouses to do the same. One common way people meet new like-minded people is by participating in activities that interest them. From attending book readings, to taking Spanish classes, to joining the biking or hiking club, it's a win/win scenario. You get to do something you enjoy, and you might meet a new friend. (And even when you don't meet a new friend, you still engage in something that interests you, which ups your happiness in life, so what's to lose?)

Army spouse Linda Beougher says, "I have found that my best friends appeared when I was doing what I loved to do. That could be taking a class in something that interests me, exercise, a trade group, spending time at my children's school, at the church, whatever. It seemed that I bonded most with people with similar interests/lifestyles more than with people in the unit or neighborhood where I always looked first."

One of Holly's greatest gifts when her twins were young was to be part of a playgroup. Gathering together with other moms who were going through the same challenges was affirming. The opportunities for her children to have fun with other children and for her to observe how they played and interacted with other children were benefits in and of themselves. There were others. She could observe how other mothers dealt with parenting issues such as disciplining, which gave her ideas for how she could approach disciplining her own children. She gathered ideas and resources, such as who were the best babysitters in the neighborhood and where to get the best buy on diapers, formula, or hand-me-down clothes. It became a fabulous support group for her as she listened and shared the ups and downs of parenting with other moms. To top it off, she met one of her dearest friends to this day in that neighborhood playgroup.

If there's not an organized playgroup right now where you are, consider starting one. Inviting another mom and her children over for a play date is the first step. Holly found other moms of young children when she moved to a new area through an international organization called MOPS (mothers of preschoolers), www.MOPS.org. MOPS also has groups for mothers of school-aged children, mothers of teens, and groups specifically for moms dealing with the challenges of military life.

Don't forget to check out the programs on post/base for families. For example, at Joint Base Lewis-McChord, you'll find The Escape Zone, and Raindrops and Rainbows, indoor activity centers where moms can gather with their children and connect with each other. The base MWR Child, Youth & School Services also hosts many programs for preschoolers through teens.

For many activities you enjoy, you will find groups already in place as you move around. It's an easy entrée into a group of like-minded folks. For example, if you enjoy knitting, check out StitchnBitch.org to find a group of knitters wherever you move. If you've been thinking about knitting, you should know they welcome beginners. Working with needles and yarn has been shown to lower stress and blood pressure, and lessen pain!

Another great place to find groups of people interested in activities you are interested in is MeetUp.com. You can search by interest to find other people in your area who are also interested in biking or volleyball or antiquing, or even "raising daughters with high self-esteem."

You don't have to attend an event. Just be open to things that interest you. Kathie has met a number of good friends by calling them up after reading an article about them in the post or local newspaper, or reading an article they wrote in the paper. She simply asks if they'd be interested in a walk and talk, or in meeting over coffee. To date, no one has said no. "You quickly know if there is any kind of connection or not in a first-time meeting," she adds. "Some of those meetings were one-time things. Others have evolved into deep, long-term friendships."

Attend activities provided by your spouse's unit. Almost every spouse we talked with for this chapter mentioned at least one good friend they met through their spouse's unit. That is indeed how we met one another—when our spouses were both attending a military school together.

"My first military friend I met through our battalion coffee group," says Army spouse Tara Crooks. "I always tell the story of me moving to Fort Hood, Texas, before Kevin was there (one year early) due to him doing his schooling. I worked for Nine West Group, Inc., in Austin, Texas, and lived in Killeen. I had never been on a post other than Fort Sill as a 'drive-by' and so I was terrified of the commissary and the PX, and had no idea what the military was all about. I spent an entire year working my tail off long hours, so I didn't have to go home because, frankly, I was lonely!!! When Kevin finally came to Fort Hood and we joined a unit, the battalion commander's wife was so wonderful! She personally called and introduced herself and invited us to her home. I think if she hadn't done that, I never would have gotten involved in coffees and other events in the battery or battalion, but thankfully, she did. I met my first friend, Erin Nauman, there. Her husband and mine worked together and, ironically, were very good friends, though we didn't know. We spent our four years in Texas hanging out and exploring with the Naumans."

"Since that time," Tara adds, "I have recognized the value of social events in the military, and I attend the spouse club, family readiness group, battery and battalion functions, balls, etc. You never know what you might find once you're there. It's definitely out of my comfort zone, but it's helpful."

Connect with Other Military Spouses During Deployments

You might want to take part in military support groups, especially during deployments. You'll connect with others dealing with the same kinds of challenges you are dealing with, and you'll get information about the unit you might not otherwise get.

Considering moving home during a deployment? You might reconsider. Marine spouse Tina McIntosh wrote in a *Marine Corps Times* newspaper essay, "I thought coming home would be easier and less aggravating. I was wrong." Tina moved home to Ohio when her husband deployed to Iraq. "I had no idea things would be this different away from a military base or that people were oblivious to world events. I assumed people respected our troops and were as educated [about deployment] as we are. I was wrong. It seems as if they don't even realize there are troops abroad in hostile environments." As she and many other spouses have learned, it can be difficult to be in a civilian environment where everyone is simply going about their lives "business as usual" as if there were no war going on and no Americans like your spouse living in daily danger.

It really does help to interact with others who are dealing with what you are dealing with. Other friends and family can be sympathetic and supportive, but nobody can really understand what you are going through unless they have done so themselves. Consider these comments from women at a retreat for spouses dealing with a year-long deployment:

- "This weekend has taught me that I'm not alone in this situation, and my son is not the only little boy that doesn't like to listen and is not so well behaved. Now I feel like I will be able to make it."

- "The best part of the weekend was spending time with other spouses who you know are feeling and going through the same thing as you are. To be able to share feelings and be able to just cry when there was the need. To have people around who understand exactly how I feel and have been feeling for a whole year!"

Navy spouse Erin wrote, "The Norfolk Navy wives are wonderful! If you need an ear or shoulder at 1:00 a.m., they are there. If a ride is needed, babysitting, a party, BBQ, or just shopping with a buddy, they are there."

When Army spouses Cathy Sterling, Clara Bergner, Carol Brooks, and Ellen Torrance lived at Fort Stewart, Georgia, they said they couldn't have made it through those months of deployments without their "walking talking" buddies. They met in the morning to walk and talk. They said they'd "solve all the world's problems" during those regular walks. They held each other accountable and supported each other. Exercise was an added bonus.

Consider doing what four Marine spouses did during a long deployment. Two of them took all the kids for an evening and overnight at one house. The other two women then had the evening to enjoy a movie and dinner with each other. The next morning these mothers would wake up on their own schedule—no children to feed or get ready. The one night and morning of no responsibilities were absolute luxuries for each of these busy moms. The next week they reversed roles.

Another great idea is to gather with other military spouses who are going through a deployment and form a book club. Read books that other military spouses have written about surviving and thriving during deployments.

One great resource is *Surviving Deployment* by Karen Pavlicin. This book helps you learn what to expect, how to prepare, and how to grow as individuals and families. It has checklists, tips and ideas, and stories of how other spouses have handled the challenges of deployment. Gathering with other military spouses as you read and talk about the book can help you turn an otherwise lonely and challenging situation into a positive experience.

There's another reason military friends can be so important during a deployment. It's common for your friends who are dealing with a deployment to almost become a surrogate family. You do so many things together—from dinner, to watching television, to spending time with your kids—that you would otherwise be doing with your spouse. When your service members return, you and the other spouses understand that the intensity and time available to spend with one another simply will not be the same. Your civilian friends might not as quickly understand that sudden change.

Being a military spouse allows you an opportunity to become part of a community that will last a lifetime. Holly talks about how this community welcomed her with open arms from the first day she arrived at Fort Riley,

Kansas, as a new bride many years ago. Although the faces changed constantly as she moved all over the world with her husband and family, the bond these military spouses felt remains rock solid even today.

She would tell others, "If we were meant to be on this earth by ourselves, we would have been put here by ourselves. We are not here by ourselves; we are not expected to go through this life by ourselves." This community believes in helping each other along the way and not worrying about whether or not we are able to repay that person who helped us during a difficult time. Our job is then to help someone else when we see an opportunity to do so. As Kathie says, "It's like the title of the book and movie, *Pay It Forward* (Catherine Ryan Hyde). That's how it works. We help other military spouses, and they help others, and the cycle of community never stops."

Don't Limit Yourself to Activities on Post or Base

It's great to have a mix of friends, both military and civilian, to enrich your life. Many military spouses have discovered what we have over time. We need our military friends because they truly understand what we are dealing with as we face a deployment or yet another move. They speak our language and can share important resources available through the military. But we also want our civilian friends, because they quickly connect us to community resources we might not find otherwise, they take us away from the constant diet of military news, and they enrich our lives by exposing us to new worlds outside the gate. Plus, we think it's important that we all connect more with the civilian community so there isn't such a divide between the military and civilian worlds.

Be open to connections as you go about your daily routine. Kathie can point out good friends she met sitting next to each other at a workshop, talking on the telephone when Kathie called a local Mac Club for computer help, and going for a chiropractic adjustment.

Army spouse Tara shares this story: "I also have a best friend who lives in the town right outside of post about thirty minutes from me now. When I lived in the same town, I shopped at the local Walmart. We were new here, about two weeks into our tour. We were both standing in line to get pictures. I had my daughter, Wrena (four years old), in the cart and she had her son, Zane, in the cart with her. It was a long line and we stood there forever. I just started up a conversation. Once she walked away I thought, man, I should have gotten her phone number. Lo and behold, two minutes later, she came back and said, 'I really should have gotten your phone number.' Turns out we're both from the Midwest, our kids love each other, our husbands are friends, and we do tons of family things together. It's great to have them here with us at Fort Stewart."

Too Shy to Speak Up?

What if you are shy? For one thing, you aren't alone. Fifty percent of Americans label themselves as shy. Like many of them have, you can learn to be more comfortable by learning new skills and behaviors and self-talk. Even those people who aren't shy can learn from this information.

Tap into resources that help you connect. One favorite is Baber and Waymon's book *Smart Networking* (formerly *Great Connections*). The book is filled with ideas for how to start conversations, join groups already in conversation, and how to get and keep connections going. The authors share how to remember names, how to leave a conversation when it's time to do so, how to help people remember your name, and how to ask questions that trigger conversations. Kathie credits their book with helping her move past her introverted nature to connect with people with each new move and in each new group situation.

Marla Paul's book *The Friendship Crisis: Finding, Making, and Keeping Friends When You're Not a Kid Anymore* is also full of great ideas. Marla first wrote an essay about how difficult it was to make new friends with her own move from Dallas to Chicago. When the essay ran in the *Chicago Tribune* and later in *Ladies' Home Journal*, the response was overwhelming. Women across the country wrote in with similar experiences. Using feedback from many of those women along with interviews with top friendship experts, Marla started writing a monthly column on the subject. That column turned into the book. It's a great resource.

For one thing, it's great to see how others have faced the same kind of friend challenges we all have at some time—from rejection of our overtures to having a clingy, too-needy, or negative friend, to having friends who never take the initiative. Following are tips from these and other resources.

Create Your Agenda

This idea from Baber and Waymon is what Kathie, an introvert, uses to help her step into any new situation where she doesn't know people, and even to help her start meaningful conversations in situations where she may simply not know people very well. Before going into a coffee or military ball or a conference, she takes the time to come up with her agenda. Taking a minute to think about who will be at that event, she comes up with three bits of information she has to share that might be of interest to people there, and three bits of information she is looking for that those individuals might be able to provide her.

"I don't always need to use my agenda," she says, "since sometimes great conversations just happen. But when we start talking about the weather, this gives me a topic to introduce that just might trigger a more purposeful conversation."

Use the Agenda Idea for a Great Unit Coffee

This is a way to get everyone talking in a purposeful manner, extroverts and introverts alike. Here's the actual flyer copy from one of Kathie's unit coffees at Fort Lewis. Their group used this a couple of times a year to spark resource sharing and conversation. Feel free to tweak it to fit your group and location. This would work well in a new neighborhood as well, to get neighbors together to connect and share.

The Monthly Coffee: Good food, great company (and, yes, let's admit it, getting to check out other people's homes)…and most importantly, great resource sharing! Join us on____at____. You can come empty-handed, but you have to bring two things in your head (and you might want a pen and paper handy). This will be an opportunity to give and get great resources. Here's how it works:

Think about who will be here: military spouses who include working women, stay-at-home moms, childless women, young women, women of a certain age, women who have lived in this area for a while or in an earlier assignment, women new to the area. You come prepared with one resource (or more if you like) to share and one to ask for.

For example, I'm happy to share: 1. A great and reasonably priced place to buy large and small pots for your indoor and outdoor plants, and 2. An even nicer place than Ruston Way to enjoy long walks along the water. Resources I'm looking for: 1. Best way/place to sell antique furniture, specifically a couch and chair, and 2. Favorite local nurseries.

> *You get the idea. Here are other possible categories to get you thinking: best free thing to do with kids in the area, best cheap eats restaurant, favorite Washington State ferry route, best home décor store, best military lodging deal in the Northwest or Hawaii.*
>
> *If we find time to share just one resource per person and to get one resource for each person there that evening, just think of all the great resources we'll all discover. And just think: no awkward small talk about the weather.*

Be Curious

Every person has a story. Learn to ask questions to draw them out—and learn to listen. Ask things like: "How did you and your husband meet?" "Is there a story behind your name (for unusual names especially, but even common names often have an interesting story behind them)?" "What's the best thing that's happened to you in the last week?" "What do you like best about this location?"

Be a Friendship Booster

Marla Paul's book shares important friendship boosters and friendship busters. The busters include jealousy and habitually canceling dates, for example. The boosters include showing up for happy and sad events, remembering birthdays, artful listening, making peace with imperfection, and helping out in a crisis.

We have always heard "a friend in need is a friend indeed." It's true. Army spouse Linda shares, "I have found that my best friends were the ones there for me during difficult times. As much as I thought I could earn a friend from helping them, it was really when I asked for help that I discovered the true meaning of friendship. One of my current best friends is another mom from my child's class a few years ago. Although I didn't know her at the time, I asked if my child could play with hers for a couple hours while I went to a doctor's appointment. It turned out I had a major illness, and she helped me get through it by taking my children a lot until I could make other arrangements. Our friendship grew. Another friend flew all the way across the US to stay with me and drive me to daily radiation appointments! Thank God for girlfriends and the sacrifices they make."

Ask For a Job

As an introvert, Kathie learned to always "ask for a job" at events and gatherings. It's much easier for a shy person to initiate conversations with others when they have a purpose: "Please fill out this nametag," "Let me show you where to put your coat," and so on. Volunteering in any community or organization is a sure-fire way to more easily connect.

Find or Create Your Tribe

Consider forming your own group for support. Support groups can take many different forms. Some of you have discovered joy and support with playgroups, Bunko groups, book clubs, or scrapbooking groups. There are movie groups and meal-making groups. Check out the book *Girls' Night Out*, in which authors Tamara Kreinin and Barbara Camens share stories of women's groups of all shapes, sizes, and ages. Also see Chapter 9 of this book, including our Dare to Dream Team concept.

The common thread these groups all share is a consistent, planned, and scheduled way to gather together for sharing and laughter. Groups help you see you aren't alone, and you aren't the only one who's ever gone through what you are going through. Groups give you support and celebration and a sanity check.

If you are isolated by circumstances, cyber groups can be a lifesaver. According to Marla, "Friendships often flourish more quickly over the Internet as some people seem more comfortable revealing themselves on computer screen than in person. It inspires self-revelation in the way of a journal or diary." And you can do this without having to coordinate schedules. There are many military spouse chat rooms. Just don't forget the dangers of cyberspace, especially spending too much time chatting and not enough time living with your family and local friends, and taking time for you.

And when your spouse isn't deployed, consider the value of groups of couples as friends. We can each point out how much more we enjoyed our assignments when we had that kind of group. We were part of one together in Fort Leavenworth, Kansas, our "four seasons group," a group of military members and their spouses. We shared dinners out and in, wine tastings, day trips around the area, 10K runs, and even a New Year's weekend away where we all joined in the Polar Bear Club swim on New Year's Day! Kathie and Greg had a group in Tacoma who shared dinners and movies out, activities such as bike riding and hiking, and who celebrated milestone events as a group, from baby showers to new jobs.

This can be as simple as finding one common interest and taking turns to take the initiative to share that activity. Army spouse Anne Melia and her husband shared regular "cheap eats nights" with another couple. "One of us would call every three weeks or so and say, 'It's time for cheap eats,'" she says. "It allowed us great conversation time and an opportunity to discover good inexpensive restaurants in the Fort Lewis area."

Find Your Battle Buddy: Tara Crooks and Star Henderson's story

The military gets it right when it assigns each individual someone to "watch their back" in military training and combat. We agree, the easiest way to navigate this system we adoringly call "military wife life" (MWL) is with such a friend by your side, someone who will watch your back. Even though the military coined the term, we have adopted it and call those kinds of friends our "battle buddies."

Having a friend who understands the life of a military spouse is important to survival. We, Tara Crooks and Star Henderson, founders of Army Wife Network, are one example of a battle buddy pair.

We have been through deployments, started a business together, and we've weathered/are weathering the life of an Army wife and motherhood of Army brats. We're real-life Army wives who have had good days and bad days, but ultimately we brave it out and are better for the experiences we've had. We've been battle buddies for seven years now. We should be set for another seven-plus years of this MWL together.

We believe that while the road is tough, it is traversable, and the journey of a military family has inherent value measured in enriched life experiences, pride, and sense of honor. All our military families need are battle buddies willing to mentor and empower them for the duration of their service.

Once you've made a friend, you'll have someone to attend events with, ask questions of, and generally feel like you're not alone in your new surroundings. Even if this person is as new to the military as you, you'll still have a battle buddy to trek the journey with you.

You may have to get creative, and may not get the opportunity to meet anyone in your situation face to face. That's what happened to Star, a National Guard wife, when she moved to a new town right before a deployment. Online resources and phone calls to people she knew were going through the same thing helped a lot. A 2:00 a.m. Internet search is what ultimately led her to Tara, then owner of Army Wife Talk Radio.

Mingle and get to know those sitting next to you or across the room, whether in the ER or the big-box store, because battle buddies can be found anywhere.

Note from Kathie and Holly: *We have been battle buddies for twenty-one years now even though we have only lived in the same place one time for ten months while our spouses attended a military school. We've been there for each other through the good times and the bad, through laughter and tears, through celebrations and venting, through successes and failures. We plan to be battle buddies forever.*

Make Time for Your Friends and Extended Family

Obviously, this is a big challenge for military spouses, especially those dealing with a deployment or a move.

One idea is to do your daily activities together. Kathie always suggests a walk whenever someone wants to get together with her. (That used to be running.) "The most consistent I ever was with a running buddy was at Fort Lee, Virginia," she says. "Pat's husband worked with my husband. With three children, one of whom had special needs, the only time she could manage consistently was very early morning before her husband left for work. We would meet and run and talk together. I can't tell you how many times we'd both have trouble dragging ourselves out of bed. We'd say 'I was hoping you'd call to cancel,' but neither of us wanted to let the other down. And we always felt better after the run."

Take a class together; schedule your manicures or pedicures together. Kathie finds the local beauty school and meets friends there for inexpensive pampering and conversation. Walk your dogs together.

"I use my Bluetooth headset for long chats with my friends," says Claire, an Air Force spouse. "I can fold laundry and pick up the house at the same time and still be very present to the conversation."

Trade out things you don't like doing. For example, three of you can help one friend clear out her cupboards or sort her photos into groupings or clean the house together. Then do a dreaded chore for another one the next week. Any chore is easier when done as a team. Good music, conversation, and laughter help you forget that what you are doing is a chore.

The Internet has been a godsend for military spouses. Now, when you first move to a new place, even before you can make new connections, you still have the support of your close friends from the previous assignment. Where you might not be able to talk by phone as often as you might need to during those early months with time differences, you can email and stay in touch through Facebook.

"Email is my favorite method of staying in touch, especially with time zone differences," says Army spouse Linda, "but I still need to hear my friends' voices periodically. I treasure Skype, allowing me to talk over my computer for free!"

Tara keeps up to date with family and friends using private groups on Facebook and her personal blog. Other spouses use family web sites to keep their friends and family up to date with their lives. One friend makes a photo collage every month or so and posts online for family and friends to see her children grow and their family activities. Others use programs like Blurb.com to create books of photos for each year's events so extended family members can see what they've been up to, and for their own family memories.

We think the Internet is wonderful to help us stay connected. However, we want to make sure you are each aware of the need for OPSEC, operational security. Make sure you limit access to what you post. We've seen spouses posting all kinds of details on where their husband or wife is deployed, the unit names, photos of their specific locations. We know it's hard to think this way, but in our current world of war and terrorism, it's dangerous to share details. Just like you don't want to announce to the world that you are home alone with a spouse on the other side of the world. Use common sense.

Family is important and, just as with friends, it can be difficult to maintain close relationships over the many miles and moves. You can use some of the same strategies you use to keep in touch with friends to stay connected with extended family. Jacey Eckhart has many good ideas in her book *The Homefront Club*. Here are ideas shared by spouses in our workshops.

One idea is to help young children know who they are talking with when their grandparents or aunts or uncles are on the telephone. Otherwise, it's a disconnected voice that doesn't have meaning to them. That's why Skype is so great. But even without Skype, you can have a photo of the person they are talking to in front of the child while they are on the phone so they make that connection.

Another spouse created a book for her daughter called *Sally's People*. In the book, she has photos of each of Sally's important extended family: grandparents, aunts, uncles, godparents. Her mom spends time going through the book with Sally telling stories, "Here's Uncle Greg. He has a dog named Ruff. He likes to play guitar." You get the idea. That way when Sally gets to spend time with her relatives, she knows a little about them.

And, of course, the key to staying connected is to make time. Value your friendships and family relationships for what they are and how important they are in your life. As Marla says, "Treat a friendship like the gift it is."

Make and Keep Friends for Life

One thing many of us have discovered as military spouses is how great it is to have friends worldwide. As we move or travel for business or pleasure, we often have friends to visit and vice versa. We noticed with military friends especially, even when many years have passed in between visits, we fall immediately into comfortable deep conversations as if no time has passed. If you've ever been to one of the military resorts like Hale Koa in Hawaii, you've probably noticed the number of obviously retired couples sitting at dinner and talking and laughing with other older couples. We always picture ourselves doing that in later years, taking advantage of military hops and military resorts to travel with our longtime military friends, as long as we keep the connections strong.

Listen to what Air Force spouse Dixie Schneider says years after her husband retired from the Air Force. "We have friends we made in the Azores during an early assignment. We have exchanged the same birthday card to each other for the past twenty-plus years. We have used every ounce of space writing notes on the card but somehow find a new spot each year. We go visit them or they come here every other year. We toured Germany with them one year, and this year we are going on a river cruise from Bucharest to Budapest."

Remember Shequita Gatlin who asked the question that prompted this new chapter? She left the book event that evening with two new friends because another spouse reached out. After Shequita stood up to ask her question, Army spouse Yuri Nardi gave Shequita her phone number. "Yuri, her friend Caren, and I went out afterwards," Shequita told us, "and we've gotten together since."

Key Points and Action Steps

▷ Find new friends through activities you enjoy and by asking existing friends to introduce you to their friends.

▷ Get together with other military spouses during deployment.

▷ Find a battle buddy.

▷ Schedule time for friends and extended family.

Resources

The Friendship Crisis: Finding, Making, and Keeping Friends When You're Not a Kid Anymore by Marla Paul (2005).

Girls' Night Out: Celebrating Women's Groups Across America by Tamara Kreinin and Barbara Camens (2002).

Make Your Contacts Count: Networking Know-How for Business and Career Success by Anne Baber and Lynne Waymon (2007). Previous books: *Smart Networking* (1997) and *Great Connections: Small Talk and Networking for Businesspeople* (1992).

Surviving Deployment: A Guide for Military Families by Karen M. Pavlicin (2003, *Second Edition* 2014). www.KarenPavlicin.com.

Chapter 15

Strengthen Your Military Marriage

Relationship Resources and Ideas

S ince strong, positive support is important to your happiness in life, it makes sense that you would want the support of a strong relationship with your spouse.

Holly's Journal

Of course, I want a strong healthy relationship with my spouse. Why do you think I got married? I love being with my husband. I didn't get married so I could wake up each morning and say, "How can I make his life miserable today?" Nor did I want to wake up to someone who was thinking the same question about me. All I want is to wake up with my husband in bed with me.

I once heard the definition of unhappiness is when your expectations do not meet reality. I had expectations of what married life would be like. You know, the kind of relationships where couples walk hand in hand, eat dinner together, dance together to their favorite music, watch movies together, and sleep together. Well, my expectations are not meeting my reality. As a military spouse, I'm facing a different picture of married life, and I don't like it. I have no one within my own extended family to turn to for advice or as a role model since no one has ever been a military spouse. I wonder if I can make it as a military spouse.

> *I get all these books on marriage, hoping to find ideas to help rekindle the romance. As I turn the pages of ideas, I find myself screaming. My screams turn to tears, because every idea is centered on having a spouse within reach. Mine isn't. He's far away—again. Ideas like playing our favorite song together and having a candlelit dinner for two are out of the question. Write loving messages on the bathroom mirror so he can see it when he gets up— not gonna happen. Are you not listening? He's not home.*

The ideas in these marriage/relationship books Holly was reading at the time she wrote in her journal were good for "normal" relationships, but military marriages are not normal. Mind you, we do think many of the key concepts and research in relationship books are important for all of us, but they aren't all we need as we build our military marriages.

Military marriages face greater challenges than marriages in general. The stresses brought on by constant moves, repeated separations, especially wartime separations, long work hours, and frequent weekend work can wreak havoc with any relationship. We need different ideas. We need to hear how other military couples have made their marriages work through this challenging lifestyle.

Holly's journal pages above are from more than twenty years ago. Her marriage survived, yet it wasn't without a lot of help from other military spouses who shared what worked and what didn't. She learned from marriage retreats put on by the military. Thankfully, more recently, there have been a number of books by military spouses who want to share ideas. Holly had to learn to take proactive steps to work on her relationship and not take things for granted. It wasn't long before she discovered YES it is possible to have a happy military marriage, a marriage full of love and respect. Strong marriages not only make a difference in our own lives, but also in our children's lives, and to other military spouses who follow us.

Shellie Vandevoorde, author of *Separated By Duty, United In Love* (first published in 2003 and updated in 2010), was one of the first military spouses to write a book specifically on relationship issues for the military couple, especially relationships challenged by deployment. It's full of lessons learned and ideas not only from her but also from many other military couples.

The Military Marriage Manual by Janelle Hill, Cheryl Lawhorne, and

Don Philpott, and *Operation Military Family* by Michael J. R. Schindler are two others, all welcome resources for a military spouse's library. The bottom line is: don't think you can do this military life by yourself. Let's learn from each other. Share what works. And remember to surround yourself with other spouses who believe in their marriage vows and want to support their spouse's service. Look for the healthiest role models.

Below are some ideas gathered over the years from other military spouses and military chaplains who have helped us see what truly wonderful marriages we can have while married to the military.

Find Something for Yourself, and Strengthen Your Relationship

If you spend all your time taking care of everyone else and waiting for your spouse to come home, it's not a healthy relationship of two equal partners. When you look to your partner for your happiness and meaning in life, that's quite a burden for your partner. Not having interests and accomplishments of your own leads to low self-esteem (and clinginess!).

As Michelle Weiner-Davis points out in the book *Divorce Busting*, "Unhappy marriages consist of unhappy people. If you are dissatisfied with your life, everything is colored by that fact. Little irritants become major crises. You've got a shorter fuse with the kids and you're more likely to respond rashly to your mate. Unless your life has definition and meaning without your mate, your relationship is doomed from the start."

When you look to your partner for your happiness and meaning in life, that's quite a burden for your partner.

Another challenge to a marriage is when one spouse doesn't have a support structure in place; he or she demands a lot of a partner. Looking to the partner for everything is especially problematic when that partner is deployed and can't be there. Depending on the partner exclusively is a problem when one person works long hours, with a work schedule that is truly beyond an individual's control, as is often the case with the military.

Kathie recalls how she used to greet her husband in tears when he got home from work at Fort Rucker. After being by herself all day, she wanted to go out; while, after being at work all day, he just wanted to stay home! She knows she isn't the first—or last—spouse to feel that way. That's why it's so important to have healthy interests of your own as well. When you have interests of your own, you usually also have a group of people involved with those interests. You aren't isolated. Military communities provide many kinds of support structures. And don't forget, you can always start your own support structure in the form of a Dare to Dream Team (see Chapter 9).

We've had people suggest when a person builds new interests, his or her spouse might be threatened by the way they are changing. We once wondered aloud how our message to spouses—about finding something for themselves—will work if they have a husband or wife who is totally unsupportive of them? When Holly's husband, Jack, heard that, he said, "Listen to what you are saying. If a spouse doesn't want his or her partner to be happy in life, there is something wrong with that relationship."

As John Gottman, long-time relationship researcher, says, "Your partner's dreams are not a threat. They are the deep desires of someone you love."

> *"Ann Dow tells me that her mother always believed that the only way to be a good parent was to be a whole person. It occurs to me that the same principles apply to a marriage—the only way to be a good spouse is to be a whole person as well." —Joan Anderson,* An Unfinished Marriage

Take Advantage of Marriage Enrichment Classes and Resources

A smart move for every military couple is to proactively work on your relationship and to consider taking relationship courses. You don't have to reinvent the wheel here; learn from other people's experiences rather than having to make the same mistakes yourself. It's interesting how most parents read many books about pregnancy and child rearing to help them figure things out. But how many couples read up on relationship-building skills and practices?

Let's face it, most of us spent more time researching and planning the wedding itself than researching and planning the long-term relationship.

Marriage enrichment programs are available through the services as well as in our civilian communities. Some programs are tailored to couples in crisis. Others offer positive tips to strengthen your relationship, effectively communicate, understand money, and renew your marriage commitment. Research the available programs to find the best match for you and your spouse.

Generally, service enrichment programs are sponsored by the installation chaplain or your family service center. Here are a few examples:

Air Force Marriage Care is a weekend retreat program designed to help airmen and their families reintegrate into family life after a deployment. Marriage Care is open to active duty, Reserve, and National Guard Airmen and their spouses.

Army program Strong Bonds offers single soldiers, couples, and families relationship-building skills to thrive within the military lifestyle. The Strong Bonds couple weekend retreat is offered by Army chaplains and is designed to strengthen relationships, inspire hope, and rekindle marriages. Strong Bonds is open to active duty Army, Army National Guard, Army Reserve and Air National Guard families. To locate a retreat near you, go to www.StrongBonds.org.

Chaplain's Religious Enrichment Development Operation (CREDO) Spiritual Fitness Division provides Coast Guard, Navy, and Marine Corps personal growth retreats, warrior transition retreats, marriage enrichment retreats, and family enrichment retreats.

National Guard and Reserve families are eligible for the service programs listed above as well as varying marriage enrichment programs within your state of assignment. For example, the Ohio National Guard offers the Prevention and Relationship Enhancement Program (PREP) as well as a follow-on to PREP called LINKS (Lasting Intimacy through Nurturing, Knowledge, and Skills).

More programs are becoming purple and welcome families from all services. If there isn't a marriage enrichment program specific to your service in your location, don't be afraid to ask a sister-service if you can attend its program.

Contact your family service center or chaplain for more information about available programs, but don't forget to look outside the gate. Local churches, nonprofit organizations, and community groups offer marriage preparation and enrichment programs. Some organizations partner with local installations to offer services to military families, especially those dealing with reintegration after wartime deployments. Operation Military Family offers workshops, retreats, and seminars in Washington State and Military Marriage Enrichment provides marriage preparation and enrichment programs in Texas. The Coming Home Project provides numerous workshops and retreats near San Antonio, San Francisco, San Diego, and Washington, DC. Project Sanctuary holds marital retreats in the Colorado Rocky Mountains. Project New Hope hosts retreats in several states. These are all free programs for military members and their families!

Unit chaplains, family service centers, or the state Joint Family Assistance Center may have suggestions for programs in your area.

Kathie sat in on a relationship class offered by Chaplain Maj. Thomas Cox at Fort Lewis's annual Parent University one year. She came out of it thinking, "Every military couple should be required to attend this session early in their marriage, with refresher courses along the way!"

Chaplain Cox shared information based on the research of John M. Gottman, PhD. For more than thirty years, Gottman has studied what makes couples successful and unsuccessful, monitoring more than sixteen thousand couples in great depth. Gottman's book *The Seven Principles for Making Marriage Work* is based on his research and is full of great information and good exercises. It's worthwhile reading for any couple.

Chaplain Cox's key point is to strengthen the friendship that is at the heart of any marriage. The more you know and understand about your partner, the easier it is to keep connected when life swirls around you. Rest assured, in a military life, you'll face a lot of swirling times. Gottman's book has great exercises to help you get to know one another better. And part of that is knowing what your spouse does in the military.

Ask questions, visit your service member's place of work, take part in bring your family to work days, and take advantage of GI Jane/Jane Wayne events. Make use of the Military 101 programs to learn the lingo (available through the family service centers or online courses).

When you don't make the effort to learn what your spouse does and vice versa, you end up living two very different and separate lives, which isn't great for any relationship.

Gottman says you can tell a strong relationship by how much each partner knows about each other. Can you both easily answer questions like: "What is his favorite childhood game? Who is her favorite uncle? What's his favorite movie of all time? What is her biggest challenge at work right now? Which coworker does he like most/least?" If you can answer these questions, you are taking time to talk and get to know each other. You are showing you care about each other's life.

Here's one fun way to get to know each other when your spouse is deployed, an idea shared by a young woman in a Marine Corps spouse workshop. She searches Google for "relationship quizzes." Thousands of fun quizzes come up. She chooses one to send to her husband. She answers the questions herself as well, and they discuss their answers by email.

Build a culture of appreciation between the two of you. One approach is to treat your spouse as well as you do your friends. "We already have the 'friend' skills," says Gottman, "After all, we don't talk to our friends in explosive, blaming ways. We have to learn to talk to our spouse like we talk to our friends." The words "please" and "thank you" aren't just words to use with strangers; we all need to hear them. We have to nurture fondness and admiration for each other, creating ways to say, "I love you." What's crucial here is that we learn to express love in the language our partner understands.

Turn toward rather than away from each other. Learn to communicate effectively and to build what Gottman calls a healthy emotional bank account. If you don't meet the emotional needs of your spouse, he or she will look to meet those needs elsewhere, and vice versa.

Be aware of the magic ratio of five to one. Gottman has found that in successful relationships, there is a ratio of five positive interactions to every one negative, since negative ones hold so much power.

It can be challenging to persuade your spouse to attend workshops like these. He or she might have reservations about going to relationship classes or wonder, "Things are just fine; why do we need a class?" With the rate of deployments and pace of training, it might be hard to make time during a workday. If it were required as part of basic training or military family orientation programs, maybe it would seem a normal part of being married. The fact is these classes are becoming much more common, offered by the units themselves as retreats for all unit members. Take advantage of them.

If no programs are available to you where you are located, use the books listed in the resource section of this chapter as a good starting point. Get a copy of Gottman's book and work through it one chapter at a time, doing the exercises and discussing them with one another. You could even do that during a deployment via email or letters.

If your relationship needs help, counseling is available through Military OneSource. You are eligible for twelve free, confidential in-person counseling sessions, and that can be you, your spouse, or as a couple. Be sure to check with your family service center to find out what is available. Offerings change all the time.

But what if your spouse doesn't want to work on the relationship—doesn't want to read any of the books or go to workshops or counseling? What can you do? Well, according to long-time relationship counselor Weiner-Davis, "Relationships are such that if one person makes significant changes, the relationship must change…You can change your marriage by changing yourself."

Chaplain Cox agrees. "Generally speaking, when spouses ask their partner to read a book about marriage, there is another message being communicated. For example, from a female perspective, they want their husband to read the book because they believe it will make their marriage better. A typical male hears the message, 'You're doing something wrong in this marriage, and this book will help you.' It is more effective for one person to read a book that speaks to them and make changes themselves. Odds are their spouse will begin to notice the change and may ask to learn more."

Learn From the Experience of Other Military Couples

Ask any spouse who has been married for a number of years what the secret to their success is, and you'll get different answers. Here are some things we've heard from other military spouses.

"Build on the strengths—don't magnify the weaknesses" is Holly's favorite relationship quote. Gottman's research backs that up. As he says, "Happily married couples aren't smarter, richer, or more psychologically astute than others. But in their day-to-day lives, they have hit upon a dynamic that keeps their negative thoughts and feelings about each other (which all couples have) from overwhelming their positive ones." After the honeymoon is over, it's all too common for couples to start focusing on what's missing in their mate and overlooking the fine qualities that are there. We often start taking our spouse's good qualities for granted.

Wayne Perry, MANning the Homefront, says,"Different strokes for different folks. Just because one person's spouse gets to call or Skype every day doesn't mean yours can. Or maybe yours isn't wired that way and doesn't want to. It doesn't mean he/she doesn't love or care about you, it just means they are different than someone else. So don't compare your relationship to what you see others as."

Start a "What I love about my spouse" list. Keep it on your computer (or in a journal), and keep it current. Once a month reread the list and relish what you've got! Every now and then share that list with your spouse. Or do what one Marine couple does. They share one item every evening before bed as in "I love you today because..." listing one specific action or attribute that stood out that day.

"Realize that sometimes in this military life," shares one Army spouse, "the feeling you get that your husband or wife doesn't even know you exist— or at least doesn't seem to care—isn't true at all. Often it's the result of the extreme stress they are under in their job at the moment, where they simply don't have anything left to give."

You thought you married a soldier, a sailor, an airman, a Marine, a Coastie, a pilot, a SEAL. You thought it was just a job. Reality will soon set in as you begin to understand the man or woman you married has chosen to take on more than a job. Holly shares how it took her years, but she finally got it that this was not a job to her husband, this was his

"You can change your marriage by changing yourself." —Weiner-Davis

calling in life, to be a soldier and to be a leader. Later, when Holly listened to Jacey Eckhart's CD, *I Married a Spartan: The Care and Feeding of Your Military Marriage*, she truly could laugh and nod in agreement with Jacey's message of insight and wisdom about being married to someone in uniform. If you are married to an individual who down to their toes believes in what they are doing and thinks it's their duty and an honor to serve their country, then you need to listen to this CD. www.JaceyEckhart.com.

Recognize and plan for the stresses that every move can put on a relationship. As Holly says, "We go to great lengths to find out about schools, housing, jobs, etc., when we move. But how many people give any thought to how it will affect the marriage? With all the millions of details to deal with, we don't usually take much time to find ways to pamper our relationship as husband and wife." As she points out, moving is listed as one of the most stressful life events. In fact, some military spouses have even named this challenge "cardboard box poisoning." Maybe we all need to add to our moving to-do list some things specifically for us as a couple: make dinner reservations as soon as possible after arriving at the new location; schedule a surprise for one another (massage, flowers, sports tickets, etc.); agree on what is off limits, in other words no arguing over small things, no yelling unless the house is on fire, and so on.

Take advantage of a powerful tool Navy spouse Sherrie learned from a *Reader's Digest* article many years ago. A marriage counselor interviewed for the article mentioned a magic question that can change a relationship for the better. The question to ask yourself on a regular basis is, "What would it be like to be married to me?" As Sherrie reports, she reads that question once a month. "It's so easy to focus on what my husband is doing wrong, or not doing. That question stops me short each time as I acknowledge lapses in my own behavior. It makes me change—at least for a while anyway—which is why I read it every month!" (And with technology, you can easily add that as a recurring event in your smart phone or computer calendar so it pops up every month.)

Recognize the reasons behind your spouse's actions may be different than you think. Capt. Rich Brown, PhD, a former Navy officer, wrote the book *Engineers in Love: Unlocking the Heart of the Technical Male.* As he says, "I use the term engineer, but the messages hold for other professions that deal with the world of logic, structure, and rules, such as the military." He has three simple things to teach husbands: "Talk to your wife. Make room for your kids. Take care of yourself. The 'what to do' is simple—it is the doing of it that is awkward, especially at first." That's why many men tend to head to work even when they don't have to. They know how to do work; it can seem easier than complicated relationship challenges at home. Realize that some men will cover up feeling scared by showing anger. "Men often use anger to cover their fear of not being able to fix the problem," says Rich. Just knowing that can change how you approach communications and interactions when anger shows up.

> *Find a way to spend time together to talk about life, not about finances or chores or your children.*

Cultivate interests in common with your spouse. Martha, an Air Force spouse, suggests that although it's important to have something you do for yourself, especially critical during deployments, it's also important you cultivate interests in common with your spouse. "It's important you spend some of your recreational time doing things as a couple," she stresses, "rather than spending all your together time doing chores or discussing the children or in separate pursuits." Here's a great idea from Della Elzie, a Marine spouse and mother of three. With each new assignment, she and her husband take on one new activity they haven't done before. "We scuba'd in Cuba, tried golf in Hawaii, and ran a marathon together in Virginia."

Recognize the importance of fun. Terry Sovinski, family and marriage counselor in Vilseck, Germany, says many times couples' problems are the result of lack of shared fun. They just can't remember the last time they had fun together as a couple. If you fall into this category, be sure to do the Simple Joys exercise in Chapter 19 with your spouse. Start adding in activities you both enjoy. And see what a difference that makes in your relationship.

Schedule regular date nights when your spouse is not deployed. "It seems crazy that you have to consciously schedule in time to be together alone," added one wife, "but that's reality. If you don't schedule it in your calendars, it doesn't happen!" Gottman's research backs this up. His recommendation is to have a weekly date with your spouse. Chaplain Cox modified that for military during the workshop. "Of course, that would be ideal, but with the OPTEMPO today, once a month might be more realistic." And that's when they aren't deployed, of course. With deployments so common now, date nights when they are here are even more crucial. He did stress the importance of choosing what you do on a date. Going to a movie doesn't really count here because it means you don't get to talk with each other. Unless, of course, you go to a movie for the stress release of laughing together at a comedy, and then take time for coffee and conversation after the show. Find a way to spend time together to talk about life, not about finances or chores or your children.

Here are date-night ideas from other military spouses.

- One couple has a date on the 27th of every month because their wedding was on the 27th. It's easy to remember, and they take turns planning what they do on the date.

- Marine spouse Kathleen Schmidt and her husband occasionally have what they call "teen date" nights. "We do what you used to do as teens to have fun together," she says, "We go for ice cream and a walk on the beach, take photos in those small photo booths, make out on the Ferris Wheel, and we act goofy and laugh, laugh, laugh."

- When your children are old enough, involve them. Holly has her twins help her set the mood for Mom and Dad's date night at home by setting the table with candles and flowers and choosing the music. Her children get pizza and a video in the family room, so Holly and Jack can have time talking together alone. (Her son has learned to set a romantic table. We think his future wife will thank Holly!)

- Marine spouse Cindy Garland always creates a "Date Night Co-op" wherever they live so couples get date nights out without the expense of babysitters. "We look for two other families with children of similar ages as our own," she explains. The first Friday of the month all the kids go to one house where the parents provide inexpensive dinner and games, while the other two couples get a date night. That rotates from house to house with the fourth Friday reserved as family night for all of them. (Plus, think of what happens here. Not only do you get a date night, but your children get to socialize with other children, and you have two other families to call in emergencies, who already know your kids.)

Access Additional Relationship Resources at Reunion Time

Kathie's mother-in-law, Naomi, always said only half-jokingly, "You two never have time to get tired of each other—you're always saying hello or goodbye." When we are talking about short TDY trips, there may be some truth to the old saying, "Absence makes the heart grow fonder." It may not be as true for long separations.

Reunions after deployments are challenging, no matter how joyful and romantic they seem at first. Problems can arise three months later. Expect that, plan for it, and take advantage of the resources and information provided by the services addressing those times. With the pace of deployments and the increased possibility of posttraumatic stress disorder (PTSD), reunions become even more challenging. Even if you've been through one reunion and one reunion workshop, don't assume future reunions will be the same. There is a big difference in the issues you face during a reunion for a generally safe peacekeeping deployment versus a reunion with a service member who has been through combat. The reunion workshops and resources provided by the services will improve as they learn more about what to expect and what can help with this challenging transition. This is one situation where you really don't want to figure this out by yourself. Tap into one of the many programs listed earlier in this section.

Pick up one of several books that address reunion challenges. One written specifically for military families is *Life After Deployment: Military Families Share Reunion Stories and Advice* by Karen Pavlicin. Families from all services share their experience in the book, including the joy and anxiety of homecoming, adjustments of living together again, and how they coped with anger, depression, PTSD, injuries, grief, and other challenges.

Key Points and Action Steps

▷ Believe that a successful military marriage is possible; surround yourself with other happy military couples.

▷ Strengthen the friendship that is at the core of your marriage.

▷ Build on the strengths, don't magnify the weaknesses.

▷ Tap into resources and programs available via your military community to strengthen your marriage.

▷ Go on date nights regularly.

Resources

Divorce Busting: A Step-by-Step Approach to Making Your Marriage Loving Again by Michelle Weiner-Davis (1993).

The 5 Love Languages: The Secret to Love That Lasts by Gary Chapman (2010). Also look for *The Five Love Languages Military Edition: The Secret to Love That Lasts* (2013) coauthored with Jocelyn Green, focusing on the specific challenges faced by military couples.

I Married a Spartan: The Care and Feeding of Your Military Marriage (2012). A CD by military life consultant, Jacey Eckhart, available on iTunes and Amazon. www.JaceyEckhart.com.

Life After Deployment: Military Families Share Reunion Stories and Advice by Karen M. Pavlicin (2007). www.KarenPavlicin.com.

The Military Marriage Manual: Tactics for Successful Relationships by Janelle Hill, Cheryl Lawhorne, and Don Philpott (2010).

National Military Family Association has important resources for you at its site, including service-specific and other marriage enrichment programs. For the cases of divorce, NMFA also spells out your benefits, how to find an attorney, and important child support information and links. www.MilitaryFamily.org.

Operation Military Family: How Military Couples are Fighting to Preserve Their Marriages, Updated Edition by Michael J. R. Schindler (2011).

Separated by Duty, United In Love: A Guide to Long-Distance Relationships for Military Couples, Updated Edition by Shellie Vandevoorde (2010).

The Seven Principles for Making Marriage Work by John M. Gottman, PhD, and Nan Silver (2000). Gottman's web site www.Gottman.com has self-help tips, relationship quizzes, and other resources.

Surviving Deployment: A Guide for Military Families by Karen M. Pavlicin (2003, *Second Edition* 2014). www.KarenPavlicin.com.

The Treasure of Staying Connected for Military Couples by Janel Lange (2004).

Chapter 16

Ask for Help, Accept Help, Offer Help in Challenging Times

Another Important Kind of Support

There are times when additional support is needed in our challenging military lives. Asking for help is a sign of strength and wisdom. We all need to accept help and can offer help, too.

Ask For and Accept Help When You Need It

A few years ago, Marine spouse Cherie found out, after the fact, that a dear friend had been going through serious depression. The woman hid it well, always putting on a positive front. None of her close friends knew. They all felt terrible when they found out. There was so much they would have happily done to lighten her load, if they'd only known!

Have you ever been there? You know how that feels. So turn it around. If you need help, and you don't let anyone know, you cheat your friends of the opportunity to help. Most military spouses happily step in to help others. You really do reap benefits for yourself when you help others, even though that isn't why you help. But, when it comes to being able to ask for help for ourselves, we are among the worst.

Holly fits right into that mold—always reaching out to help others but not as good about asking for help when she needs it. As a single mom with twin infants while her husband was deployed, that trait came to a head one day. One of her four-month-old twins was sick and not sleeping for days on end. Holly was so sleep deprived she couldn't think straight.

Julie Woods and Beverly Young, two Army wives who lived on Holly's street, stopped by that day to see how Holly was doing. In just minutes, they realized Holly was at the end of her rope. They decided to step in and take over with the kids and told Holly to go to bed. Julie even got someone to fill in for her at work so she could help Holly. Of course, Holly started protesting immediately. What is it about us that we can't just accept needed help graciously? When someone really wants to help you, thank him or her and accept the help.

We've heard many stories during the Iraq and Afghanistan deployments of spouses who had to go into the hospital for a procedure or even a birth, who didn't let anyone know. They went on their own, in some cases with small children in tow, rather than asking help of their friends and neighbors. Everyone around them felt terrible after they found out.

We think this sometimes happens because we all know people who ask for help all the time, too much of the time, the ones who seem to expect everything to be done for them. You've all met someone like that. They are the ones complaining all the time, demanding that the military take care of them. They complain about the military but don't access the resources provided. You don't want to be like that, so you end up not asking for help that is reasonable to ask for, help you really need. Think about this. You know how we joke about people who won't ask for directions when they are lost? Well, it's just as ridiculous to not ask for help when you need it.

Pay It Forward

When someone helps you, it's natural to think, "How can I repay you?" But you don't have to repay that person. You can help someone else in the future. That's how life works. At the time, you probably can't repay the person who helps you, but you can pay it forward by helping someone else at a later date.

Dorothy Wilhelm is an Army widow and mother of six with two sons and one son-in-law who are career military. She learned the lesson about forward payment early in her military life. Her story:

It was Christmas. I was alone in the maternity ward of a big Air Force base hospital in California, facing months in bed as the result of a complicated pregnancy. My husband had taken our infant daughter to get settled with his mother until the new baby was born—and doctors weren't optimistic. They told us the expected child almost surely wouldn't live. I lay in the starkly furnished hospital ward, with twenty-two women, all happy new mothers, and I was not able to keep back the tears. I was only twenty-two years old. Without warning, a small tornado whirled into the room. Her name was Mary Ann, and her husband was part of my husband's Army ordnance company. That was all I knew. I'd been on her mind, she said. She couldn't bear to think of my spending Christmas alone, she told me. I wasn't too crazy about the idea myself, I admitted.

"You're coming home with me," Mary Ann announced in a voice that brooked no argument.

This young mother had plenty of other things to do during the hectic holiday season with her own three small children and a dog, but she took care of me, confined to bed, as if it was the one thing she wanted to do. As in all good Christmas stories, her family made room for the stranger in its midst.

Despite the medical opinion, my baby didn't die. In the spring, I wrapped my healthy new son in a blue blanket and went back to say thank you to Mary Ann. We already had orders to a new post, so I'd have no chance to repay her or even to see her again. "I just don't know how I can pay you back," I said. Mary Ann looked at me as if I weren't quite bright, something I was to become used to over the years ahead.

"You can't do anything for me," she said. "You'll do it for somebody else."

Those six words have followed me down the years—the motto for military families everywhere—we do it for somebody else.

One time reprint rights granted by Dorothy Wilhelm. This column originally appeared in the Tacoma News Tribune.

Contact Dorothy: www.ItsNeverTooLate.com

Here's how Vivian Greentree, Navy wife and member of Blue Star Families, responded to Wilhelm's story:

"I love the 'pay it forward' mentality," she wrote us, "I had a similar experience when I was in school and Mike was deployed. There were a few times I had to go in early and my babysitter couldn't get here to watch the kids in time, and I couldn't find anyone to cover for me. She told her mom, a Navy wife, too, who called me and told me to bring them to her house to wait for her daughter to get home from school. She wouldn't take no for an answer or accept any money. She said another Navy wife had helped her when her kids were young and she went back to work, and she was 'paying it forward' with me. When I kept saying thank you, she said, 'don't worry, you'll do it, too, when you see another wife in need.'"

Greentree also emphasized the importance of knowing your neighbors before you need their help. It is nice to have online support and ability to talk to people, however, there might be times when you physically need someone to come over and check on your house or watch your kids so you can go to the ER, either by yourself or with one of your kids.

"I developed a kidney stone while driving back from South Carolina with my two boys," wrote Greentree. "We were returning from a trip to see Mike before he left for Iraq. I drove all the way home (six hours) to make sure I could have my boys at home before I went to the ER. I had to get a neighbor to watch them for me, so I could get to the hospital. I'm just so glad I already knew my neighbors and had their numbers at home. I know it is hard to do, but it really is something we should do, in base housing and off. Get to know your neighbors so you can ask them for help if you need it. They can watch your house when you are gone, loan you sugar so you don't have to drive to the store with the kids, etc. It makes the whole deployment thing that much easier. Plus, you feel safer and more connected."

And, of course, it's a two-way street. You can offer help to your neighbors when they need it.

Consider Co-oping Tasks

Army spouse Star Henderson shares, "Think of economies of scale. Maybe one spouse loves to do a ton of baking, but could use help with laundry. The bulk of laundry is down when your husband is deployed, so why not do another family's laundry for a couple batches of cookies or a special cake when you need it for kids' school or a coffee."

Using economies of scale, capitalizing on and bartering your own skills, will save you much time and aggravation. "It's a bonding experience, and helps you gel that relationship over everyday things," says Henderson, "so your relationship is prepped for the down-right dirty and difficult things. Make it a co-op for things like babysitting, baking, errands, gardening."

Be Specific in Your Offers of Help

When you do offer help, don't just say, "What can I do to help?" A lot of us can't easily verbalize what we need. That question often results in the polite but untrue answer of, "Oh nothing, I'm fine."

Be specific. Here are some of Holly's favorites from deployment.

- "I made dinner for my family and I made an extra plate for you. Can I bring it over?"
- "I'm going to the commissary. Do you need milk or anything?" What a gift. Getting two babies ready and shopping at the commissary was an insurmountable task at times, especially when it was just for one or two items.

Army spouse, Linda Beougher, dealing with challenging medical problems, shares some things that helped her during that time.

- Other parents took my two girls for play dates or sleepovers, so I could get the sleep I was supposed to be getting to heal.
- Since I wasn't able to drive, and my husband couldn't take any more time away from work, friends drove me to doctor's appointments and drove the girls to their activities so they could keep some routine going.
- Neighbors gave us dinner coupons for local restaurants—especially helpful were those restaurants that delivered.

Star shares, "If you want to help arrange for meals for a grieving family or a new mom, or any family who might need help getting meals over a short period of time, there is an easy and free way to set up a schedule with your friends and neighbors without a lot of extra work and phone calls. Check out FoodTidings.com or MealTrain.com." These programs are free and they send reminder emails to those scheduled to bring a meal.

A great source to help you figure out how to best offer help to friends in need, whether they are dealing with a challenging time or with the loss of a loved one, is Barbara Glanz's book, *What Can I Do?* It was triggered by her own experience after the loss of a child and the loss of her husband.

"People would ask me, 'What can I do?'" she said, "but I didn't know what to ask for or felt awkward asking, so they did nothing because they were afraid it wouldn't be the right thing, which left me feeling so alone." Glanz interviewed thousands of people around the globe as she traveled doing her speaking business, asking those who had suffered losses, "What helped the most?" Her book is full of solid ideas.

Asking for help and offering effective help aren't always automatic skills we have. Like many other skills, we develop them over time.

Journal and Listen to Positive Recordings

Journaling and listening to positive recordings are both great ways to help yourself. While many people use blogs or computer programs to record their thoughts, putting pen to paper and journaling longhand can be a powerful life tool toward self-awareness and spiritual growth. Journaling is a nonjudgmental and all-accepting friend. As a matter of fact, it is possibly the cheapest therapy you will ever get.

There is increasing evidence to support the notion that journaling has a positive impact on physical and emotional well-being. James Pennebaker, a psychologist and researcher from University of Texas at Austin, contends that regular journaling strengthens the immune cells. According to Pennebaker, writing about stressful events helps you come to terms with them, thus reducing the impact of those stressors on your physical health.

Consider the following benefits of journaling noted by Pennebaker and Maud Purcell, a psychotherapist and researcher.

- Journaling helps clarify your thoughts and feelings. Do you ever seem all jumbled up inside, unsure of what you want or feel? Take a few minutes to jot down your thoughts and emotions (no editing!). You will quickly get in touch with your internal self.
- Journaling assists you in knowing yourself better. By writing routinely, you will get to know what makes you feel happy and confident. You will become clear about situations and people who are toxic for you, important information for your emotional well-being.
- Journaling reduces stress. Writing about stressful events helps you come to terms with them, allowing you to feel calmer and better able to stay in the present.
- Journaling helps you solve problems more effectively. Typically, we problem solve from a left-brained, analytical perspective. But sometimes the answer can only be found by engaging right-brained creativity and intuition. Stream-of-consciousness writing

unlocks these other capabilities and helps us think of unexpected solutions to seemingly unsolvable problems.

- Journaling assists in resolving disagreements with others. Writing about misunderstandings rather than stewing over them can help you to understand another's point of view. And, you may come up with a sensible resolution.

Kathie has journaled for years and can't imagine figuring out her life or dealing with challenging times without it.

"I read back over my journals once a year on or near my birthday—it's my gift to myself. I often discover good decisions I made but never implemented, so I can then choose to make the change. I've learned the power in working things through in my journal before sending off an angry email response or telephone call. And, I discovered that journaling can help get out those thoughts that otherwise keep circling in my head, especially at night."

Journaling is possibly the cheapest therapy you will ever get.

We heard from a new Air Force spouse who found out how helpful journaling was as she and her husband went through their first move together. "It was a soothing way to express myself through the move when my husband couldn't offer any words of advice," says Tracey McNamee, "it was a good place to express my fears and anxieties."

One handy resource is a personal journal for anyone whose spouse is deployed, *Deployment Journal for Spouses: Memories and Milestones While My Loved One is Deployed* by Rachel Robertson. In this journal, there are gentle writing prompts and inspirational sayings to guide you through deployment and homecoming. There is even a Keeping Track section to remind you to write about milestones and special moments.

It may seem counterintuitive, but writing down your fears and anxieties really does help to lessen their impact in your mind.

Kathie is by nature a high anxiety, catastrophizing worrier, a trait that gets plenty of fuel in this military lifestyle. Early on, with her husband's first dangerous deployment, she realized she needed help. She couldn't get her mind to stop the "worst case scenario" thoughts, especially at night, which meant she wasn't sleeping well. Lack of sleep just added to her anxiety level.

A friend recommended some tapes for her to listen to. These recordings first talk you into relaxation and then repeat positive affirmations, from reducing your anxiety to increasing your positive feelings of self-confidence.

"The tapes helped me a lot," says Kathie, "I would listen to them as I fell asleep at night, and they really helped me fall asleep. I'd also listen to them during the day as I went about my work." They helped shift her into more positive thinking. Called *The Love Tapes*, they are available through ELS Audio Publishing, www.EffectiveLearning.com.

"May sound 'woo-woo,'" says Kathie, "especially the title *The Love Tapes*, but they work for me."

Access Military Family Programs

Part of asking for help is asking about and accessing help provided by the services. One of the biggest frustrations of the people coordinating family programs is the small number of people who take advantage of them. Don't assume you know everything that is available just because you've been married to the military for a while. New programs arise regularly, especially as greater needs arise. A few examples:

- Many posts/bases provide free respite care, taking care of children so that Mom or Dad get time for themselves during deployment.

- Some units have overnight "lock-ins" with activities, fun, and supervision for the kids so Mom or Dad gets a night to themselves.

- Operation Purple, a joint effort of Sears and National Military Family Association, provided free summer camp for children of deployed military during the summers of 2004–2013, hopefully to be repeated in future years. Also Operation Purple Family Retreats and Operation Purple Leadership Camps for teens.

- At Operation Homefront, OperationHomefront.net, communities step in to help families of deployed military with everything from car repairs to home repairs.

- YMCA provides respite care camps/nights and reduced membership for families who can't take advantage of a local post, such as Guard/Reserve families during a deployment.

- DoD has arranged free membership to www.SitterCity.com, with access to babysitters, dog walkers, housecleaners, and the like.

Make Use of Military OneSource

Military OneSource, as we've mentioned, is a key military benefit. Even if you've heard of it, you might not appreciate the magnitude of help available to you through this service, including:

- Childcare availability in a particular area. Phone counselors provide a list of providers on and off base as well as whether or not they are licensed. (There are online locators for childcare, eldercare, massage practitioners, etc.)
- School reports, with teacher/student ratios at schools and SAT scores of the schools located near a particular base.
- Exceptional family member services available in an area.
- Support for parenting issues, even potty training toddlers.
- Where to get car repairs done.
- Landlord/tenant problems.
- Relationship problem solving.
- Dealing with relocation stress.
- Adoption assistance.
- Gambling addiction or eating disorders.
- Pet care availability.

Families can request a Know Your Neighborhood report, based on Zip-code, providing information about your current or move-to community.

You can get twelve free confidential in-person counseling sessions through this service (available to the military member, spouse, or child).

At MilitaryOneSource.mil, find online self-assessments, CDs on stress and deployments, free TurboTax software, and free home baby-proofing kits.

Another thing to be aware of is the fact that simultaneous translation is available over the telephone for about 150 different languages. You can even fax in a doctor's bill or utility bill for translation (the fax service is available free through family service centers on base.) They'll interpret forms at school or help a non-English-speaking person go through forms and procedures for a myriad of processes: medical, educational, career, etc. Imagine how extra challenging this military life is when English isn't your native language. If you know a spouse in this situation, let them know about the translations available through Military OneSource.

What a gift to individuals. And what a gift to unit leaders, FRG leaders, key volunteers, ombudsmen, and family service staff members. Now when you are asked a question or faced with a situation you have no experience with, you have an instant place to turn to get helpful information.

This service is available online or by phone 24/7, 365 days a year, and to families who are living away from a military installation. It solves the problem of family members who work and can't access the nine-to-five services available on base. The people who answer the phone are all masters' level consultants and the service can be used anonymously. The policy is that a telephone must be answered within three rings, and you don't have to jump through the kind of "push 1 for, push 2 for" hoops some companies make you deal with. Military OneSource is available to all active duty, Guard and Reserve members (regardless of status), their family members, installation helping agencies, Individual Ready Reserve (IRR) and Department of Defense civilians who live overseas.

Talk about an easy and accessible way to ask for the help you need!

Military OneSource is not available to Coast Guard spouses since it's a Department of Defense program. The Coast Guard equivalent is Work-Life at www.USCG.mil/WorkLife.

Get Professional Help for Depression

There is another kind of help that needs to be discussed—getting help if you are depressed. It's something we don't talk about openly enough. People who need help—who need counseling or therapy or maybe even drug therapy—often won't ask for it because of military culture and reality. In some cases, people don't recognize they are depressed.

"I just couldn't get myself out of bed," one spouse told us. "I dragged through each day doing the bare minimum of things that had to be done. I procrastinated on everything, even important things. I just couldn't seem to care."

Cheryl, an Air Force spouse, described her experience with depression. "I kept thinking, what's wrong with me? I have nothing to be depressed about. My husband isn't deployed to Iraq like so many of my neighbors' husbands are. If anyone deserves to feel depressed right now, it's them, not me. I have a good life, a great relationship with my husband, good friends. What do I have to be depressed about?" That kind of thinking kept her from asking for help for months. Finally, her uncontrollable crying, constant insomnia, and feelings of failure and helplessness drove her to get help.

The National Institute of Mental Health estimates 18.8 million adult Americans suffer from depression during any one-year period. Two thirds of those do not get the help they need. Eighty percent of people who are treated show significant improvement, but many people do not even recognize they have a condition that can be treated, or if they do, won't go for help.

There is a social stigma. Susan Fletcher, PhD, who has worked with adult depression in private practice for more than sixteen years says, "Many people grew up hearing 'Get over it—life's not that hard.'"

Depression is one of those things many of us don't talk about, in society at large, but especially in our military world. People who need help often won't ask for it because of military culture. This applies to both the spouse and the military member.

A service member thinks, "If I go for counseling, it goes on my record and affects my promotability and security clearance." The Defense Department study on posttraumatic stress and other mental disorders among soldiers and Marines returning from Iraq and Afghanistan, reported this attitude in the *New England Journal of Medicine*. Of the troops whose responses indicated they had a mental disorder, only between 23 and 40 percent sought professional help. Troops said seeking mental health care would kill their careers—that their command climate was to just "suck it up."

The civilian spouse of a military member has related fears. "If I go for counseling, it will go on my spouse's record and affect the way he is seen by superiors—'Can't you control your family? If you have problems at home, you most likely aren't as effective a leader or team player at work either.' And that can affect our family livelihood. Am I really prepared for that?"

Plus there's the whole confidentiality thing. The on-post community is small. Who is going to go for counseling on post if they fear their neighbors will know about it? Yes, we know counselors are supposed to maintain confidentiality, and we expect most do, but that doesn't mean we don't still have the fear that a counselor won't. It may be an irrational fear, but who ever said you are fully rational, especially when you are depressed?

For many males, there is a macho/strength factor, with depression seen as weakness. In fact, the National Institute of Mental Health started a "Real Men, Real Depression" campaign to bring more attention to that subject.

We have a similar challenge as military spouses. We have a bit of the "pioneer" mentality. We say, "We are strong and can handle anything thrown our way. At least that is what everyone else seems to manage, so what is wrong with me?" or "No matter how bad my situation is, there is another military spouse who has it worse. I've had to move too much, every three years, sometimes after only one or two. But that family had to move three times in two years!" or "My husband deployed into a danger zone for six months. But our neighbor's been in three major deployments and did an unaccompanied tour in Korea" or "I'm struggling here being the 'single' parent of two babies. But my neighbor is managing with five kids while her spouse is deployed." "How can I complain? What's wrong with me that I can't handle it? Why can't I just 'snap out of it,' have a positive attitude, get moving?"

People who need help often won't ask for it because of military culture.

There may well be spouses who move smoothly through this military life. We've met them—so have you. They seem to take it all in stride. In fact, some thrive on crisis and change. It makes us wonder, why can't we?

We judge based on our perceptions of how others are doing, based on what they show to the outside world. Who knows what the reality of their lives really is?

Another thing to consider is this. We are all so different in our energy levels, in our basic mood levels, in our organization habits, and in past experiences that have taught us or not taught us effective coping skills. Some people inherit a tendency for depression. Just because one person can easily handle a tough situation doesn't mean we all can.

Depression can happen because of many different things, from life experiences to chemical imbalance. Experts tell us psychological stresses that can bring on depression include loss or major life changes—positive as well as negative ones. Well, if anyone faces major life changes and loss on a recurring basis, it's military spouses! Experts say most people will show signs of depression at some time in their lives. It can be a minor illness that lasts a short time and goes away by itself. It can be a major illness that severely limits how you function and requires treatment.

You can make confidential calls to Military OneSource for advice and referral for twelve sessions of free counseling off-post.

The first step is to know the signs of depression so we might recognize it in ourselves, in our spouses, or in our friends. Sometimes when a person is deeply depressed, they can't take action to get help. It can mean a friend stepping in to help them get the help they need.

If more people are open about their need for counseling, it will become more accepted. Hopefully, like other outdated "rules" of military life, we can eventually get rid of the stigma that keeps people from getting the help they need, spouses and service members alike.

As for Cheryl, she finally saw her doctor, who prescribed a mild antidepressant medication. With that, increased exercise, and getting involved in activities again, things shifted. She said, "I feel like I have my life back!"

Terri Barnes wrote about depression in her Stars & Stripes *column "Spouse Calls: Messages from a Military Life" (excerpted with permission):*

Diana Hartman said there are six things that should be given to every depressed person: regular and appropriate doses of medication, therapy, comedy, light, a creative outlet, and physical activity.

"These should not be suggestions, they should be prescriptions," she said. She speaks from years of experience as a patient and—in the years since her recovery—as a volunteer counselor with depressed and suicidal people.

Her advice to someone suffering in the darkness of depression like she did: "I know you've endured a litany of people who were supposed to help you and didn't, and some of them even made it worse. I know you feel helpless, listless and dreary, apathetic, disgusted, and defeated. Get help anyway. I know it's hopeless. Do it anyway."

An important resource to know about: Suicide Hotline 1-800-273-TALK (8255). Veterans or those calling on behalf of veterans can dial the same number and press 1.

Recognize the Signs of Depression

These can all be symptoms of depression:

- Feeling down, blue, hopeless, sad, or irritable.
- No longer feeling pleasure when you do things that would usually be fun.
- Having low self-esteem ("I'm not a competent person"), negative thinking ("I'll never feel better"), and trouble concentrating.

- Feeling less energy.
- Seeing changes in your appetite, weight, sleeping patterns, or having more physical pain.
- Feeling bad enough that you are having trouble doing your normal activities at work or at home.
- Abuse of alcohol or drugs.

Based on the above list, if you answer yes to the following three questions, it's time to get help.

1. Do you have some or all of the symptoms listed above?
2. Have you had them for two weeks or more?
3. Are they getting in the way of your normal life at home, school or work?

Ask for Help Following Combat Assignments

Combat engagements can increase rates of depression, PTSD, divorce, and suicide. For many spouses, anticipatory grief and secondary PTSD are a stark reality. It's even more important than ever to seek help when you believe there may be a problem.

We've listed under Resources several web sites and books published for military families and for counselors working with military families that focus on reunion and the effects of wartime deployments.

There is much research going on to figure out how best to identify and treat issues that result from war, especially from extended war and back-to-back deployments. In many ways, this is new territory. Researchers are studying warriors, family members, and children. We hope robust, effective programs will result.

Key Points and Action Steps

▷ Asking for help is a sign of strength and wisdom. Don't hesitate to ask for help when you need it.

▷ Journal to clarify your thoughts and reduce stress.

▷ Recognize signs of depression and know that you are not alone. Reach out for help.

▷ Familiarize yourself with the benefits of Military OneSource.

Resources

After the War Zone: A Practical Guide for Returning Troops and Their Families by Matthew J. Friedman, PhD, and Laurie B. Slone, PhD, (2008).

At Ease, Soldier!: How to Leave the War Downrange and Feel at Home Again by Gayle S. Rozantine, PhD (2011).

Blue Star Families, www.BlueStarFam.org.

Deployment Journal for Spouses: Memories and Milestones While My Loved One is Deployed by Rachel Robertson (2008). (Robertson also has deployment journals for military children and for service members' parents.)

Deployment: Strategies for Working with Kids in Military Families by Karen Petty, PhD (2009).

Families Under Fire: Systemic Therapy With Military Families (Routledge Psychosocial Stress Series), edited by R. Blaine Everson and Charles R. Figley (2011).

Finding My Way: A Teen's Guide to Living with a Parent Who Has Experienced Trauma by Michelle D. Sherman, PhD, and DeAnne M. Sherman (2005).

A Gift From Within, web resource dedicated to PTSD survivors, partners, and mental health professionals. Founded by Frank Ochberg, MD, professor of psychiatry at Michigan State University and former associate director for the National Institute of Health, who has studied PTSD extensively. The site has information on various therapies, how to find counseling, and a roster of survivors willing to take part in a network of peer support. www.GiftFromWithin.org.

Her War, Her Voice started as a way to connect spouses dealing with depression or facing PTSD with their spouse's return from war. It evolved to a place to connect and find your own voice as a military spouse, no matter what you are dealing with. The purpose of Her War, Her Voice has been to ensure no military spouse ever feels alone. www.HerWarHerVoice.com

Hope for the Homefront's goal is to reach and restore all women touched
     by the life and service of a combat veteran through their retreats,
     seminars, publications, webinars, social networking, and peer group
     support and mentoring. www.HopeForTheHomefront.org.

Life After Deployment: Military Families Share Reunion Stories and Advice
     by Karen M. Pavlicin (2007). www.KarenPavlicin.com.

The Love Tapes, www.EffectiveLearning.com.

Military OneSource, www.MilitaryOneSource.mil.
     US: 1-800-342-9647
     Overseas: 800-3429-6477
     Besides the availability of free, confidential, in-person counseling, the
     site has many resources about depression, from articles to free CDs.

National Association of Child Care Resource and Referral Agencies
     (NACCRRA) / Child Care Aware of America works with DoD to help
     families find and afford quality childcare. There is free assistance in
     many cases. www.NACCRRA.org or www.ChildCareAware.org.

National Center for PTSD, www.PTSD.va.gov.

National Institute of Mental Health, www.NIMH.nih.gov.

*New Light on Depression: Help, Hope, and Answers for the Depressed and
     Those Who Love Them* by David B. Biebel, DMin, and Harold G.
     Koenig, MD (2004).

Not Alone Community. For warriors and family members dealing with
     combat stress and PTSD, providing programs, resources, and services
     through a confidential and anonymous community.
     www.NotAlone.com.

The Real Warriors Campaign is an initiative launched by the Defense
     Centers of Excellence for Psychological Health and Traumatic Brain
     Injury to promote the processes of building resilience, facilitating
     recovery and supporting reintegration of returning service members,
     veterans and their families. www.RealWarriors.net.

Tragedy Assistance Program for Survivors (TAPS). A support network for
     the surviving families of those who have died in service to our country.

800-959-TAPS (8277). Mentors available to help you through this time, along with seminars, retreats, and camps. www.TAPS.org.

Writing to Heal: A Guided Journal for Recovering from Trauma & Emotional Upheaval by James W. Pennebaker, PhD (2010).

What Can I Do?: Ideas to Help Those Who Have Experienced Loss by Barbara A. Glanz (2007).

Wounded Warrior, Wounded Home: Hope and Healing for Families Living with PTSD and TBI by Marshéle Carter Waddell and Kelly K. Orr, PhD (2013) and When the War Comes Home Don't Retreat retreats, www.WhentheWarComesHomeRetreats.com.

Chapter 17

Have Faith

Faith, hope, and gratitude are essential to your overall sense of happiness in life. Faith is defined as the firm belief in something for which there is no proof. Our interviews with military spouses, as well as the research on happiness, indicate that having a belief in something greater than yourself provides a sense of hope, optimism, gratitude, and purpose, which is key to greater life satisfaction.

Recently, more and more scientific research has been published on the beneficial relationship between religion, spirituality, health, and happiness. The research does not point to any specific religion; the focus is on having a higher belief.

Harold G. Koenig, MD, codirector of the Center for Spirituality, Theology, and Health at Duke University Medical Center, has published extensively in the fields of mental health, geriatrics, and religion. He has diligently documented the faith-medical initiative, which promotes a holistic approach of body, mind, and spirit in healing.

In the book *Handbook of Religion and Health*, Dr. Koenig and other researchers examined twelve hundred separate research studies conducted over the past century. Their work is considered the most comprehensive book of its kind. The book reviews and discusses the extensive research on the relationship between religion and a variety of mental and physical health outcomes.

The research in this book reveals that people who have faith and who are involved in positive religious activities are more likely to experience:

- Well-being, happiness, and life satisfaction.
- Hope and optimism.
- Purpose and meaning in life.
- Higher self-esteem.
- Adaptation to bereavement.
- Greater social support and less loneliness.
- Lower rates of depression and faster recovery from depression.
- Less anxiety.
- Less psychosis and fewer psychotic tendencies.
- Lower rates of alcohol and drug use or abuse.
- Less delinquency and criminal activity.
- Greater marital stability and satisfaction.

When we are able to develop a strong spiritual faith during peaceful times, that faith will be there to support and sustain us through times of crisis. There aren't very many other lifestyles as challenging as the military, especially in the midst of terrorism and war. As military spouses, when we allow our peace of mind to be affected by the external happenings of the world, it is almost impossible to quiet our souls and connect our hearts with our heads so we can nurture our spiritual health and grow. Finding some practice that allows us to quiet our minds and grow in our faith can help us get away from the constant thoughts of worry and fear. Having a strong faith and spiritual health helps remind us that even in times of turmoil, there is a place we can go for peace, a peace we can always rely on.

Finding your spiritual center and developing your faith is an internal event, not an external one. This means slowing down and listening within for guidance.

How can we strengthen our faith in the fast-paced, challenging military lifestyle? It's a lifestyle that leaves very little room for reflection time. When we interviewed military spouses and asked them to share ways in which they were able to develop their faith and spiritual heath, they provided us with the following ideas.

Pray and Meditate

Holly likes to compare our lives at times to a wild storm at sea, with waves crashing against the shores and ships tossing back and forth. Yet even in the midst of the storm, if you go down to the depths of the ocean, you will find centers of calm and stillness. The waves and what's on top of the water represent our outer lives, constantly busy and sometimes absolutely crazy wild. Yet, like the depths of the ocean, we, too, have a stillness and quiet within us that we can get to even in the midst of a storm. Individuals who have a strong faith and regular spiritual practice, who allow themselves to get quiet and go within on a regular basis, find they touch a center of calm that helps carry them through the stormy times.

Learning to be still is one of the most valuable ways to nurture your soul. Start your meditation by repeating a mantra or prayer to help settle your busy mind. Whether it's something like "Om" or "Let go, let God," a mantra can quiet that nonstop monkey mind many of us have. Then spend time in silence, gently using your breath to re-center yourself when your mind gets active again. For some people, using chanting CDs helps them quiet their mind and stay focused. Kathie's current favorite is *Embrace* by Deva Premal. She also often uses Jon Kabat-Zinn's *Guided Mindfulness Meditation*. The key is, it's important to find one that speaks to you. For others, focusing on a candle in complete silence works best.

The military has tested the efficacy of meditation training for its warriors. A November 2010 *Men's Journal* article, "Meditation Fit for a Marine," reported on one such program conducted by the Marine Corps. "The results of the Marines' experiences, published in the peer-reviewed scientific journal *Emotion*, showed that the men who embraced meditation walked out of predeployment training with minds that were more agile than those who didn't. They also reported improved athletic performance, relief from anxiety, better sleep, and stronger memory."

The institute that conducted that training is currently doing research with soldiers. Mind Fitness Training Institute conducts Mindfulness-based Mind Fitness Training (MMFT) for individuals in high-stress situations. Military members at war, and their families on the homefront, certainly fall into that category. Meditation can help.

Regardless of the precise nature of its origins, prayer has long been a feature of virtually every living religion, from Christianity to Buddhism.

Prayer is an act of communion with God, with spirit, such as in devotion, confession, praise, or thanksgiving. Prayer may be oral or mental, secret or social. Prayer's major purpose is to give us an additional, effective way to draw near to and harmonize with our God, with our Higher Spirit.

Cheri Fuller, mother of a Marine, is an award-winning author of more than forty books. Cheri's passion is encouraging women and inspiring and equipping people of all ages to connect with God in their busy life and impact their world through prayer. Her book *A Busy Woman's Guide to Prayer* offers creative ideas to weave prayer into the fabric of your day.

Cathy Sterling, an Army spouse, shares this great idea on how to create a way to spend more time in prayer. "In the book *Practical Prayer* Anne Tanner suggests making physical and mental space for God within your home. Find a space where you can be in silence, relax, and be comfortable. At the bazaar last fall, I saw a church kneeler (*prie-dieu*) in one of the antique booths and was intrigued, thinking that might help me focus better in my prayer life. There is something about kneeling in prayer in church that I always find comforting and focusing. Someone else bought the kneeler before I decided I really wanted it, so I've been wanting one ever since. Two of my friends went to a flea market and surprised me with one the other day. It is beautiful and inviting and comfortable to kneel at. I put it in my bedroom and see it as I wake up every morning and go to sleep at night, so of course, it invites me to come kneel and say some prayers."

Similarly, Kathie created a space in her bedroom for meditation. She covered an antique trunk with a colorful cloth and added statues and heart stones and quotes that inspire her. Her favorite candle holder is inscribed with the words of Julian of Norwich: "All shall be well, and all shall be well, and all manner of things shall be well," words that always help to slow down her breath and mind.

Create a space that works for you, that invites you to slow down and sit in prayer or meditation.

Read Inspirational Stories and Devotionals

Military spouses of all faiths have walked through the loneliness of deployments and have found comfort in knowing others have gone through some of the same challenges they have endured. We have seen a growing number of books, as well as online faith-based support organizations emerge, specifically for military spouses and their families. Their stories inspire us and continually remind us we are not alone.

Kristin Henderson, Marine spouse, is a brilliant writer. We found comfort in reading her personal story of her struggles to reconcile her Quaker beliefs in pacifism, with her strong feelings about the terrorist attacks on America, and her husband's deployment to war. In her book *Driving By Moonlight*, it is in her faith (and her dog, Rosie), where she finds peace and learns the freedom that comes with letting go.

Alison Buckholtz, Navy spouse, also has a talent for writing and has shared her story of deployment in her book *Standing By: The Making of an American Military Family in a Time of War*. In her book, Alison shares the importance and the struggles of practicing their Jewish faith as they move with the military.

Sara Horn, Navy Reserve spouse, first experienced the military as a journalist, covering stories in Iraq the first year of the war. Her second visit to Iraq was to gather material for her first book, which she wrote with Oliver North, *A Greater Freedom: Stories of Faith from Operation Iraqi Freedom*. Following her husband's first deployment to Iraq, she reached out to military wives by starting a military wives support organization, Wives of Faith, www.WivesofFaith.org. One of the benefits of connecting with other military wives through online message boards or groups like Wives of Faith is sharing stories with one another. Sara saw the need to write her book *God Strong: The Military Wife's Spiritual Survival Guide* to help military spouses realize they are not alone, that there is a greater strength to rely upon.

Army wife Shannon Burrous created F.R.A.Z.L.E.D. Military Wives Christian Network, www.BlogTalkRadio.com/FrazledMWCN, an online radio show to help military spouses embrace military life, feel comfortable asking questions about their faith, and keep their focus on God.

Marshéle Carter Waddell is the wife of a career Navy SEAL. Together with their three children, the Waddells have endured many lengthy separations and frequent deployments for combat duty, special operations training, and real-world conflicts for more than two decades. Her husband is a disabled combat veteran with PTSD and multiple traumatic brain injuries (TBIs). Her first two books, *Hope for the Home Front: Winning the Emotional and Spiritual Battles of a Military Wife* and its companion Bible study, *Hope for the Home Front Bible Study*, were so successful she and her team at Hope for the Homefront began offering When the War Comes Home retreats for military spouses who are dealing with the challenges of living with a wounded warrior. Her most recent book is *Wounded Warrior, Wounded Home*, written with a military veteran and counselor, Kelly K. Orr, PhD. When a combat veteran struggles with PTSD and/or TBI, every member of the family experiences the effects. This book shares insights from dozens of families and research, offering readers a hope-filled way forward.

Holly likes to turn to inspirational devotionals to inspire her spiritual growth. One book of devotionals for military spouses she highly recommends is *Medals Above My Heart*, written by two military spouses, Brenda Pace and Carol McGlothlin.

Other books that have received great praise are *Faith Deployed: Daily Encouragement for Military Wives* and *Faith Deployed…Again: More Daily Encouragement for Military Wives* written by former Coast Guard spouse Jocelyn Green, along with fourteen other military spouses from all branches of service. Her latest accomplishment is the *NIV Military Wives' New Testament with Psalms & Proverbs*. This book includes ninety special devotions written by military wives and edited by Green. Their words of help and hope encourage you as you serve our country in your own way.

Most military communities offer ways to enjoy the treasures of fellowship, religious study, and spiritual growth through the chaplain's office. You'll find a myriad of activities, from church services to weekly Bible studies, as well as assistance in identifying resources within the local civilian community. Seek out opportunities for spiritual growth.

Practice Yoga or Tai Chi

Another possibility for quieting and centering is practicing yoga. Yoga helps you become more aware of your body's posture, alignment, and patterns of movement. It makes the body more flexible and can help you relax, even in the midst of a stressful environment. Most people start practicing yoga for the physical benefits, to feel fitter, to be more energetic and peaceful. Yoga was created in ancient times, however, to help individuals develop the flexibility to be able to sit in meditation. Sitting in meditation creates conditions where you are not affected by the happenings around you. This, in turn, creates a remarkable calmness and positive outlook that can carry you through stressful times. Tai chi is another physical practice that quiets your mind. It's often been called "moving meditation." In order to move through the movements, you have to focus only on the movement. Your mind can't wander off into worries or planning.

Cultivate Quiet Time in Simple Activities

When the mind is engaged in simple daily activities that are effortless for you, you are better able to connect with your spiritual center.

Nancy Boatner, an Army spouse, finds her quiet time while she vacuums! When we first heard she vacuumed her house twice a day, we admit to thinking immediately that she's a bit over the top, but then we talked with Nancy and found out her secret of the vacuum.

"Hey, I have three young children at home and a husband who is away," she told us many years ago. "How much 'me' time do you think I get? When I'm vacuuming, the children see and hear I am busy, and they have to play until I am done." Vacuuming gave her time to let her thoughts flow, to turn off the many questions and demands of her young children, to just "be" for a time. The fact that she ended up with a clean house was icing on the cake.

Whatever works for you, carve out quiet time to get to your core.

Now that we know Nancy's secret, we've been sharing it with other moms over the years. Just think of the benefits of vacuuming: exercise, semi-alone time, and a clean floor. Pretty smart, huh?

Linda Beougher plays the harp. She's found that if she plays the harp, especially favorites such as "Somewhere Over the Rainbow" as her girls are falling asleep, they sleep better, and she calms her mind at the same time.

Cathy Sterling is a weaver. She sets up her loom in whatever quarters they get, even if the only space is in the middle of the living room. When she's weaving, she enters a state of flow, letting all the other stuff go for that time. Monica Dixon has a similar experience when she quilts.

For you, it might be knitting, gardening, scrapbooking, woodworking, sewing, bread making, working on cars. Whatever works for you, carve out quiet time to get to your core. The centering and quieting that results from these activities will help carry you through the stressful, chaotic times.

Spend Time in Nature

Enjoying nature, walking or hiking, watching a glorious sunset or sunrise, noticing the celestial rays shine through the trees in the woods, or listening to the waves of the ocean are all ways to stop and take stock in the power of the universe—and to step away from the busyness of daily life to get quiet within.

When you allow yourself to get away from the constant thoughts of worry and fear, and from the litany of things you still have to do, you will be amazed at the strength and knowledge you already have within that you may not have ever tapped into it before. Developing a strong sense of faith and spiritual health during peaceful times will support and sustain you through times of crisis.

Key Points and Action Steps

▷ Create a space where you can slow down and relax, pray or meditate.

▷ Read inspiring stories.

▷ Practice yoga, tai chi, or similar mindful exercise.

▷ Carve out "me time" in simple daily activities and while enjoying nature.

Resources

A Busy Woman's Guide to Prayer by Cheri Fuller (2005).

Driving By Moonlight: A Journey Through Love, War, and Infertility by Kristin Henderson (2003).

Faith Deployed: Daily Encouragement for Military Wives by Jocelyn Green and others (2009); *Faith Deployed… Again: More Daily Encouragement for Military Wives* by Jocelyn Green (2011); and *NIV Military Wives' New Testament with Psalms & Proverbs: 90 Days of Encouragement and Hope* (2013).

F.R.A.Z.L.E.D. Military Wives Christian Network, www.BlogTalkRadio.com/FrazledMWCN.

Full Catastrophe Living: Using the Wisdom of Your Body and Mind to Face Stress, Pain, and Illness (2013) and other books and recordings by Jon Kabat-Zinn, PhD.

God Strong: The Military Wife's Spiritual Survival Guide by Sara Horn (2010).

Guided Mindfulness Meditation CD by Jon Kabat-Zinn (2005).

Handbook of Religion and Health, Second Edition by Harold G. Koenig, MD, Dana E. King, and Verna Benner Carson (2012).

Hope for the Home Front: Winning the Emotional and Spiritual Battles of a Military Wife by Marshéle Carter Waddell (2006), and *Wounded Warrior, Wounded Home: Hope and Healing for Families Living with PTSD and TBI,* coauthored with Kelly K. Orr, PhD (2013).

Medals Above My Heart: The Rewards of Being a Military Wife by Brenda Pace and Carol McGlothlin (2004).

Mind Fitness Training Institute, www.Mind-Fitness-Training.org.

Practical Prayer: Making Space for God in Everyday Life by Anne Tanner (2002).

"Research on Religion, Spirituality and Mental Health: A Review." *Canadian Journal of Psychiatry,* 54 (5), 283-291, by Harold G. Koenig, MD (2009).

Standing By: The Making of an American Military Family in a Time of War by Alison Buckholtz (2013).

Thanks!: How Practicing Gratitude Can Make You Happier by Robert A. Emmons, PhD (2008).

Wives of Faith web site, connecting, supporting, and encouraging military wives, www.WivesofFaith.org.

The Woman's Book of Yoga and Health: A Lifelong Guide to Wellness by Linda Sparrowe with Patricia Walden (2002).

Chapter 18

Experience the Power of Gratitude

Our signature prop in our workshops is a pair of colorful rainbow glasses. When you look through these glasses, everything you look at is surrounded by rainbows. Seeing rainbows changes our attitudes. The rainbow glasses are a fun, colorful, playful reminder for all of us to look for the good in other people and in situations.

Negative things are going to happen to you in life, guaranteed. When something negative happens, you have two choices. You can do what Kathie used to do: focus on the negative, wallow in the negative, and obsess about the negative. When you do that, we guarantee you'll become more negative, your situation will become more negative, and what's even worse, you'll attract negative people to you.

The opposite is also true. When something negative happens you can choose instead to look for the good. It may be that it's a tiny, tiny nugget of good or of value, but just the fact that you look for the positive shifts your focus out of the negative. If you choose to do that consciously and consistently, we guarantee you'll become more positive, your life will become more positive, and what's really wonderful is that you'll attract other positive people to you. You'll change your overall experience of life.

Part of that choice of joy and looking for the good includes being grateful for what you already have. A study by the University of California–Davis, ("Counting Blessings Versus Burdens," Emmons and McCullough, 2003), found that people who reflected on things they were grateful for, either through journaling or by making lists, "were healthier, less stressed, more optimistic, and more likely to help others." In Emmons' book *Thanks!: How the New Science of Gratitude Can Make You Happier,* the author bridges scientific research with the works of philosophers and theologians to confirm that being grateful leads to a happier, more satisfying life.

Stacy Miller, an Army spouse, wrote to us and said gratitude is a value she holds dear. "It's important to me that I show gratitude for the many blessings I have and receive."

While Stacy's husband was deployed, she chose to focus on the good. One of those focal points was being grateful for the many friends and neighbors who helped her make it through that tough time.

"When my husband returned, I felt like I needed to do something for everyone who helped me by raking leaves, watching my children, making us dinner, etc.," Stacy explained. "I decided to have a Valentine's Day cookie social. It's kind of like a cookie exchange, except I did all the baking. It was a great opportunity to thank people again, and for my husband to thank people for helping take care of us during his absence."

Taking the time to switch our focus to what we are grateful for can make a difference in how we experience and approach our situations.

Your choice of focus can affect your children as well. After hearing James Crupi, PhD, speak at an Army Morale, Welfare, and Recreation conference, Kathie has been sharing something he said that really struck her. "If you go home at night and complain about change, you will raise kids who fear change. If you sit around the dinner table and everything is negative, you will raise kids who are negative." Try starting your dinner conversations with the question, "What's one good or funny thing that happened to you today?" rather than diving into the more common litany of complaints.

Here's one simple example of how your focus and attitude can change a negative experience. Joan is an Army spouse who wrote us this card after attending one of our workshops: "I attended your seminar last week and wanted to thank you and share a story that happened as a result of what I learned from you two. I've just moved here and since my husband is deployed, I get to do this move all by myself. So I'm sitting in the midst of these boxes, feeling quite angry. I opened one box and all these pictures fell out all over the place. Normally, I'd have said a few choice words, stuffed them into a folder and plodded on. Instead, I took to heart your advice from the seminar and savored the moment. I called the kids down, and we spent an hour tripping down memory lane. It put us all into a better mood, and I even got them to help me do some more unpacking—hoping to find more treasures like the photos. Thanks for a great day and a different perspective on boxes!"

Holly's Story

I had heard about grateful journals from friends, watching Oprah and reading books. I started my own when I began reading Sarah Ban Breathnach's book Simple Abundance. Writing in my grateful journal helped me come up with my new mantra "Focus on the Good Road."

We all have good roads and bad roads to travel in life. It's a guarantee. The funny thing about life is that the good and bad roads run parallel with each other. Sometimes, the bad road seems a bit wider and longer than the good road, but nonetheless, the good road is always running alongside the bad road. We just have to turn our heads and notice all the good.

Identifying all the things I am grateful for honestly does make me see more clearly how wonderful my life really is overall. I took this approach one step further during a time when the twins were preschoolers and Daddy was gone again for long periods of time. Sound familiar to anyone? I began individual grateful journals with each child. We purchased colorful journals and each night before they went to bed, I spent time with each child and wrote in their journal what they were grateful for that day. Some of the entries were simple "I am grateful for the ice cream we ate tonight." Others were lengthy entries about all the fun things they did that day.

Doing this every night allowed us to end the day on a positive note. I can't explain how it happened, but the empty feelings and anxieties we all were experiencing while Daddy was away seemed to fade. The children slept better. I slept better, knowing my children did have things to be grateful for, and their little lives were filled with joy even though Daddy was far away, being a soldier. I felt better as a mother that I was helping my children early in their lives to turn their heads and Focus on the Good Road.

We have both kept gratitude journals for many years now. We don't always record in them daily, but we have the habit of at least reviewing what we're grateful for when we're falling asleep at night. We find ourselves turning to our gratitude journals every couple of months if we are going through a bit of a slump. Reading through the list and adding to it puts us right back into a feeling of abundance. You can start with one of these methods.

Method One: Sit down and write down one hundred things you are grateful for. Small and large. Even if you don't reach one hundred, just working toward that will throw you into that "wallowing in abundance" mode.

Method Two: Make a list of ten things for which you are grateful. Each evening for thirty days, read the list and add one more. By the end of thirty days you'll be living in abundance thinking.

Here's an idea for the whole family: Set up a big jar in your living room. As you think of it, jot down on pieces of paper something good that happened that day. Read these on New Year's Eve to end your year on a great note. This may sound simplistic, but make no mistake, it's powerful.

As military spouses, we are fortunate to get perspective as we move around and live and travel in different places. We are often more aware than many Americans of living conditions in other countries, as we read about and watch on television reports of the conditions of the areas of the world our spouses deploy to. We know we live in one of the most (if not the most) abundant places in the world. It's helpful to remind ourselves of that on a regular basis.

Key Points and Action Steps
▷   Learn to consciously shift your focus to gratitude, to look for the good.
▷   Create your own gratitude list and add to it or review it frequently.

Resources
"Counting Blessings Versus Burdens: An Experimental Investigation of Gratitude and Subjective Well-Being in Daily Life." *Journal of Personality and Social Psychology,* 84 (2), 377–389, by Robert A. Emmons and Michael E. McCullough (2003).

Simple Abundance: A Daybook of Comfort and Joy by Sarah Ban Breathnach (2009).

Thanks!: How the New Science of Gratitude Can Make You Happier by Robert A. Emmons, PhD (2007).

Chapter 19

Rediscover Simple Joys

Happiness research reveals that our experience of happiness in life, to a great deal, is made up of simple daily joys. It's a matter of learning to be in the moment enough to enjoy simple pleasures as they occur. Many of us have a lot of joy in our lives, but often we race right by what is good as we move on to the next task, to the next item on our daily to-do list. We can greatly improve our daily quality of life and our energy by taking time to participate in and appreciate simple joys. Quite frankly, if you are a military spouse acting as sole parent while your spouse is deployed, short simple joys might be all you get. They can change your daily experience if you let them.

Simple joys can bring us happiness and energy. Could you use a bit more energy in life? Start with this simple exercise.

Make a List of Joyful Activities

Get your pen ready and do this exercise quickly, as fast as you can. Write down as many things as you can think of that bring you joy. Keep going until you run out of ideas.

_____

_____

_____

The research for this came from *You Don't Have to Go Home from Work Exhausted!* by Ann McGee-Cooper, PhD, and her colleagues out of Dallas. This is a book we highly recommend, whether you work outside the home or not (we think stay-at-home moms need more energy than anyone!). It is full of great ideas to increase your daily energy. One thing the authors discovered was that most busy adults, when asked, "What do you do for fun?" usually come up with ten to fifteen items before running out of ideas.

Researchers did this with ten-year-olds. Ten-year-olds easily came up with fifty-five items before running out of ideas! We had a fourteen-year-old boy in one of our sessions and he came up with thirty-two items, so we think there's a pattern here, a transition that takes place, as we grow older.

So what does that say to us as adults? The responses we get from audience members include:

- "It means we are boring."
- "We have forgotten how to have fun."
- "We don't have time; we have too many responsibilities."

There are two common problems for most adults. The first is that some of us actually have forgotten what is fun. We are so caught up in our work and chores and responsibilities, we have forgotten to have fun. And the second is that many of us don't allow ourselves to have fun. We say things like, "I'd really like to do that, but I should do the laundry," or "I'd really like to do that, but I should mow the lawn," or "I'd really like to do that, but..."

There's another problem for us as busy adults. Look back at your list right now, and circle items that would take you only five to ten minutes to do and enjoy. When we ask audience members how many have the majority of their items circled, we rarely get hands raised. This is typical of most busy adults. When asked what they do for fun, most adults come up with items that take an hour or longer or a half day or longer to do.

Now think about your typical day. When you have free time in your busy day, does it come in big chunks of time of one hour or longer or a half day or longer? For most of us, any free time we have comes in five minutes here, ten minutes there. That applies even more so during deployments.

If you have short breaks in your busy day, and you don't know fun things you can do in that time, what do you fill the time with instead? Well, some of us complain to neighbors or coworkers. We join the Ain't it Awful club. Some of us, and we know this because we used to do this, make lists of things we still have to do. Right? And then we worry about them, which is not a very energizing break.

The fact is, if you take a five- or ten-minute break and fill it with something that is not fun for you, you are going to return to your work or chores with less energy and joy. Research shows that if, instead, you fill your short break with things you enjoy doing, you will return to your work and your chores with more energy. If you fill your break with something that is playful or that makes you laugh, you come back with more creativity and problem-solving ability, as well as added energy.

Here are ways to increase your list of short, fun items.

Share your list with others. When you hear others' ideas, you'll hear things that you enjoy, too, but you just forgot. You can add those to your list. You may also hear things you just never would have thought of. We were sharing ideas in Heidelberg, Germany, at a conference for drug and alcohol counselors. A gentleman sitting in the front row quickly raised his hand to say, "The first thing I thought of and wrote down was to jump up and down." We were thankful we weren't having our session videotaped that day, because we know our faces gave away what we were thinking. "Oh…really…that's nice; that's…interesting." But then, we decided to try it out, and we discovered he was right! Since then, we've done this with every audience. We get them jumping up and down. And everyone agrees. It raises your energy. Most folks can't help but laugh, so your joy and creativity rise as well.

Fill your break with something that is playful or that makes you laugh, and you'll return to your work with more creativity and more problem-solving ability, as well as added energy.

Lest you think this idea is silly, read the email we received from one Army spouse a few months after our workshop in Vilseck, Germany: "When you told us the jump up and down story, I didn't take it seriously. How could I jump up and down in the middle of a store? But the other day in my kickboxing class, the instructor told us to do something new. She wanted us to do full jumps, arms in the air and all the way back to the ground. She suggested we try for two minutes. I don't think we even got to thirty seconds before the whole class was incapacitated because we were laughing so hard. That was the most fun class we ever had, just because we 'jumped up and down.' I think I might be doing it a little more often—at home anyway. Thanks, Jennifer."

Here are short, simple joys other spouses have mentioned:

- Take a quick walk outside. A ten-minute walk increases your energy for one full hour. (And best of all, researchers at Northern Arizona University found that just ten minutes of exercise is all it takes to improve overall mood!)
- Pet your dog or cat.
- Use the Tingler (a fun head massager).
- Write a postcard to a friend. You have the joy of thinking about them, and they have the joy in receiving a note from you. And, it has greater impact than an email.
- Sing out loud or dance around the room.

Break longer items into smaller ones. Look at those things that take longer, and figure out what piece of that activity you could do in five to ten minutes. For example, how could you find a way to enjoy golfing in five to ten minutes? You could putt, practice your swing (with or without a club), look through a golf magazine, or call a friend to schedule a tee time. Or you could close your eyes, talk yourself into relaxation, and then visualize yourself playing golf on a gorgeous day on your favorite course. Any one of those things would be a more energizing break than worrying or complaining.

Go to the toy store with yourself in mind. (We're talking about the exchange toy section or Toys 'R' Us or Walmart.) Don't think about your kids or nieces and nephews or grandkids, just you. Find toys you loved as a kid, such as Slinky or Etch-a-Sketch. Find new fun toys that didn't exist when you were younger. There is a saying: "You don't stop playing because you grow old. You grow old because you stop playing!" Even business guru Tom Peters says, "An office without a toy is like computer without software." We all need play, laughter, fun, and the chance to lighten up in our lives.

Let's face it, during a deployment, especially, if you are acting as a single parent handling all the chores, all you have time for are short, simple joys. You need all the energy and problem-solving ability you can get, so consciously add in fun things. We know how natural it is to think, "How can I do fun things even in small doses when my spouse is in danger?" The fact of the matter is that during deployments especially, you have to incorporate these small joys, for your energy and for your sanity!

Doing this Simple Joys exercise as a group or family is a great idea. We've seen this successfully done in family readiness group meetings, key volunteer groups, clubs and office meetings, as well as within families. Once you understand this concept of filling your day with simple joys, you will see that it is the accumulation of these simple joys that bring you that sense of overall happiness with life.

By the way, don't forget to use the items on your list that take an hour or longer. Compare lists with those of your spouse and your children. Schedule in things you enjoy doing together on a regular basis. If we don't plan and schedule these things, they often don't happen.

It's important for your relationship to consciously add in fun. As Terry Sovinski, a family counselor in Vilseck, Germany, told a group of military spouses during a family readiness group orientation, one of the main things he sees in couples that are in trouble is a lack of shared fun. We come together through activities we enjoy doing together. You've heard the saying, "No one on their deathbed ever said, I wish I spent more time at the office." Well, we think no one on their deathbed ever said, "Boy I wish I'd kept a cleaner house," or "Boy, I wish I'd watched more television." Make time for fun in your life. Plan for it. You'll increase your joy and your energy. The research proves it.

Holly's Story

My hardest lesson: Letting go! Enjoying the moments!

You would think someone as playful as me would have fun playing with my children each day. Sadly, not so. I would feel the weight of daily responsibilities, managing a home, community involvement, disciplining, and work deadlines always hanging over me. It made me feel stressed and unhappy with my role as a parent. I was well aware of the fact that the lives of my children were flying by, and I wanted to cherish those times, but it seemed I often let other responsibilities take over. The "joy of parenting" just wasn't there for me.

The Wall Street Journal had a regular column called "A Balanced Life" in which a controversial discussion between working mothers and nonworking mothers arose. (Don't you think "nonworking mothers" is an oxymoron?) One letter hit home. "One of the key things overlooked in this battle is that

the success of the stay-at-home mom is perhaps best measured by how little she accomplishes, not how much. When she is truly connecting with her
child/children, she is not doing laundry, dishes, cooking, yard work, driving,
etc. (and I add volunteer work). She is doing nothing except hanging out and
being with her kids. This requires a tremendous mental shift from her former
career where success meant getting things done. Success with kids means
not getting things done, except the bare minimum, because only when you
are hanging out in the hammock, watching the leaves fall . . . are you giving
them the absolute, undivided attention they crave. Most people have not
made this mental shift."

I certainly fell into this category, as I was notorious for making to-do lists
and expecting to get the majority of the items done. I was continually disap-
pointed at the end the day when I only accomplished one or two things on
my list. Why did I continue to punish myself like this? Why couldn't I learn to
just let go and enjoy this time with my children, let alone take time to care
for myself?

Some people have an easier time letting go than others. My mental shift
is a work in progress. One step I took toward letting go was to make a to-
do list with my children at breakfast or the night before. I wrote the items
or the children drew pictures of what we were going to do that day. Each
child got to put down what s/he wanted to include. At the time we started
this, my twins were four years old and 99.9 percent of their items included
Mommy playing with them. (For example, play dolls with Mommy; play cars
with Mommy; go to the park with Mommy.) They wanted my individual and
undivided attention. Doesn't every child? Completing this list with the children helped them understand there are things Mommy wanted to get done
that day, and it was also a visible reminder for me to stop and play with each
child. As their mother, this is exactly what I wanted to be doing—every day!
Furthermore, it helped them know Mommy was going to spend time with
them that day. After we completed an item on the list, we got to cross it off.
The feeling of accomplishment made me feel like I was doing a good job.

One particular morning, my daughter's item was to pick dandelions
with Mommy, lie on the grass, and watch the clouds together. Children are
so wise, if you just listen. They understand the concept of simple joys! My
daughter certainly does!

So, simple joys can bring you energy as well as happiness. Take a few minutes now to go back to your list and identify a few more things that bring you joy—things that are fun for you—big and small.

We love to watch the birds outside the window at the bird feeders and birdbath. We love to watch movies, in the theater or on video, as we eat popcorn. Kathie and her husband love to kayak—the peaceful paddling kind. So, what is it for you? Do you enjoy playing with your kids, throwing a Frisbee to your dog, traveling, hiking, biking, listening to a favorite song, reading a joke of the day, or something else?

Key Points and Action Steps
▷ Make a list of simple activities that bring you joy.
▷ Spend five to ten minutes each day doing fun things that energize you.

Resources
You Don't Have to Go Home from Work Exhausted!: A Program to Bring Joy, Energy, and Balance to Your Life by Ann McGee-Cooper, with Duane Trammell and Barbara Lau (1992).

Chapter 20

Increase Your Energy and Decrease Your Stress

"Go for my dreams?" people ask. "I wish I could, but I can hardly get myself out of bed in the morning. By the end of the day, I'm dragging. About all I can manage is to slump in front of the television to relax a bit, get to bed, and start all over again the next day. I don't have any energy left to get going on something new, especially something as big as my dreams!"

Sound familiar? We hear this all the time. Let's look at how to increase your energy on a regular basis. If you are tired and running on empty, the last thing you will do is move toward your dreams. You won't even have the energy to get excited about the idea! You must address self-care first.

When Holly was a new mom of twins and dealing with her husband being deployed, she was low on energy herself. Giving all her energy to take care of her children and her community, she would often say, "If I can comb my hair and brush my teeth in the same day, it's a good day." That is all she could give to herself. Something had to change!

The first thing that had to change was her mindset. For most women, especially mothers and especially military spouses, self-care is not even on the radar screen. With all the demands on your time, especially if you are dealing with a move or a deployment, time for yourself just doesn't happen. And it won't ever just happen. Like Holly, you have to change your thinking about the importance of taking care of yourself.

You are no real use to others if you are running on empty. Oh sure, you can manage it for a while. We all do. But keep running on empty, and you'll end up crashing. If you are lucky, it will only be something like getting sick and having to stop for a short while. If you aren't lucky, it can be even more.

Holly's Story

I went to great lengths to work in exercise and time with my girlfriend, Cheryl Crosswaite. Both being moms of toddlers and preschoolers, we complained that our days were filled with work, maintenance, chores, and child-care duties. There never seemed to be time in the day to be able to talk as friends, let alone exercise. My three-year-old twins no longer wanted to sit in a stroller while I pushed them for exercise. Taking them out on their tricycles didn't work, either. As any mother of twins will tell you, whenever you let go of twins' hands they immediately go in opposite directions—guaranteed. Cheryl was having similar problems with her children, ages two and five.

We decided to take action. We took our four children to the local high school track, which had a big fence around the entire area. We put the children in the middle of the field with toys, balls, a wagon, a pop-up tent, (even a potty chair for those toilet-training moments). We told the children they were to play in the middle of the field while we exercised for thirty minutes. (For those of you who don't have children, I am sure you are laughing at this point, asking, "Why is this such a big deal?" Those of you who have or had toddlers and preschoolers know this is a big deal—asking toddlers to stay in one area while Mommy walks away from them.)

But it did work—with a little effort and determination on our part. At first, Cheryl and I were only able to walk/run halfway around and then back as to not be too far away from the children. We started out with fifteen minutes and increased our time with each successive day. Cheryl brought a timer and set it for thirty minutes so her five-year-old could understand when we would be finished exercising. There were times when the children would cry and want to run alongside us. We were consistent in telling them they could run with us, but we were not going to stop exercising until our thirty minutes were up. We helped each other be consistent and continued to increase our time. The children began to play more and more independently and even started cheering us on as we ran around the track.

I loved those times I had with Cheryl. We talked about our dreams, we brainstormed for each other, we held each other accountable, and we were friends helping the other person become the best she could be. Everyone won in this scenario. Because Cheryl and I felt better about getting time to talk with a friend and to exercise our bodies, we felt better about our overall outlook on life. Our husbands even commented on the difference. We were happier and we had more energy for life—energy for our dreams, our husbands, our children, and ourselves.

You have to make the decision that self-care is important and a priority. After one of our workshops, we got an email from an Army spouse whose husband deployed, leaving her with two young children. She said we had given her the permission she somehow needed to hire a sitter once a week, so she'd have some time to herself.

Hey, if you need permission, we hereby grant it to you.

Let's think about this—from whom are you waiting for permission? Your spouse? Your kids? Your community? As Dr. Phil (McGraw) says: "Obviously, a top priority is to be a good mother. If you really care about your kids, you will take care of their mother." This is also true of fathers, but mothers somehow have a harder time with the concept.

Dr. Pamela Peeke, author of *Fight Fat After Forty*, points out, "I tell my male patients that they have to get out and exercise, and they do it. I tell my female patients the same thing, and they start talking about their children." She points out to these mothers that if they don't do regular exercise to reach the ongoing calming effect exercise provides them, they are choosing to be a cranky, stressed-out parent, ready to scream at the slightest provocation. Which kind of parent do you think your kids really want?

One woman we know finally got this concept as her two boys grew a bit older. "I used to love to take ballet class—before children," she says. "I'm no good at it, but it just plain energizes me and makes me grin from ear to ear." Recently, she started classes again. "I can't afford childcare," she adds. "So I told my boys, 'You can either sit on the sidelines quietly and draw, or just sit and watch Mommy, just like Mommy always sits and watches you at swimming and soccer.'" She figures it's important they understand that Mommy is a person, too, with interests of her own.

Learn to Live Strategically

Everything has energy: the foods you eat, the music you listen to, the people you spend time with, the things you read, the kinds of shows you watch on TV, your home environment, even the clothes you wear. Think with each, "Does this support me and give me energy and vitality, or does this suck my energy and reinforce negative energy?" It's all a choice.

Remember, knowing what works and doing what works are two different things. We've both been there and still get to that same place sometimes—that place of knowing your daily actions are adding to your already high stress level, but you are not making any changes. The starting point is to at least know what works and what doesn't when it comes to effectively managing your energy and stress levels.

You might want to think of this as living strategically. You don't have to give up all the things you enjoy; that might not be the best thing for you. What you can do, instead, is give up things for certain periods of high stress when you know you need to be at your best. It's that 80/20 concept. If you make smart choices in activity and nutrition 80 percent of the time, that 20 percent of cake and coffee and chocolate won't harm you in the long run.

We've asked lots of military spouses—especially those with the added time challenges of childcare—what works for them to keep their energy up and stress down. Here are the things we hear most often.

Learn to Say No

Learn to build your "no" muscle. Not using this muscle seems to be the main obstacle keeping military spouses from putting themselves first. When you get clear that self-care is your priority, it is easier to say no to a request.

We are fully aware of the responsibilities that come with parenthood and know there are many requests that can't be ignored. We are also aware that there are many important community projects you may choose to take on, and friends and neighbors you'll choose to help out. But there are just as many times in your day when you are asked to do something you really don't want to do, to which you can say "no." You have a choice. Awareness is the first step. Pay attention to how often you do things you'd rather not do. Stop and pause before responding to a request. The key here is to learn to say no to the things you don't want to do, so you can say yes to the things you do want to do.

Let your family know that you are going to make your self-care a priority, and you may say no to some of their requests. We heard veteran military spouse Susan speak at a conference. She described how she finally understood that she needed one evening a week for herself. So she held a family meeting to discuss this. As she said, "After all, what were they going to do, fire me?"

Don't you think it's time we start modeling to our children that each individual is important, including Mom and Dad? Saying no brings up the fear of disappointing or hurting others, of missing opportunities, and of making mistakes. But saying no means saying yes to you! No one else can do this but you.

> *Learn to say no to things you can say no to, so you can say yes to the things you want to do.*

Breathe

"I stop and breathe" is one of the most common things we hear from others when we ask them how they deal with stress.

An entry by Lisa Wolfe, "Burying Zebra," in *Oprah* magazine, made us both laugh out loud: All mothers know how to do deep breathing if they went through Lamaze. "I remember my prenatal breathing. Those long deep breaths may have been useless during labor, but they sure do come in handy years down the road when you want to whack your kids, but know you can't."

Effective, conscious breathing is important for all of us. Most of us live on shallow chest breathing, holding our stomachs in and limiting our oxygen. We deprive ourselves of added energy that results from simple, effective breathing. Take a deep breath, not just filling up your lungs, but actually taking a deep belly breath, feeling your ribs expand as your lungs expand, and let the air out slowly. Say to yourself, "Stop and be present, take a deep breath, go slow." As you exhale, you might say the words, "Let go and relax" or simply "calm." Do this right now. Close your eyes. See how you feel after stopping to take a deep breath.

We can all do that. It's an easy step that takes very little time. The hard part is to remember to do it. Holly wrote the word "Breathe" on three-by-five cards and put one in her car, one on her bathroom mirror, one on her kitchen windowsill, one on the telephone, and one above her computer. She found out quickly that her whining toddler was not going to suffer if Mom stopped, stepped back, and took a deep breath. Everyone benefits when Mom takes a moment to stop and breathe.

Kathie has the following sign on her computer:

> *Breathing in, I calm body and mind*
> *Breathing out, I smile.*
> *Dwelling in the present moment,*
> *I know this is the only moment.*
>
>   —*Thich Nhat Hanh,* Being Peace

You can use external triggers to remind you to breathe. Have you noticed how often you hold your breath as you go about your work? It's not uncommon to find yourself literally holding your breath as you concentrate on something you are doing. That raises your stress level and decreases your effectiveness in getting that job done.

When the telephone rings, purposely take a deep breath before you pick it up. For one thing, you'll be more present to the caller that way, and it's a chance to remind yourself to breathe. Do the same thing with stoplights when you are driving the car. A red light means stop, take a deep breath (or two or three) and do shoulder shrugs to release tension.

For those times when you need a little extra stress reduction, stop to breathe and take a whiff of aromatherapy. The essential oil of lavender reduces stress, while peppermint raises energy. Find what works best for you.

You can use your breath and your thoughts in combination to help deal with extreme stress. Linda Beougher is an Army spouse who went through brain tumor surgery to remove a golf-ball-sized tumor pressing against her brainstem. When we asked this mother of two young girls how she managed her fears during that time, she shared a yoga breath exercise that helped her. It's an exercise we have both used many times since and have shared with spouses dealing with fears during wartime deployments.

As you breathe in, say to yourself, "I breathe in trust, energy, lightness, faith" or whatever words speak to you. As you breathe out, say to yourself, "I breathe out fear, anxiety, fatigue" or whatever thoughts you want to be rid of. It seems simplistic, but this exercise can have a powerful effect on your day. Start and end your day with this exercise as a way to help keep fear and anxiety at bay. Linda reminds us, too, that this exercise is great for any time. Simply change the words and say, "I breathe in creativity, joy, abundance. I breathe out self-doubt, negativity, lack." Kathie always makes sure to end up with the "in breath," so the positive words are the last ones her mind and subconscious hear.

Dr. Martin Rossman is a physician, author, and educator known as a pioneer in the field of guided imagery, especially for cancer patients. According to Rossman, when you worry about possible negative outcomes, that is imagery and it negatively impacts how you feel. Using positive guided imagery or a simple breath exercise can put you in a place of peace for a time, lowering your overall anxiety.

Take One Day at a Time

Many military spouses share this tool for how they manage this crazy lifestyle. When they plan their day, they schedule their self-care first and then work the rest of the demands and chores around their self-care time. That way it is never last on the list. Last things often get dropped, so put yourself first.

Stick to the motto: "Just for today, I can take care of myself. Just for today, I can make healthy choices when eating. Just for today, I can drink lots of water. Just for today, I can get to bed earlier. Just for today…" Do not think about tomorrow or of losing ten pounds or of adding a full-fledged, long-term exercise program, or giving up television or extensive Facebook time forever. What can you do today that will help you take care of yourself? Make that your priority for the day.

Add Movement to Your Day

Self-care is not about working out or losing weight. It is about taking care of you. When your life is packed with activity, the thought of adding a workout into that schedule sounds impossible. For one thing, the word itself sounds like work, like one more chore. Instead, say to yourself, "I want to add more movement into my day." You can do that for one day—just one day at a time. Just move!

We promise you: If you add some movement to your life, your energy will increase, your stress will decrease, and you will find yourself better able to handle the challenges thrown your way.

Here's added reason to get moving. Gallup research shows that people who exercise at least two days a week are happier and have significantly less stress. In addition, these benefits increase with more frequent exercise. They found that each additional day of exercise in a given week—at least up to six days, when people reach a point of diminishing returns—continues to boost energy levels.

It might seem counterintuitive, but one of the best ways to combat fatigue is by exercising or moving your body.

One experiment revealed that just twenty minutes of exercise can improve your mood for several hours after working out. Those who exercised for just twenty minutes had a significant improvement in mood after two, four, eight, and twelve hours when compared to those who did not exercise.

On days when you don't have twenty or thirty minutes to exercise, a mere eleven minutes of lifting weights or ten minutes of doing yoga stretches have been shown to increase metabolic rate, which helps you burn more fat throughout the day. And, you feel better. Any exercise is better than an entire day with no vigorous activity.

Here are some simple and fun ways to put more movement in your day:

- Get up from the computer, television, or from your chores and Hula-Hoop! Hey, it gets all the kinks out. One woman in our seminar told us her doctor advised her to Hula-Hoop to get her waist back after giving birth. It worked for her. It works for us to pump up our energy in a short amount of time. You'll be amazed at what fun hoop dancing, as they call it these days, can be. Check out some of the YouTube videos on hoop dancing. It's Kathie's new favorite activity, fun and playful. She even started a group that meets once a week at the local gym to hoop dance to fun music.
- Turn on your favorite music and dance around the house. You can do this by yourself or with your children. Get your kids dancing and picking up their toys at the same time—what fun!
- Park farther away from the store and walk to the entrance.
- Do something fun for you that has movement built in. From riding a bike, to playing Frisbee with your dog, to inline skating, fun movement beats working out every time.
- Keep toys in the trunk of your car. After picking up your children from school, stop at a park and play with them for a bit. You'll help them get some energy out, they will have fun with Mom or Dad, and you increase your energy for the rest of the day.

- One of the best things to do for your physical and emotional health is to walk and talk with a good friend. Think of it as "moving therapy."
- Use a pedometer and move. The pedometer keeps you honest about how much walking you really are getting in your day, and it's an incentive to increase that amount.

Sneak exercise into your day. Make it a game. Do squats while you blow-dry your hair or while you watch your kids practice soccer. Walk around the soccer field; you can still have your eyes on your child. Use the bench at the field for triceps dips or angled push-ups. Use the monkey bars for pull-ups. If you feel conspicuous doing that by yourself, enlist another parent to join you. You may start a trend.

For great ideas of things to do in short amounts of time, read *Gotta Minute?: The Ultimate Guide of One-Minute Workouts for Anyone, Anywhere, Anytime* by Bonnie Nygard, MEd, and Bonnie Hopper, MEd. It's a short book full of ideas for simple things you can do at your desk, watching television, or while doing chores. Or check out the FitDeck cards created by a Navy SEAL, with exercises you can do in one minute, www.FitDeck.com.

Dump Your Time and Energy Drains

If your life is so packed full that you think, "I can't add movement or weight training or meditation on top of all this," you are probably right. Your life is too full. Take something else off your list to make space. It's your health, longevity, and sanity we are talking about here.

The kinds of things you might remove from your list include:

- Watching television. We aren't asking you to quit watching a great, funny program that makes you laugh. We don't mean to cut out those shows that teach you new things, or movies that allow you a good laugh or cry. We suggest cutting out the kind of mindless TV watching that often happens, especially when you are tired, where you just sit as one show follows another, whether or not you are even interested, often finding it difficult to get up to go to bed and get the rest you so desperately need. More than any other activity, watching television promotes lethargy and passivity. You see it in your children. It happens to adults, too. You just don't feel like doing anything! The average American adult watches four-to-six hours of television each day. Cut out two or three of those hours, and switch that time to healthy self-care and your dream project.

- Endless surfing of the Internet. Granted, there are great resources on the web. In fact, we share many in our resource list and wonder how we'd survive without email connection with our friends and Internet access for research. But, maybe you are like us and have experienced the negatives attached to too much surfing. We have both at times ended up surfing the net late at night when we are already dead tired. "I'll just get on and check my email," we think. We surface hours later without any helpful new information, now totally exhausted with few hours left to sleep. Monitor your use! One idea is to set a timer to go off at a specified time so that you stay aware of how long you are on, or use time tracking software to keep you fully aware of how you spend your time online.

One Army spouse said she knew she couldn't handle a constant diet of television or Internet news while her husband was deployed, but she also didn't want to miss important news. She asked family members to do the surfing and let her know when they found an article about his unit.

- Endless rambling telephone conversations. Of course, you need to connect with your friends and family. But you know when you've been on the phone too long, especially if you have fallen into gossiping and complaining about life. It's often a procrastination trap that keeps you from doing what you say you really want to do. If you need to talk, go outside and walk and talk with your friends. Turn an energy drain into an energy gain. Or do what Kathie does—hoop dance while you talk on the phone!
- Shopping out of boredom. This is especially problematic to those who truly are addicted to shopping, getting that high from buying. Your energy level and your checkbook don't need that. Try exercise or a creative pursuit instead. Or find art exhibits or museums to wander in rather than stores full of temptation.

Other common energy drains: clutter, procrastination, hanging out with negative people, unresolved conflicts, appliances that need repair, putting off important tasks such as updating your will, and so on.

From Kathie's Journal

I recently took action in one area that was taking over my life and draining my positive energy. My email inbox was overflowing, always! A good portion of the emails were blogs or newsletters or store sale notices that I had actually signed up for at one time. Or maybe I was automatically added because of a purchase. I constantly felt overwhelmed and spent hours each day trying to plow through it all. Even though I often deleted many of the newsletters, I had this sense of guilt in not reading them. What if I missed something important?

It seemed easier to simply delete things rather than dealing with them, but even just reading the subject line and hitting delete takes time. It adds up. So one day, I took twenty minutes to go through my delete box and open up these items to click the "unsubscribe" button, often a one-click process. Sometimes it took me to a web site where I had to enter my email to unsubscribe. I easily unsubscribed from forty different email feeds that day. Over the next few weeks, each time a new item came in, I made a conscious choice and hit unsubscribe on many.

Certainly, I have blogs and newsletters I kept coming. But now, I have time to read those. My inbox is manageable. I feel like I can breathe again!

We all have our own energy drains. The key is to identify them and find ways to eliminate or limit them. It takes awareness and conscious choice. We recommend further reading on the issue of energy drains. Cheryl Richardson's book *Take Time for Your Life* has a great explanation in chapter three. She says, "What you may not know is that actions you don't take use energy—mental energy, emotional energy, energy that could be better used in a positive way." She includes a comprehensive checklist for you to identify your own energy drains.

Tune In to the Power of Sound

In one workshop, we split people into two groups. We asked one group to brainstorm words that bring up images of unwanted sounds, discordant sounds, sounds that grate on your nerves. The other group brainstormed yummy sounds, pleasant sounds. Just read through the two lists below yourself. How does each one make you feel?

List one: screeching tires, car alarms, hate-filled voices, slamming doors, smashed glasses, constant criticism, deep bass woofers pounding out rap music, police car and fire sirens, lawn mowers, leaf blowers, the constant ringtone of a Blackberry as messages come in.

List two: birds singing, bees buzzing over flowers, wind humming in the trees, leaves rustling, pleasant wind chimes, babbling brooks, the quiet in and out lapping of the surf, a purring cat.

If you are like us, just reading the words elicits a different reaction in our bodies. Reading the first list causes us to tense up. Reading the second relaxes us, slows our breath. If just reading the words can impact your stress level, imagine what the sounds themselves do to us.

The key is to figure out what negative sounds you can cut out or at least muffle, and what positive sounds you can add into your environment on purpose. This can be as simple as closing the door on the laundry room so you don't hear the washer and dryer going. Or choosing the music you listen to as you go about different activities.

One woman wrote how she spent a portion of each lunch hour sitting in her car with the oldies station blasting, singing at the top of her lungs. "With a full time job and two kids at home, this is my daily stress release, singing music I love," she says.

Music can rev you up or slow you down.

One study showed that music caused a positive effect on the mood of 92 percent of people. The key was that it was music of their choice.

Music therapist Louise Montello, PhD, author of *Essential Musical Intelligence*, reports that listening to the right music helps your body's natural rhythms synchronize and harmonize. You can slow down your heart rate and breathing to a more relaxed state.

Kathie uses music strategically. Her favorite soundtrack to clean house to is *The Big Chill*; it elicits a high-energy response. Her favorite music to relax to is *Cristofori's Dream* by pianist David Lanz. Listening to that CD causes her whole body to relax. She's also learned to use ear plugs to cut out or at least diminish irritating noise that she can't control, like a neighbor's leaf blower, especially when she needs to concentrate on a piece of writing.

We can't control all the sounds in our environment, but we can certainly control many.

Turn Interests into Energy!

It's true. When you pursue your interests, you increase your energy level. Energy begets energy. Watching life on television does not beget energy. Participating in life does. Staying in your pajamas all day does not beget energy. Getting yourself dressed and out the door does. Waiting for the perfect circumstances or some future date does not beget energy. Taking action does.

This crazy military lifestyle is full of richness and possibilities, but your self-care needs to come first before you can even start to live life to its fullest. Take your first steps in saying yes to yourself—yes to self-care!—one step, one day at a time.

Key Points and Action Steps

▷ Make a list of things you can say no to.

▷ Find ways to add movement to your day.

▷ Identify energy drains.

▷ Add positive, calming sounds to your day.

Resources

Breathing: The Master Key to Self Healing by Andrew Weil, MD (1999).

Fight Fat After Forty: The Revolutionary Three-Pronged Approach that Will Break Your Stress-Fat Cycle and Make You Healthy, Fit, and Trim for Life (2001) and *Body-for-LIFE for Women: A Woman's Plan for Physical and Mental Transformation* (2009) by Pamela Peeke, MD, MPH, FACP.

FitDeck card packs, www.FitDeck.com.

Gotta Minute?: The Ultimate Guide of One-Minute Workouts for Anyone, Anywhere, Anytime by Bonnie Nygard, MEd, and Bonnie Hopper, MEd (2000).

Guided Imagery for Self-Healing: An Essential Resource for Anyone Seeking Wellness by Martin L. Rossman, MD (2010).

HoopGirl.com. Hoop dancing information and resources.

How to Say No Without Feeling Guilty: And Say Yes to More Time, More Joy, and What Matters Most to You by Patti Breitman and Connie Hatch (2001).

Softpower! How to Speak Up, Set Limits, and Say No Without Losing Your Lover, Your Job, or Your Friends by Maria Arapakis (1990).

Strong Women Stay Young by Miriam E. Nelson, PhD and Sarah Wernick PhD (2005); *Strong Women Stay Slim* (1999) with menus and recipes by Steven Raichlen; and other books by Miriam Nelson, www.StrongWomen.com.

Take Time for Your Life: A Personal Coach's 7-Step Program for Creating the Life You Want by Cheryl Richardson (1999). Plus, her book *The Art of Extreme Self-Care: Transform Your Life One Month at a Time* (2012).

Time Management for Unmanageable People: The Guilt-Free Way to Organize, Energize, and Maximize Your Life by Ann McGee-Cooper with Duane Trammell (1994).

Chapter 21

Use Strengths for the Greater Good

T he research suggests and our experience and interviews with many military spouses confirm that the greatest high in life comes from using your strengths to serve a greater good. There really is such a thing as a "helper's high" similar to the "runner's high," where the release of endorphins, the feel-good brain chemicals, increases your experience of happiness. The most lasting experience of happiness occurs from using your strengths in service to others. That can be one on one with a child, with coworkers in the workplace, in a volunteer situation, or with a stranger on the street.

Coast Guard spouse and mother of three, Maria, works on the marketing team at Costco. She also serves on the board of directors for the Lower Columbia Hispanic Council in Astoria, Oregon, providing services for the Hispanic community.

"We help with banking, filing taxes, credit, and anything we can help with. I serve as an interpreter at work and in the community," explains Maria. With fifteen years as a military spouse, she is accustomed to adapting to new communities. She learned English herself at fifteen and has worked hard to perfect her language skills, even joining Toastmasters and later serving as president of Toastmasters International in Astoria. She's found ways to use her strengths for the greater good, bringing herself great joy in the process.

Like so many military spouses, Army spouse Cathy Sterling tells us the helper's high is what keeps her going. Cathy has volunteered countless hours, year after year, in the different military communities where she has lived. Cathy says, "I know I have a choice of where I use my strengths, and I want to be involved in my community, knowing I might be helping others through my actions. The bottom line is that I feel a sisterhood with other spouses, and they are the ones that keep me going."

> *"Above all, we must realize that each of us makes a difference with our life. Each of us impacts the world around us every single day. We have a choice to use the gift of our life to make the world a better place—or not to bother."*
> —Jane Goodall

It took Cathy a while to realize that finding your purpose or calling could be as simple as recognizing that you may already be doing what you are supposed to be doing. Often, our purpose in life is right in front of us, if we just stop to notice.

Just talk with any of the spouses we've profiled in this book. So many of them are using their strengths in a way that helps others. That can be in a volunteer position, but is just as likely to be in a business or career. Many military spouses use their strengths in quieter ways, helping neighbors; raising creative, responsible children; and mentoring others in their workplace. They use their strengths, engage in life, and make a difference, creating a path to happiness.

Use Your Strengths for the Good of the Military Community

Often things happen to us in this military life that really don't make sense at all, things that affect other military spouses.

We mentioned earlier that we recommend not joining Ain't it Awful clubs, groups of negative people who can pull you into their negativity. However, there is one type of Ain't it Awful club that works. It's when a group of people come together to acknowledge something is wrong; and rather than simply complaining, they step up to take proactive steps to initiate important change. Maybe we could call them Change the Awful clubs.

Many spouses have stepped up and used their strengths to advocate for changes that affect us and all military families in the future. Talk about leaving a legacy. Just think how these individuals feel when they reflect on what they did.

One example we should all know about as military spouses is National Military Family Association (NMFA). NMFA was organized in 1969 as the National Military Wives Association by a group of military wives and widows. At that time, if you were married to the military and your spouse died in retirement, his retirement pay stopped. You got nothing despite the many sacrifices you had made. How unfair was that! Because of the efforts of these women who stepped up to protest that situation, the Survivor Benefit Plan came into being.

Since then, NMFA, a nonprofit association, continues to educate military families about our rights, benefits, and services. NMFA promotes and protects the interests of military family members by influencing the development and implementation of legislation and policies that affect us. NMFA is a big part of our voice to Congress; many of the benefits we take for granted came about because of NMFA, such as:

- The comprehensive dental plan for active duty families.
- Student travel allowances for families stationed overseas.
- Increased active duty survivor benefits.
- Cost of Living Allowance (COLA) for service members stationed in areas in CONUS with exceptionally high cost of living.
- Adoption expense reimbursement for active duty military families.

During wartime, NMFA expanded help for military families. The organization created Operation Purple Camps for children dealing with military deployments, Operation Purple Family Retreats to allow families to reconnect after a deployment, and Operation Purple Healing Adventures for wounded military members and their families.

NMFA is pushing for research to help the services better understand how to help military members transition back from war and to help them and their families adjust and deal with post-deployment challenges.

The Army's Family Action Plan (AFAP) is another great example of spouses asking for change for all of us. Army spouse Joyce Ott convinced the Army to have the first Army Family Symposium, which continues today as AFAP.

Every year through AFAP, community members of every post get to raise top concerns, asking for what they want changed. Many of the issues get solved locally. Others are raised to the Department of the Army level. In fact, since the program started in 1983, hundreds of changes have been made to legislation, Army policy and regulations, and programs and services. More than half of AFAP issues benefit all of the Department of Defense, not just the Army. Things have changed for the better for all of us—because someone stepped up to ask!

Marine Corps spouse Vivianne Wersel stepped up to make a difference. One week after her husband's safe return from a stress-filled tour in Iraq, he suffered a fatal heart attack. Since his death occurred in the US and not in Iraq, his family was not eligible for enhanced benefits. They would receive about $12,000, a far cry from the $238,000 the family would have been eligible to receive if he had died under the same circumstances while in Iraq.

Change happens because someone chose to believe change was possible.

Vivianne believed "all deaths in the Marine Corps should be ruled equal." She took her fight to Congress, to senators, even by email to the president. Her efforts, with the support of NMFA, Gold Star Wives of America, and others resulted in an amendment to the Senate version of the National Defense Authorization Act, which passed and became law. Her efforts paid off for her family and the many others who had suffered the same fate since the war began.

This war has seen other changes for military families. For example, families' presence at the arrival of caskets at Dover Air Force Base, Delaware, is relatively new. The military only started paying travel and lodging expenses for relatives to travel to Dover in 2009. Because the policy was new, there were no facilities for families at Dover itself.

When Suzie Schwartz, spouse of the Air Force chief of staff at the time, stood with her husband to pay respects to these families, she was shocked to see the cramped, no-frills waiting area at Dover. Though nothing can soften the blow of what these families are dealing with, she believed private, calming spaces for the families were the least the military could do to ease their pain. She took on the project to fix it. In late 2009, the Center for the Families of the Fallen opened its doors. This $1.6 million, 6000-square-foot space gives families a place to assemble privately before being taken to the flight line. There are several private rooms, a kitchen, a children's room with a crib and toys, and areas for meditation. A Fisher House hotel for military families was added in 2010, and a playground for children of the fallen was added in 2012. All because as Susie Schwartz said at the dedication, "This comes about from those of us willing to say 'let's figure out how to do it better.'"

These are just a few of the stories of military spouses using their strengths for the greater good. It's the path to the highest level of happiness, even though that wasn't the driver for any of these spouses. As military spouses, we are part of something bigger than ourselves.

As one military spouse said when she called into a *Navy Wife Talk Radio* interview: "When I'm eighty years old, I'll know I really lived life and my family made a difference."

Use your strengths for the greater good in some way, and you'll be able to look back on your life knowing you made a difference.

Key Points and Action Steps

▷   Refer back to the strengths you identified in Chapter 5. Is there a program or community need you are passionate about where you could apply one or more of your strengths?

▷   What are some other ways you can step up to make a difference for the greater good?

Chapter 22

Tap into the Richness of Military Life

O f course, we think it's important to acknowledge and address the challenges of this life. It's just as important to make sure we acknowledge and take advantage of the benefits this military life offers us. This life provides many positive things. As Army spouse Kris says, "It is so overwhelming at times, especially the moves, but as my grandma used to say, 'I'll take the roller coaster over the carousel any day!'"

Here are the benefits mentioned over and over again by military spouses who opened their eyes to possibilities with every move.

Cherish Patriotism, Pride, and *Esprit de Corps*

Neither one of us can attend a military parade, listen to "The Star-Spangled Banner" being played in a military theater, or watch a reunion ceremony without choking up or dabbing away tears.

One thing our military life has given us is a deep sense of pride in the men and women who serve in the military. You really get to see how professional and dedicated they are. As spouses, you are part of that dedication, professionalism, and the sacrifices made for our country and to help other countries. Military spouses are part of something much bigger than ourselves, something most other people never get to experience.

When we've been involved with deployments, especially, we've felt the deep connection to group. There is a connection among military spouses bonded by our experiences. We both have many civilian friends we admire, but we don't know too many who have had to overcome and thrive in the kinds of challenges military spouses deal with regularly.

We love each of our soldiers, airmen, sailors, Marines, Coasties, and National Guardsmen, and we are proud to stand beside them. Cherish that sense of pride, patriotism, and *esprit de corps.*

From Kathie's Journal

Months after the terrorists crashed into the World Trade Center, I read interviews with New Yorkers who were in the city at the time. They described how they dove in to help in any way they could, even if it was making sandwiches. Person after person said the same thing, "It was a horrendous event, but I have to say I've never felt more alive than when I was helping out." Why? They were part of something greater than themselves. That is something we experience over and over again as military spouses.

Get to Know Our Country

For many people, the first chance to really get to know this vast country of ours is when they retire, invest in an RV, and hit the road. As military spouses, we have that opportunity much sooner.

"One highlight of military life for me," says Army spouse Linda Beougher, "is moving around the country and finding out what we truly like about an area as we discover it through 'infant eyes.' I lived in places for short periods of time and would delve into the museums, monuments, history, etc., and was often told by locals that I knew their home better than they did."

It's true. Kathie always laughs at how often she introduces locals to things in their own town that they aren't aware of.

We have the advantage of knowing we will be moving on. Locals always feel like "I can get to that another time," but we know we might not. Add to that the fact that locals tend to travel in circumscribed paths, driving on automatic, while we see our new environment with open, curious eyes.

Many military families have discovered parts of the country they prefer over where they originally lived, something they might never have done without the journeys provided by military moves.

Get to Know the World

One thing we heard over and over from spouses: "Get out and explore the world!" Take advantage of living in a different country for a few years. Many of the places you get to live are places other Americans save up to visit for just one brief vacation in their lifetime. You get to experience other countries through all seasons, which means you get to experience all kinds of different festivals and customs, if you open up to them. Learn to relish the differences as you move around, rather than being one of those "ugly Americans" who just keeps talking about missing Costco or Walmart or their favorite fast food place. Get out of the food court and explore.

From Kathie's Journal

When I reminisce about life in Europe, I often mention how much I love the German bakeries. We could walk over in the morning and get a mix of breads and pastries for house guests or ourselves. We could stop by and get a great loaf of bread for dinner. Great breads, lots of variety, including my favorite—delikatusbrot—full of hazelnuts, walnuts, and other nuts and seeds. Imagine my surprise to hear a comment from another woman who lived in Germany as a military spouse. She hated the experience. One of the first examples she gave of the deprivation of life there was the German bakery!

"Imagine," she complained, "the breads had no preservatives, so you had to go buy them every other day or so."

What I had seen as such a positive experience, something I missed back home in the US, stood out in her mind as a big negative. It just goes to show you, it's not what happens to us, it's not what we experience or where we live, it's how we view that experience. Our attitude. You really can find the positive or the negative in just about anything. It's your choice.

Overseas assignments truly are one of the benefits to military life. We've seen the world and really experienced foreign cultures. You want to take advantage of this benefit your civilian friends rarely experience. And, you don't want your memories of overseas tours to be dismal housing and on-post bowling alleys, Burger King, and Popeyes!

You probably know military families who hated their assignments overseas. Often you find out after talking with them further that they never left their base or post! Sure, it's a little scary to go off-post in a country where you don't speak the language and don't know the customs. Take advantage of the orientation programs offered in many military communities overseas. Befriend a military spouse who does know the language or at least already knows her way around. Plus, it's easier to go exploring with someone else, unless you happen to be one of those who loves to do that on your own.

Take advantage of inexpensive MWR trips and tours, and learn about great opportunities from other military spouses. In Germany, for example, be sure to read a copy of *Never a Dull Moment* as soon as you arrive. This book is updated regularly by military spouses and sold as a fundraiser for the Americans Working Around the Globe. It lists places to shop, eat, and stay throughout Germany. You can get a similar book for Italy. Check

> *"Travel is more than the seeing of sights; it's a change that goes on, deep and permanent, in the ideas of living." —Miriam Beard*

with the spouse club and other military spouses you meet when you get to a new assignment to find out what's available there. Ask other military spouses and families for suggestions on what to do and see, where to eat out, what activities you or your kids might enjoy. We've both had great experiences we would have missed if we hadn't had the advice and guidance of other military spouses.

"I think the biggest benefit to military life is all the travel!" says Marine spouse Lori Cleymans. She describes how she did not enjoy Okinawa at first, until she started to explore and learn about the culture, language, and traditions. "While in Okinawa, we took a trip to China and Kyoto, Japan. Again, we would have never done that while living in the States. We went to China as part of an ITT tour group and it was a blast! I saw the Great Wall, the Forbidden City, the Terracotta Army, and so many wonderful sites."

Listen to what Marine spouse Amy Fetzer says: "I've been able to do things most people never get the chance to do, just because I was married to a Marine. How many people can say they've ridden in an armored personnel carrier, rappelled down a cliff in Okinawa to scuba dive, or had lunch in a Chinese junk floating on Fragrant Harbor in Hong Kong?"

Ask military spouses to list some of the highlights of their lives, and they often come up with activities that would have been difficult (or cost prohibitive) to do in another environment. Here are some we heard:

- Four-day hut-to-hut hike in Austria provided inexpensively by MWR Heidelberg—awesome scenery that can only be accessed by hiking or mountain biking.
- Attending the World Harp Congress in Prague. "If we hadn't been living in Germany, an affordable train-ride away, I could never have done that. My US harp colleagues are green with envy."
- Running a marathon on the Great Wall of China!
- An all-inclusive family-oriented Center Parcs resort in Germany. "Better and more affordable than Disney World. I wish they had those in the United States. Best family vacation we ever had."
- A barge vacation in France. "It was affordable for us because we could drive there from where we were stationed in Germany. We split the cost with other military families. We drove the barge and did our own cooking."
- Touring Paris with my children. "My children have vivid memories of the Louvre and Notre Dame. We camped to make the trip affordable, but that added to the fun."
- Having friends literally all over the world!

You gain a lot from living in so many different states and foreign countries. You become more open to different customs and cultures than many of our countrymen who have never left the country or, in many cases, have never left their own states. You are more interested in international news and more aware of world situations, because your life has been and can always be closely affected by those situations. As the world community becomes more globally connected, this becomes more important to all of us.

We've noticed that our international experiences allow us to hold our own in conversations with people of all levels and backgrounds, a definite plus in the business world. Many of the experiences we've been blessed

"Over the years as a military spouse, I was exposed to other cultures and lifestyles. I learned that we all have differences, but we are all individuals first. As I was exposed to more people, I stopped being so close-minded." —Mollie Gross, author of Confessions of a Military Wife

with because of this military life are experiences that only the wealthy have had access to in the past. We don't know about you, but much as we don't love the actual moving part of this life, we've loved the living in and experiencing so many different worlds. It's made our lives much richer overall.

Open the World to Your Kids

Hope Gibbs moved six times as a child because of her dad's Navy career. Each move was an adventure for Hope and her sister because of their mother. "Mom always made it sound like wherever we were going was the best place on earth," says Hope. "She would research what interesting sights there were to see, and find out about youth groups, schools, and churches, so we would already feel a little at home by the time we got there."

Ask any military brat about his or her experiences growing up, and you'll hear the negatives brought on by constant moves. But you'll hear about amazing opportunities as well, experiences that greatly expanded each individual's worldview to encompass the global community.

- "I got to take my elementary school photo in a kimono. Sure stands out from those other school photos."
- "We got to graduate from high school in the ruins of an ancient temple in Turkey."
- "I got to go on a student cruise with visits to Egypt and Morocco."
- "I attended a German–American school, which started my interest in international relations and gave me a good base on a second language."
- "My American friends are amazed that our family trips included places like Amsterdam, Paris, and hiking in Japan."

Some of the disadvantages of military life can turn into long-term advantages. Nancy was an extremely shy child who had a hard time dealing with change. Moving with the Air Force, starting new schools, and having to make new friends was always excruciating for her. She now sees those experiences as valuable skill-building ones that helped her more easily step into new situations and create new communities as an adult.

As Army spouse Linda says, "We were able to have our girls attend a German school for a while. They learned some of the German language and customs, but more importantly, it opened their minds to differences in the way other people think and do things—they learned that no one is more or less correct, just different!"

Seek Out Unique Opportunities, Compliments of Uncle Sam

During a workshop in Germany, as we had folks running around to get ideas and resources for their dreams, one woman's label read "horse farm." She clarified for us that she eventually wanted horses—something not possible for her in Germany. *Au contraire*, we thought to ourselves. "Have you connected with any local German horse people?" we asked. No, she hadn't. She was just waiting until they moved back to the United States. That might be three years of not pursuing her passion.

As military spouses, it's key to realize opportunities exist everywhere—in Germany or Japan or Turkey, even in a remote site in rural Georgia, even when you think you are stuck in the "middle of nowhere." The challenge is to look for and take advantage of those opportunities. Many of them are not just amazing opportunities; they are experiences you will find nowhere else in the world.

Ask the questions, "What is available here? What is unique to this place that I can use in my dream development? How can I make use of this situation?" Asking those questions sets off light bulbs in your head, at least much more so then when you stick to the mantra of, "If only we weren't sent here…" (We know; we've tried it both ways!)

Here's an idea that made this woman's face light up in our workshop: Interview horse places where she's living. Enlist the help of a military spouse who speaks German. Write an article for the post paper for all those other horse lovers. It's a win/win. She'll learn tips on managing horse farms, make valuable contacts, and find places to ride. She'll get to experience how the horse world in a foreign country differs from the one she knows. She'll provide a service to other military members. And, she'll provide marketing to German horse stables, connecting our two communities, which enriches all of our lives.

Turning our thinking around about military life can open amazing opportunities. Rather than complain about another move (okay, we give you time to complain about the moving process itself), we can thank Uncle Sam for a free trip to do research for our dreams and our lives. Sandee Payne decided to think of PCS (permanent change of station) in a more positive light by changing the acronym meaning to "positive change in surroundings." What a great way to approach each move.

Help your children with this kind of healthy approach. Army spouse Niledy Casiano is the mother of three. Her family has moved with the military four times in nine years. "Rather than saying we are PCSing," Niledy tells us, "we always say to our kids, 'We are starting a new adventure!'"

Sound Pollyanna-ish? Well, what's the alternative? Wishing you lived someplace else doesn't get you very far. We know. We've tried that. Besides, have you noticed how limited some of your old friends' lives can seem—the ones who've never lived any place different or traveled anywhere? The ones who hang out in the same places and talk about the same things they did in high school? The ones who still work at the same companies where they've worked for the past twenty years, including many who hate their jobs? There are advantages to moving around. Why not focus on the benefits instead of focusing on what's missing? What we focus on really is our choice to make.

Army spouse Linda Beougher made that choice begrudgingly at first, but now sees the benefit. "I've found a harp teacher relatively nearby everywhere we've lived," she says. "At first I was a bit perturbed that I kept having to switch teachers so frequently, but over the years I've learned that each mentor had different strengths. It has been a true blessing to work with many very talented individuals, each teaching me something different."

Consider this:

- What artist wouldn't love to live in Europe or the Far East and interact with international artists?
- What graduate school student couldn't add depth and dimension to his or her thesis by interviewing topic matter experts in other states and countries?
- What cook wouldn't love to try foods and cooking techniques in places as varied as Italy, Korea, and Turkey?

What's your dream and where are you located? Write us or email us, and we'll see what ideas we can come up with to take full advantage of unique possibilities in this latest trip provided to you, courtesy of the military.

Take the Opportunity to Reinvent Yourself

During a workshop for Marine spouses in Okinawa, one woman told us this story. She had been working in city management at one location and had just been offered a promotion. Of course, that is when they got orders to move. A coworker said to her, "How do you deal with that? Just as you have this great opportunity, you have no choice but to give it up and move on." We were impressed with the woman's reply.

"Well, that is one way to look at it," she said, "but just think, how many times in your life have you had the chance to reinvent yourself? As military spouses, we get that chance on a regular basis."

We've often had this discussion with civilian friends who have lived in one place forever. It can be very hard for someone in that situation to take on a new project or career. Friends and neighbors already have a set perception of who you are and what you are capable of. When we move to a new place, those preconceived ideas don't exist. We start fresh. You can even take on a new style as you move. We know one Marine Corps child who chose to change his name with one move.

So, think of each new move as an opportunity. You may choose to reinvent yourself. What a gift!

Discover New Interests

Kathie's Story

My husband, Greg, and I are avid sea kayakers. We even own our own kayaks and have kayaked all over, in Alaska, in Baja, on lakes and rivers and bays. We have many plans for future trips.

My family and childhood friends from the suburbs of Northern Virginia find that hard to believe. They knew me as a shy, quiet, nonathletic bookworm and a chicken when it comes to physical activities.

If we hadn't moved with the military to the Northwest, I doubt I would have ever tried kayaking or hiking or gardening, all things that are central to my world these days. Every time we kayak in the water in the Northwest, surrounded by nature, I thank my lucky stars I no longer live in the suburbs of Washington, DC, as most of my high school friends still do. The suburbs were never a good fit for me. I've discovered new interests here as well as an environment that "makes my soul sing" as my friend Sarah says.

We hear the same from so many military spouses. They often discover passions and places through this military life experience that they would never have had the opportunity to experience in most other lives. We've talked to spouses who became enamored of riding horses when they were stationed in Texas. Others have taken up surfing in California, water-skiing in Alabama, flower arranging in Japan, exotic cooking in Turkey, or antiquing in Georgia.

Moving around so frequently opens you up to many new opportunities. Much of it is free or inexpensive because it's provided through the military. Open the pages of any post/base newspaper and browse through the available classes and trips.

As military spouses, we grow and evolve as our personalities develop. You might move to Arizona or New Mexico and suddenly find you have a passion for Native American art. It's just an aspect of your personality that was waiting to be explored, that you might never have discovered staying in one place.

When Janette Thomas's husband was assigned to the Marine Corps Mountain Warfare Training Center in Bridgeport, California, she knew her husband and boys were going to love this assignment. She thought she would hate it. To someone who used to work in shopping center management and who thrives in urban settings, a remote site in the mountains, located two hours from the closest store of any size (and that being Target), loomed as a bleak assignment.

Since she had to drive her sons to school every day in a forty-minute round trip, Janette started volunteering at the school. Her volunteer job turned into a paid position to create an art appreciation program for the school, something she had never considered getting involved in. Using the Internet to research ideas, she created a program that brought the students and her great joy. Now she's pursuing that line of work, something she would never have even thought of in the past. That assignment turned out to be a good one for her, as well as for her husband and kids.

Relish the Opportunity for Personal Growth

Every spouse we talked with mentioned the incredible personal growth that results from this military life. And yes, a lot of that comes from facing and dealing with challenges. In order to survive and thrive, you have to step outside your comfort zone and take on new skills.

Army spouse Susan Agustin comes from a small town in Pennsylvania. "I guess it was a good place to grow up," she says, "but I'm glad I was able to leave and experience other things. You become so empowered as you move with the military," she says. "You take on challenges, learn new things, and meet new people. It's amazing what you get to experience." Compared to the lives of her peers back home, hers is rich indeed. "I wouldn't trade my life for any of theirs," she adds. We hope you end up saying exactly the same thing.

"I know for sure I would never change any of the hard times I went through in my life. Because it was in those times that I grew the most and gained the most perspective. It's our challenges and obstacles that give us layers of depth and make us interesting. Are they fun when they happen? No. But they are what make us unique." —Ellen DeGeneres

By the way, this life can also result in personal growth for our children.

Marine spouse Kelly Thompson described this in an essay in *Marine Corps Times*. As she had to become more independent and resilient during deployments, her daughter watched her and learned. "Now, when a doorknob is loose, our ten-year-old will pick up a screwdriver and fix it herself. The kids have learned to troubleshoot their own problems."

One of the reasons we partnered with two other military spouses to write our book *1001 Things to Love About Military Life* was to shine a light on the many positives of this military life, to remind ourselves and to share with the nonmilitary world the many things we are so proud of. We included journal entry spaces throughout that book to encourage you to write down the specific experiences and memories that make this military life rich for you and your family.

Key Points and Action Steps

▷ Make a list of unique experiences you've had because of this military life.

▷ Look at this current assignment with fresh eyes. What is unique to this place that you and your family might try? Check with the family service center and the recreation center on your post or base to find out what classes and trips are available. Ask other spouses what they recommend as "not to miss" places and experiences.

▷ When you move to your next assignment, make finding new experiences a conscious, proactive part of the moving plans.

Chapter 23

Start Today to Create a Life
that Works for You

Don't stop the momentum. You've read this book. You've done the life exploration exercises. Now it's time to take action. We don't want you to get the idea that you have to take everything in this book and apply it right away. That would be impossible. We both made many of the changes we describe in this book over a long time, and we continue that lifelong process today. The key is to make conscious choices about what you want in your life, and then take action toward your vision, one step at a time. Don't wait for some-day. Start now.

You can craft a life that works for you as you move with the military, and it can be a rich, full, satisfying life. Start today!

Start by identifying at least one area in which you'd like to make a change. Maybe it's in your energy level or in your immediate environment. Maybe it's identifying what's important to you so you can set goals to work toward those things, or maybe it's identifying some simple joys you might add in immediately.

Here's what we know for sure. Once you figure out your priorities and start to set goals to take action in those areas, you'll see success. And once you see success with one small goal, you gain the motivation to move to-ward the next one. Taking action, taking responsibility, and taking control of things you can control, in a military life full of things you can't control, gives you great satisfaction. Identifying your interests and becoming engaged in life will change your experience of life itself.

You can craft an authentic life that works for you as you move with the military, and it can be a rich, full, satisfying life. Start today!

Create an Action Plan

1. Identify one area of your life in which you'd like to make a change.

_____

_____

2. Write down one thing that's important to you, such a special goal you want to achieve or a simple joy you want to add to your regular routine.

_____

_____

3. What are some of the skills you need, the people you need to meet, or the steps you need to take to make this change happen or achieve what's important to you? Below, list three actionable steps you can take.

_____

_____

_____

- Pick one small action item (e.g., get a book out of the library, research available grants, schedule an information interview, or research the professional association tied to the goal) and schedule an appointment with yourself for next week to do that one item.
- Use your battle buddy as your accountability partner. Ask her/him to call you on a specific date to confirm you took action.

4. Track your progress. Maintain a reflection journal. Include the contacts you make, motivational quotes, and key successes.

- Review the resources listed in this book. Are there organizations that align with your interests? Connect with them. Ask for help.

Use Key Topic Resources

We share resources at the end of each chapter, specific to that topic. But realize it would be impossible for us to share every resource that might be specifically useful to each one of you. We hope some of the resources we list will inspire you to locate others that fit your own unique needs and goals.

Learn how to effectively search the web for resources. Get to know your reference librarian. Librarians can help you find what you need and often have access to directories you can't access alone.

The key is to learn to ask, ask, and ask again. New programs, web sites, and books come out all the time.

Attend Military Life 101

Every service has great resources for military families and they keep improving. Ask what is available. You can save yourself a lot of time and frustration as a new spouse by taking one of the Military 101-type programs available through each service:

Air Force Heart Link
Army Family Team Building
Navy COMPASS
Marine Corps Family Team Building L.I.N.K.S.
Coast Guard Work-Life

These programs provide you with a foundation of knowledge about this life and give you a chance to meet other spouses. You'll learn military terminology and programs that will help you from day one. You can take many of the classes online. We have found these programs to be user friendly. They are not just for new spouses; even veteran spouses will learn useful information. Check with your family service center on post or base.

Bookmark Key Web Sites

There are so many web sites, and they change frequently, so we chose not to attempt to include an exhaustive list of useful sites here. We've included a few that are good gateways to further resources.

Blue Star Families supports military families through the unique challenges of military service and asks the larger civilian population to help. The group connects military families regardless of rank, branch of service, or physical location, and empowers them to create the best personal and family life possible for themselves. Volunteer leaders oversee local chapters throughout the world and help military families have a voice in their local communities. www.BlueStarFam.org.

Military OneSource provides information and assistance in such areas as parenting and childcare, educational services, careers, finances, civilian legal advice, eldercare, crisis support, relocation, and counseling services. www.MilitaryOneSource.mil.

Every military spouse should be a member of National Military Family Association, so you can keep up with and give input to Congress on issues concerning military families. Plus, this is a great central source of information and resources you can trust. www.MilitaryFamily.org.

Military spouse Benita Koeman created Operation We are Here after her family's experiences during her husband's three deployments. Wanting to help other families access important resources, and help civilian communities provide useful resources, she offers practical suggestions to churches, communities, and individuals on how to support and encourage the military home front, and provides a list of resources for families/loved ones of deployed military personnel. www.OperationWeAreHere.com.

Read Books for Military Spouses

Thankfully, there is now a long list of books specifically for military spouses (and others for military children and parents of service members).

When we first tried to get our book published, one publisher said to us, "There is already a book out there for military spouses—we can't see supporting another one." That's like saying, "There is already one parenting book, there is already one dieting book, there is already one cookbook...no need for another." As if one book could cover everything we need to know about military life!

We couldn't possibly cover everything you need to know for your military life in one book. Our focus is on what you can do to craft the best life for you throughout the moves and deployments and other aspects of military life—how to take control of your own happiness in life—how to make conscious choices and take action toward your dreams and your own well-being. We touch on other important topics to point you toward awareness and resources. Other authors have focused entire books on topics such as moving and dealing with deployments.

New books are being published all the time. Check web sites such as: www.ArmyWifeNetwork.com and www.MilitaryFamilyBooks.com for updated lists.

We, along with other military spouses, have been trying for years to get the exchanges to stock robust military spouse and military children's book sections, similar to the Professional Military Reading sections. Marine Corps exchanges are leading the way. We hope to see the same in all the service exchanges.

When you can, buy these books at the exchange. A percentage of all exchange sales go back into our military communities for important Morale, Welfare, and Recreation programs. This isn't small change. As an example, in FY 2011, $42.7 million went to these programs from the Navy exchange, $47.5 million from Marine Corps exchange. In the past ten years, AAFES has contributed more than $2.4 billion to quality of life programs such as youth services, child development centers, armed forces recreation centers, aquatic centers, golf courses, and more. Shop your exchange for savings AND to help push money back into our military community.

Browse Magazines, Newspapers, and Newsletters

Your post/base newspaper is an important source of news about changes in military service benefits, resources, local workshops available to you, and in-service information that might impact your spouse's career or assignment. Each of the services has an equivalent to the Associated Press service that provides important service-wide information and articles in your local post/base paper.

*Air Force/Army/Marine Corps/Navy Time*s newspapers are published by Gannett Government Media. The primary audience is military members, but they are useful publications for spouses to read as well. They give you a good understanding of what's happening around the military. Some articles are specifically geared to family members.

Military Money online magazine provides financial advice specific to military families. www.MilitaryMoney.com. For years we wrote a mobile careers column for *Military Money*. Articles are archived on their site.

Military Spouse magazine, the original brainchild of two military spouses, is available in your exchange on base/post and in many other stores near large posts or by subscription. www.MilitarySpouse.com.

A number of military publications have military spouse columnists or bloggers, such as Terri Barnes with "Spouse Calls" at *Stars & Stripes*; Janet Farley writing a JobTalk column for *Stars & Stripes* and the Homefront column for Military Officers Association of America; and Jacey Eckhart managing SpouseBuzz at Military.com. *USAA* magazine also runs regular features and important news items for military spouses, and military spouse experts blog online at USAA.com.

Choose any one of these resources as a starting point. Take any one of the steps you identified in your exercises. Or start with just one idea you gleaned from reading this book. See the possibilities. And begin living the life you want today!

GO!

LIVE your dreams!

Acknowledgments

We thank the thousands of military spouses we've had the honor of meeting at workshops and book signings, talking to on the telephone or corresponding with by email. We especially thank the many of you who have come up to us personally at events or written to us and said, "Here's what I've done because of your book or workshop," or "You've changed my life!" It's those moments that keep us going in this work. We continue to be in awe of the resiliency and determination of military spouses everywhere. We thank you for your stories and resources that continue to add to the program we present to other spouses. We all learn from each other.

We want to thank all of the wonderful program managers, FRG leaders, and key volunteers we've met, and the ones who work tirelessly to bring in helpful programs for military spouses where they are stationed.

Thanks to the many other military spouse authors, bloggers, talk show hosts, and speakers who share resources with spouses and with each other, whose hearts and missions really are all about helping other spouses with this challenging life.

Thanks to our writing friends and Dare to Dream Team members and success groups. If we listed everyone by name after all these years and moves, that would take quite a few pages. You know who you are. We couldn't have done this work without your help and encouragement.

And most importantly, thanks to our families. The time we spend planning and packing, traveling, writing articles, and the marathon time spent editing this book, all take away from family time. We couldn't have done this work without your patience, understanding, and support.